RITES AND RANK

RITES AND RANK

HIERARCHY IN BIBLICAL REPRESENTATIONS OF CULT

Saul M. Olyan

PRINCETON UNIVERSITY PRESS   PRINCETON, NEW JERSEY

Library of Congress Cataloging-in-Publication Data

Olyan, Saul M.
Rites and rank : hierarchy in biblical representations
of cult / Saul M. Olyan.
    p.   cm.
Includes bibliographical references and index.
ISBN 0-691-02948-2 (cloth : alk. paper)
1. Social stratification in the Bible. 2. Worship in the Bible. 3. Bible.
O.T.—Criticism, interpretation, etc. I. Title.
BS1199.S59 O49   2000
221.6—dc21   99-045170   CIP

This book has been composed in Sabon

The paper used in this publication meets the minimum requirements of
ANSI/NISO Z39.48-1992 (R 1997) (*Permanence of Paper*)

www.pup.princeton.edu

Printed in the United States of America

10   9   8   7   6   5   4   3   2   1

TO THE MEMORY OF MY COUSIN

Michael Eisenberg⎯⎯⎯⎯⎯⎯⎯⎯⎯⎯⎯⎯

Contents

Acknowledgments _____

A NUMBER of individuals and institutions deserve my thanks at this juncture, and as always, it is a great pleasure for me to acknowledge each of them. Stanley Stowers, Lynn Davidman, Burke Long, Peter Machinist, Edward Greenstein, David Konstan, David Brakke, Bernadette Brooten, Carolyn Dean, and Kathryn Tanner each provided helpful suggestions on the initial project proposal out of which this book grew. I would also like to thank the following friends and colleagues, each of whom read portions of the manuscript in its penultimate or earlier forms and provided valuable critical feedback and/or bibliographic suggestions: Lynn Davidman, Stanley Stowers, Maud Mandel, Victor Hurowitz, Theodore Lewis, Shaye J. D. Cohen, and Wendell Dietrich. Burke Long, Peter Machinist, Edward Greenstein, and Martha Nussbaum were kind enough to write letters of recommendation to granting bodies in support of this project. I would like to express my gratitude to the University of Pennsylvania's Center for Judaic Studies for providing a generous yearlong fellowship and an excellent work environment that made the writing of this book possible, and to Brown University for matching funds that allowed me to accept the fellowship. I was fortunate to have the opportunity to present materials from chapter 3 at the fellows' seminar of Penn's Center for Judaic Studies in December 1997 and the faculty seminar of Penn's Department of Religious Studies in April 1998. I owe a special thanks to participants in both seminars for their suggestions, especially Barry Eichler, Victor Hurowitz, and Robert Kraft. Deborah Malmud, of Princeton University Press, has been an enthusiastic supporter of this project since the day she visited the Center for Judaic Studies in September 1997. I would like to thank her not only for her interest, but also for her helpful critical suggestions at various stages in the development of the manuscript. I am pleased to acknowledge both Douglas Knight and Tikva Frymer-Kensky for their critical and constructive feedback during the Press's review process. Both were kind enough to identify themselves to me and provide further suggestions after the review process was complete. A small section of chapter 3 appeared in somewhat different form in the article "What Do Shaving Rites Accomplish and What Do They Signal in Biblical Ritual Contexts?" *Journal of Biblical Literature* 117 (1998) 611–22. Much of chapter 4 is derived from my article "'Anyone Blind or Lame Shall Not Enter the House': On the Interpretation of Second Samuel 5:8b," *Catholic Biblical Quarterly* 60 (1998) 218–27. Material from these articles is reprinted here by permission of the Society of Biblical

Literature and the Catholic Biblical Association of America. I am pleased to acknowledge the assistance of Tracy Lemos, who checked references for me during the final stage of the preparation of the manuscript. Finally, I would like to thank John Choly for agreeing to move to Philadelphia for nine months and helping to make our time there immensely rewarding.

Saul M. Olyan
Providence, Rhode Island, 1999

Abbreviations

The following is a list of abbreviations used throughout the text and notes.

AB	Anchor Bible
ABD	D. N. Freedman et al., eds. *The Anchor Bible Dictionary*. 6 vols. New York: Doubleday, 1992.
AJSL	*American Journal of Semitic Languages and Literature*
Ant.	Flavius Josephus, *Jewish Antiquities*
AOAT	Alter Orient und Altes Testament
ARM	A. Parrot and G. Dossin, eds. *Archives royales de Mari*. Paris: Imprimerie nationale, 1950–.
ASOR	American Schools of Oriental Research
b.	Babylonian Talmud, followed by tractate
BASOR	*Bulletin of the American Schools of Oriental Research*
BBB	Bonner biblische Beiträge
BHT	Beiträge zur historischen Theologie
BZAW	Beihefte zur Zeitschrift für die alttestamentliche Wissenschaft
CAD	A. Leo Oppenheim et al., eds. *The Assyrian Dictionary of the Oriental Institute of the University of Chicago*. Chicago: Oriental Institute, 1956–.
CahRB	Cahiers de la Revue biblique
CAT	Commentaire de l'Ancien Testament
CBQ	*Catholic Biblical Quarterly*
CBQMS	Catholic Biblical Quarterly Monograph Series
D	Deuteronomistic School, Deuteronomistic work
DBSup	L. Pirot et al., eds. *Dictionnaire de la Bible, Supplément*. Paris: Letouzey and Ané, 1928–.
E	Elohist, work of the Elohist
Eng.	English
EM	U. Cassuto et al., eds. *'enṣîqlōpedyâ miqrā'ît*. Jerusalem: Mossad Bialik, 1965–88.
FRLANT	Forschungen zur Religion und Literatur des Alten und Neuen Testaments
G	Greek
HAR	*Hebrew Annual Review*
H	Holiness School, Holiness Source
Hag.	Hagigah
HAT	Handbuch zum Alten Testament
ICC	International Critical Commentary
J	Yahwist, work of the Yahwist
JANES	*Journal of the Ancient Near Eastern Society of Columbia University*
JBL	*Journal of Biblical Literature*
JNES	*Journal of Near Eastern Studies*

JBS	Jerusalem Biblical Studies
JSOT	*Journal for the Study of the Old Testament*
JSOTSup	Journal for the Study of the Old Testament, Supplement Series
Kraeling	E. Kraeling, ed. *The Brooklyn Museum Aramaic Papyri: New Documents of the Fifth Century* B.C. *from the Jewish Colony at Elephantine*. New Haven: Yale University Press, 1953.
LH	Laws of Hammurabi
LXX	Septuagint
m.	Mishnah, followed by tractate
MAL	Middle Assyrian Laws
Mek.	Mekilta deRabbi Ishmael
Midr. Rab.	Midrash Rabbah
MT	Massoretic Text
NCB	New Century Bible
NJPS	New Jewish Publication Society Version
OBT	Overtures to Biblical Theology
OTL	Old Testament Library
P	Priestly School, Priestly Writing
PEQ	*Palestine Exploration Quarterly*
Q	Qumran sigla:
1QM	War Scroll: Qumran, Cave 1
1QS^a	The Rule of the Community: Qumran, Cave 1
11QTemp	The Temple Scroll: Qumran, Cave 11
RA	E. Ebeling and B. Meissner, eds. *Reallexikon der Assyriologie*. Berlin: de Gruyter, 1928–.
RB	*Revue biblique*
RSV	Revised Standard Version
SBLDS	Society of Biblical Literature Dissertation Series
SBLSP	Society of Biblical Literature Seminar Papers
Syr	Syriac (Peshitta) Version
SJLA	Studies in Judaism in Late Antiquity
THAT	E. Jenni and C. Westermann, eds. *Theologisches Handwörterbuch zum Alten Testament*. 2 vols. Munich: C. Kaiser, 1971–76.
Vg	Vulgate
VT	*Vetus Testamentum*
VTSup	Vetus Testamentum, Supplements
ZAW	*Zeitschrift für die alttestamentliche Wissenschaft*

RITES AND RANK

Introduction _____

BINARY oppositions, or dyadic pairings of terms such as good/evil, clean/unclean, rich/poor, and self/other have long been of interest to philosophers, linguists, classicists, and social scientists, among others.[1] In recent decades, discussion of dyadic modes of thought and discourse among such scholars has affected theoretical work in other fields. In religious studies, for example, treatment of polarities has been notable especially in ritual theory and in analyses of ritual practice.[2] Yet, with few exceptions, those who study the Hebrew Bible, ancient Israel's literary legacy, have done little work with binary oppositions.[3] This is somewhat puzzling, for the binary opposition is not simply an imported theoretical construct with little or no resonance in surviving textual witnesses to Israelite culture. On the contrary, binary oppositions are deeply embedded in the Hebrew Bible's own discourse; they are evidenced across the spectrum of extant literature, in numerous biblical contexts. The dyadic contrast unclean/clean forms the basis of the Hebrew Bible's purity rhetoric, and the opposition of holy and common sets cultic space and items apart from their common congeners. Other polarities play a part in descriptions of the nature of Yhwh, Israel's national deity, as in 1 Sam 2:6–7: "Yhwh kills and allows to live, he causes one to descend to Sheol and he brings up. Yhwh dispossesses and makes rich, he debases and exalts."[4] Binary pairings are central to the articulation of the contrast between the antithetical ritual states of mourning and rejoicing, as in Isa 61:1–4: "The spirit of my lord Yhwh is upon me . . . to bring tidings to the afflicted he has sent me . . . to comfort all who mourn . . . to give to them a headdress in place of ashes, oil of joy in place of mourning, a mantle of praise in place of a diminished spirit."[5] Oppositions are present from the beginning of the narrative in Genesis 1, producing a series of contrasting phenomena that categorize and order creation (for example, heavens and earth, light and darkness, day and night, evening and morning).[6] In a word, binary oppositions pervade much of what survives of the discourse of ancient Israel, including the discourse related to the cult; they are employed by biblical writers as a common strategic device to divide, categorize, and order reality.[7]

My primary goal in this study is to investigate the manner in which hierarchical social relations are realized in biblical cultic and quasi-cultic contexts. Working from the limited collection of extant biblical legal and narrative texts, I argue that a set of discrete, socially constructed, and culturally privileged binary oppositions generates social difference in the sanctuary and in ritual contexts outside of the cult in which purity is required (=quasi-cultic settings). Ritual, in my view, is not simply a reproductive activity in which social distinctions are mirrored, but also a productive operation in which social difference is realized. Rites shape reality for participants; they do not simply reflect some preexisting set of social arrangements brought into being elsewhere.[8] Privileged oppositions produce hierarchy by bounding or restricting access to ritual contexts such as the temple, the Passover table, and the war camp feast. Within such cultic and quasi-cultic settings, privileged oppositions generate unequal social relations by limiting access to particular ritual space, actions, and items that are associated with high status, prestige, and honor. They do so also by establishing an order of precedence in ritual action that privileges certain groups (such as priests, heads of household) over others. The contrast between clean and unclean creates a boundary around cultic and quasi-cultic loci, as do other oppositions (such as circumcised/uncircumcised) according to certain texts. Other dyadic contrasts such as priest/nonpriest, whole priest/blemished priest, or household head/non–household head generate boundaries within the sanctuary and related contexts, limiting access to privileged physical space (such as the holy of holies), privileged rites (such as presentation of the deity's sacrificial portions, blood manipulation), and privileged items (such as holy foods). By creating distinctions among groups and individuals, the bounded sanctuary and related ritual sites become primary contexts for the production and reproduction of a hierarchical social order. The establishment of boundaries and the generation of hierarchy in cultic and quasi-cultic settings depend upon two movements: (1) the determination that certain binary pairings (over against others) are relevant to cultic access and social differentiation; and (2) the privileging of one member of the pair over the other within each relevant polarity. In contrast to both the privileged oppositions that produce boundaries around the sanctuary sphere and those that generate boundaries within it, other binary pairings extant in biblical texts are relevant neither to cultic access nor to status differentiation in cultic settings (tall/short, right-handed/left-handed, thin/fat, wise/fool).

A number of anthropologists have argued that binary oppositions may be employed by cultures to communicate totality and to generate hierarchy.[9] Totality is communicated by a dyad understood to be all encompassing; hierarchy is produced when one member of an opposition is privileged over the other.[10] Some dyads may communicate only a sense of totality, with no hint of hierarchical privileging of one member of the pair over its opposite; others may privilege one of the members, thereby generating a difference of rank while also communicating a sense of the whole. The biblical evidence lends support to the notion that binary pairings may function to communicate totality and to construct hierarchy. Some oppositions communicate totality with no suggestion of hierarchy. Eccl 3:1–8 represents the rhythm of human life with a series of dyadic contrasts:

> To everything there is a season, and a time for every matter under heaven: A time to be born and a time to die; a time to plant and a time to pull up what is planted; a time to slay and a time to heal; a time to pull down and a time to build; a time to weep and a time to laugh; a time to mourn and a time to dance; a time to cast stones and a time to gather stones; a time to embrace and a time to refrain from embracing; a time to seek and a time to make stray; a time to keep and a time to throw away; a time to tear and a time to sew; a time to be silent and a time to speak; a time to love and a time to hate; a time of war and a time of peace.

The fourteen oppositions in this text are introduced by the statement "to *everything* there is a season and a time for *every* matter under heaven." There is no sense in this passage that "a time to be born" is better than "a time to die," only that each is a component part of the human condition.

Similarly, the formulation "knowledge of good and evil" in Genesis 2–3 suggests only what might be called the totality of culturally specific normative behaviors, just as the common biblical geographic expression "from Dan to Beersheba"[11] suggests the whole territory of Israel; in no sense do these particular oppositions communicate any notion of hierarchy. Dan is not superior to Beersheba nor Beersheba to Dan, but when brought together as a binary pairing, they communicate the totality of Israelite territory, north to south. Likewise, "knowledge of good" is not privileged over "knowledge of evil" in the particular context of Genesis 2:4b–3:24; it is simply one component of a dyad intended to communicate the whole range of what can be known.

In contrast, other oppositions attested in biblical materials accord greater worth or higher status to one member of the pairing over against the other, thereby generating a relationship of unequals. Eccl 9:2 presents a series of binary pairings in which the first term is conventionally privileged over the second, only to make the subversive point that all come to the same end anyway: "For all there is one fate: for the righteous and for the wicked, for the good and for the evil,[12] for the clean and for the unclean, for the sacrificer and for the one who does not sacrifice. The good person is as the sinner, the one who swears as the one who avoids oaths." The dyad holy/common is another example. Though all space, objects, or persons might be categorized as either holy or common in texts concerned with the cult, holy space, objects, or persons possess a status clearly distinct and superior to that which is common, or lacking holiness. In certain texts, the contrast circumcised/uncircumcised is used to categorize the male population and bestow concrete cultic and social privileges on those who possess the privileged characteristic, circumcision, while marginalizing those who do not. Thus, a variety of biblical texts illustrate both the totalizing function of binary modes of thought and discourse and their ability to generate status difference.

Some caveats must be given here. I do not imagine that cultic and quasi-cultic boundaries were unchanging, nor do I think that the hierarchical social relations produced and signaled in ritual contexts went uncontested. On the contrary, evidence suggests that the boundaries around and within the cult could shift over time as historical and social circumstances changed, with newly privileged or reconceptualized oppositions generating new boundaries. Certainly some groups advocate such change in some of the narratives that survive. Texts also suggest that nonprivileged groups might challenge their status through ritual action of their own. A prime example is Num 16:1–17:5 (Eng.,16:1–40), the Priestly Writing's narrative of the Levitic and congregational challenges to Aaronid priestly hegemony. Unlike some others who have worked with binary oppositions (e.g., some scholars taking a structuralist approach), I do not seek to reduce complex, dynamic social relations to immutable, static structures; I am not looking for the universal, the innate, the transhistorical. Rather, I am interested in uncovering and illuminating the complexities of social differentiation as surviving biblical texts represent it, and I do so through an investigation of the employment of sets of socially constructed and culturally privileged binary pairings by those texts.

Though I believe binary oppositions are the primary rhetorical tool by which biblical texts express totality and hierarchy, I want to emphasize that these may be articulated in other ways as well. The list of household members and associated dependents that appears in texts such as Exod 20:10; Deut 5:14; 16:11, 14 is an example of a nondyadic device intended to express totality and rank within the household. The head of household is listed first ("you," masculine singular), followed by his son, his daughter, his male slave, his female slave, and the Levite, resident outsider, fatherless person, and widow, who are in some manner associated with the household.[13] All who follow the household head in the list are his dependents; all possess a status inferior to his. The order of the list of dependents probably expresses rank among them.[14]

Triadic constructions, though much less common in biblical texts than binary oppositions, are another way in which hierarchy and a sense of the whole are expressed.[15] In biblical contexts, triadic constructions are generated out of and dependent upon binary oppositions and function similarly to them, in that they divide and classify reality, often imposing a hierarchical order upon it. Several examples of triadic constructions illustrate my argument. The Priestly Writing, Chronicles, and a number of other biblical sources divide society into three groups or strata, each with distinct rank and privileges: the priests, the Levites, and other Israelites. A second example is Deut 14:21, which presents a triadic construction that distinguishes Israelites from resident outsiders on the one hand and from nonresident aliens on the other: "You shall not eat any carcass; to the resident outsider (gēr) who is in your towns you shall give it, and he will eat it, or sell it to the (nonresident) alien (nokrî), for a holy people are you to Yhwh your god."[16] Both of these triadic constructions are apparently the result of secondary development out of an underlying binary contrast, priest/Levite/Israelite from the opposition priest/nonpriest, and Israelite/resident outsider/nonresident alien from the polarity Israelite/alien. In each case, one member of the initial opposition has itself been divided: the category nonpriest gives rise to the categories Levite and Israelite; the category alien generates the categories resident outsider and nonresident alien. If binary oppositions are a rhetorical strategy to differentiate, triadic constructions provide a context to do so to a greater extent, articulating hierarchy in more detail.

It is therefore somewhat surprising that triadic modes of thought and discourse are not more common in biblical materials. Biblical texts do, however, bear witness to another secondary development out of the binary opposition that functions similarly to a triadic construction. This is what I will call the secondary binary opposition, and an example is the contrast most holy/holy. Most holy/holy presupposes the polarity holy/common, and therefore must have been generated secondarily from it, but in passages where most holy is contrasted with holy, there is no mention of common or concern with it. Therefore, most holy/holy is best described as a secondary binary opposition rather than a component of a triadic construction. The dyad most holy/holy allows for distinctions to be made among things holy, just as the triadic construction Israelite/resident outsider/nonresident alien allows for differentiation within the alien class. I should also mention the secondary binary opposition high priest/priest, which generates distinctions among priests but without reference to nonpriests.

Status and Hierarchy

Status and hierarchy are terms drawn from the discourse of the social sciences, as are social differentiation and rank. I use these terms and others of the same etiology to describe the social relationships of groups or individuals as biblical materials represent them. Biblical texts are replete with representations of social inequality, which is, in the words of L. A. Fallers, "inherent in sociocultural differentiation in all its dimensions."[17] G. D. Berreman, speaking of India and other contemporary societies, provides an apt characterization of social stratification, elements of which also characterize Israelite social hierarchy as biblical texts represent it: "A society is socially stratified when its members are divided into categories which are differentially powerful, esteemed, and rewarded. . . . [Stratification is] perpetuated by differential power wielded by the high and the low, expressed in differential behaviour required and differential rewards accorded them, and experienced by them as differential access to goods, services, livelihood, respect, self-determination, peace of mind, pleasure, and other valued things."[18] Idioms of honor and shame, suzerainty and vassalage, patronage and clientship are frequently employed in biblical texts to communicate status differences and hierarchical social arrangements among individuals and groups. Access to privileged cultic space, privileged rites, or privileged items is a cult-specific way that biblical texts represent the realization and communication of social differentiation.

Social scientific literature tends to distinguish "birth-ascribed" or simply "ascribed" status from "non-birth-ascribed" or "achieved" status.[19] Where non-birth-ascribed (or achieved) status is often associated with such characteristics as income, education, or occupation, birth-ascribed status may be determined by such considerations as gender, race, or ethnicity. Birth-ascribed social hierarchy is frequently associated with non-Western societies, while non-birth-ascribed stratification is more often than not linked to Western, capitalist contexts.[20] This, however, represents at best only a very rough generalization, for social hierarchy in various contexts tends to be characterized by both birth-ascribed and non-birth-ascribed elements. B. S. Turner observes that "it is empirically and historically the case that class and status as axes of inequality and stratification are usually mixed within social systems," though he notes that one tends to dominate the other in particular social contexts.[21] Turner goes on to argue that theories of social stratification must therefore account for both birth-ascribed and non-birth-ascribed variables and, following G. Lukács, M. I. Finley, and others, asserts the relevance of this approach even for classical antiquity.[22]

Another, complicating, dimension of social hierarchy in many contexts dominated by birth ascription is the presence of (often) ubiquitous individual relationships between patrons and clients. Unlike birth-ascribed status, which by definition is immutable, clientage could provide opportunities for social betterment to ambitious, talented individuals with the right connections. As C. Geertz has so eloquently stated with respect to patron/client relations in nineteenth-century Bali, "[C]lientship provided a way in which to forge ties across the fixed boundaries of status and consanguinity as well as to realign relationships within them."[23] Thus, a society dominated by birthascribed status differences could nonetheless offer persons of ability and drive opportunities to improve their social standing in certain respects. Clearly, charting the components of social hierarchy, even in contexts in which birth ascription plays a central role in shaping hierarchical social relations, is no easy task and must be approached with care.

It is not surprising that biblical representations of social differentiation tend to emphasize distinctions made on the basis of certain immutable, birth-ascribed characteristics. These include lineage (for example, priestly or nonpriestly, native or alien), birth order (for example, firstborn male or laterborn male), and gender. However, privileged birth-ascribed characteristics in no way exhaust the criteria that contribute to the production of social hierarchy according to biblical sources. Other immutable characteristics such as age/life stage (for example, a woman of childbearing age or postmenopausal woman; minor, dependent male or head of household) or physical condition (for example, a body constructed as permanently blemished versus whole) also play a significant part in shaping social difference, as do alterable characteristics such as male uncircumcision (see, for example, Exod 12:43–48). The contrast between slave and free is yet another relevant and complicating factor. Slavery may be temporary or permanent, involving either Israelites (for example, debtors and/or their dependents) or foreigners. Individual patron-client relationships, evidenced in a number of biblical texts, provide opportunities for individuals to improve their lot in terms of prestige and tangible assets.[24]

In addition, there are other economic dimensions to social hierarchy. According to biblical texts, the cult center receives and redistributes wealth in an uneven manner, enriching a high-status group such as the priesthood at the expense of those bringing sacrifices and offerings. Among worshipers, some are more well-to-do than others, and a number of texts distinguish between required and optional sacrifices of persons of varying degrees of wealth.[25] There is some evidence in extant texts of conflict between groups with respect to the allotment of valued assets and high-status roles. A prime example is the Levitic claim to holiness in Num 16:1–17:5 (Eng., 16:1–40), which is rebuffed in the strongest possible terms by the text's Priestly authors. In addition, there are the various Priestly and Holiness texts reserving certain cultic privileges and emoluments exclusively for priests or Levites and enforcing these restrictions by threat of death or lineage extirpation for any potential offender. Similarly, conflict between status groups over "the distribution of specific rights and privileges" has been observed by M. I. Finley for the classical world.[26] Turner and others before him have emphasized the conflict dimension of stratification based on ascribed characteristics.[27]

Cultic and Quasi-Cultic Settings

Distinctions between individuals and groups are frequently made and publicized in ritual settings.[28] The royal court, processions in the street, communal fasts, assemblies, judicial proceedings, the war camp, and the sanctuary are among the many possible public contexts in which rites create and recreate social difference in biblical texts, often expressed through the idiom of honor. The home is yet another setting where such rites might occur and where honor might be bestowed or removed. Among these various settings for status-differentiating ritual action are cultic and quasi-cultic contexts. Cultic settings in my usage are sanctified loci in which purity requirements are enforced and sacrifices and offerings to the deity are processed and redistributed. The range of biblical cultic settings includes temples, high places, and the tabernacle of the wilderness wanderings as described in Priestly narrative. What I am calling quasi-cultic contexts are illustrated best by the Passover celebration in the home as it is described in the various narratives of Exodus 12. Though this is a nonsanctified ritual setting, situated outside of a sanctuary context, sanctuary-like rules of purity and other cultic regulations apply.[29]

Cultic and quasi-cultic contexts are the ritual settings that will be the focus of my analysis. I devote my attention to these particular ritual settings for a number of reasons. Extant texts suggest that cultic and quasi-cultic rites were particularly significant to the lives of Israelites. Persons praised and petitioned Yhwh, the national god, fulfilled vows, corrected transgressions, and consumed most of the meat in their diet in cultic contexts.[30] The rehearsal of central, founding events in the nation's past is associated with the Passover meal in the home and may also have played a part in the festivals of the sanctuary.[31] For a majority of the population, those without access to the royal court and other arenas of administration and diplomacy, the sanctuary was very likely the preeminent public ritual context in which rites shaped social relations. This process must also have occurred in the context of domestic rites such as the Passover. At all events, surviving texts give this impression. Finally, I note that cultic and quasi-cultic rites are more richly represented in the biblical anthology than are those of other ritual settings (such as the reception of foreign ambassadors at court, or birth-related rituals), and therefore, there is more material with which to work.

Rites and Rank

A variety of texts suggest that ritual action in cultic and quasi-cultic contexts shapes social configurations, inscribing status on participating individuals and groups (such as priests, heads of household, dependents of household heads). In the context of the sanctuary, priests lay claim to holy foods and elite portions of offerings shared with worshipers. They perform rites, such as blood manipulation or fat burning, that are constructed as most prestigious and exclusively under their control. Their ritual actions and their claim to elite offerings and sacrificial portions realize and signal their privileged rank vis-à-vis worshipers and other cultic servants. Among worshipers, heads of household (elders) create and re-create their superior status to others in their households through ritual action in cultic and quasi-cultic settings. Elders are portrayed choosing and slaughtering for their clans and households the sheep to be used for the Passover offering; they also place blood on the lintel and doorposts of their homes to mark them as Israelite (Exod 12:21–22; cp.12:2–7). These rites of choosing, slaughtering, and blood daubing make and mark the privileged position of elders. The manipulation of blood, though performed outside of the sanctuary by the elders rather than in the sanctuary by priests, nonetheless recalls priestly blood manipulation at the altar and so underscores elder privilege in yet another way, by allowing the head of household to play a priest-like role in the context of his household's celebration of the Passover. Sanctuary rites at family pilgrimages are represented similarly. The one biblical text that describes the rites of family pilgrimage in any detail, 1 Sam 1:3–5, portrays the head of household slaughtering the sacrifice. This leads me to imagine the elder also performing initial rites of the sort described by the Priestly Writers in a text such as Lev 1:4–6. In that text, the offerer of the sacrifice strips the skin off the slaughtered animal and divides it into portions. The components of the sacrifice are then passed to the priests for further processing. In the narrative of 1 Sam 1:3–5, the sacrifice is one to be shared by the worshipers, and so the household head receives back portions of cooked meat to distribute to his dependents, creating and inscribing status differences among them as he does so. The acts of passing on the partially processed components of the sacrifice to the priests and receiving back from the priests the cooked meat for distribution realize and communicate the status of the elder vis-à-vis the priests on the one hand and his dependents on the other. He stands midway between the priests and his dependents, privileged to represent his household through the performance of initial sacrificial rites, but compelled to give up the partially processed animal to the priests who will complete the rites of processing at the altar. The order of the distribution of food items among dependents is hinted at in 1 Sam 1:4–5: wife (Peninnah), sons, daughters, then second wife (Hannah).[32]

I shall discuss two final examples of rites conferring rank. In 1 Sam 9:22–24, Saul, whom Yhwh has chosen to be king, is seated by the priest-prophet Samuel at the head of a table of notables[33] who have gathered to partake of meat in the context of a sacrificial rite at a local sanctuary. Saul is not only given a place of honor at the table, but also presented with an elite portion of meat that had been set aside especially for him according to Samuel. Both Saul's placement at the head of the notables and the meat portion he receives establish and communicate his high status. A second example, 1 Samuel 20, describes mealtime in Saul's court at the New Moon as a ritual context in which status differences are realized among Saul's courtiers. Each participant has his assigned place at the table, suggesting a hierarchical arrangement, and all are expected by the king to be present. To occupy one's assigned seat and participate in the meal realizes and communicates one's place in the hierarchy of status; in effect, the courtier states through his presence and his participation that he is loyal to his overlord, the king, and accepts his position in the status hierarchy of the court. To be absent, for whatever reason, raises questions, and it may offend the king and be perceived as threatening to the present order of things, as it is in the case of David's absence in this text (vv. 18, 24–30).[34]

The dominance of binary thinking and rhetoric in the production of social difference in the cultic and quasi-cultic contexts described by biblical texts has led me to organize this study around four privileged dyads: holy/common, unclean/clean, native/alien, and whole/blemished. I have chosen to focus on these particular oppositions for several reasons. Two—holy/common and unclean/clean—are indisputably crucial to any consideration of the workings of the cult and generate a variety of significant social distinctions in its biblical representation. I have chosen the two other focal oppositions because each finds frequent explicit expression in biblical texts, each plays an important part in generating hierarchical differentiation, and sufficient evidence survives for each to construct an extended discussion. I integrate my examination of other privileged polarities into these four chapters as relevant. I explore the important contrast priest/nonpriest in some depth in chapter 1. The mainly implicit but central opposition male/female is the focus of discussion in several of the chapters that take up gender issues. And I incorporate into my study at various points the contrast between the head of household (elder) and his dependents. Thus, I investigate the various privileged oppositions that construct social hierarchy in biblical cultic and related contexts by focusing on four dyads while making frequent reference to several others.

Some readers might wonder why I have chosen not to devote a separate chapter to the gender dimension of biblical representations of hierarchy, given its obvious importance. Early in the development of this project, I had planned to write such a chapter, focusing on the dyad male/female. But I found that gender issues were pervasive throughout the book, to the extent that they play a role in each chapter's analysis, and a particularly important role in chapters 1, 2, and 3. Thus, I abandoned the idea of a gender chapter because it would have been redundant, simply repeating material from the previous chapters and offering little that was new. Also, I find appealing the idea of mainstreaming gender issues, discussing them in each chapter rather than segregating them in a single chapter. In my view, mainstreaming the gender dimension of hierarchy serves to underscore gender's importance to this project; in no way does it diminish the centrality of gender, as some might be tempted to think at first blush.

A final word must be said about the problem of the data's limitations. In this investigation, I speak frequently of *biblical representations* of ritual action and the production of social hierarchy in cultic and quasi-cultic contexts. I have chosen my words carefully, in order to remind myself as much as the reader that we are dependent on a circumscribed set of varied and often difficult texts that do not often lend themselves to confident historical reconstruction and generalization. Some of these texts are narrative representations of cultic ritual action in an ancestral or exodus setting,[35] often of varying and disputed date and provenance. Other texts are prescriptive in nature (for example, Leviticus 1–7); their date, origin, and purpose vary, and they are frequently subject to debate. Some of the material relevant to this project is drawn from prophetic texts, some from texts that are conventionally assigned to reconstructed works such as the Deuteronomistic History (Deuteronomy–2 Kings), or the historical literature of the "Chronicler" (Chronicles, Ezra–Nehemiah).[36] Ancestral and exodus narratives probably tell us something about ritual practice in the monarchic, exilic, and post-exilic communities from which they derive, though the potential influence of idealization and even hyperbole must constantly be kept in mind when working with them. The same applies to texts describing rites set in the monarchic era or later. Prescriptive texts may reflect a utopian or revisionist program more than actual practice at any particular time or place (for example, Ezekiel 44), though I do not doubt that some prescriptive texts reflect some community's practice at some point in time. The problem is identifying who, where, and when. As the extant material is so varied in its nature, purpose, and origin, and often is in dispute with respect to date and even provenance, I will focus this investigation primarily on how the texts themselves represent rites and the generation of hierarchy rather than attempt to concentrate on reconstructing ritual practice and social differentiation in Israelite communities at any particular point in time. I will, however, speak of such reconstruction when I feel the evidence warrants it, as it sometimes does. In choosing this approach to the data, I locate myself between representatives of what I believe are two interpretive extremes that are difficult to defend: on the one hand, those who treat texts such as the Priestly Writing as if they somehow provide the historian with an unproblematic window into the quotidian workings of the Israelite cult, and on the other, those who believe that we can learn little or nothing of a historical Israel and its religious life from biblical texts.

1

Foundational Discourse: The Opposition Holy/Common

Two related binary pairings are present in virtually all texts concerned with the cultic life of Israel: holy/common (qōdeš/ḥōl) and clean/unclean (ṭāhôr/ṭāmēʾ).[1] Though mainly implicit in biblical texts,[2] the Holiness Source and the Book of Ezekiel speak explicitly of both of these oppositions, and they speak of them often in tandem. An example is Lev 10:8–11, a text of the Holiness School concerned with the prohibition of alcohol to priests serving in the sanctuary. It states that the priests are obligated "to distinguish between the holy and the common, and between the unclean and the clean," and teach Israel Yhwh's statutes.[3] Ezek 44:23 is similar: "My people they [the priests] shall teach (the difference) between holy and common, and (the difference) between unclean and clean they shall make known to them." When the priests fail to fulfill their obligation to distinguish and to teach distinction with respect to holiness and purity, the whole cultic enterprise unravels. The result is the unacceptable profanation of Yhwh himself: "Her priests have done violence to my teaching and have profaned my holy things; between holy and common they have not distinguished, nor have they made known (the difference) between what is unclean and clean; my Sabbaths they have failed to observe, and so I am profaned in their midst" (Ezek 22:26). A number of texts speak of the punishments to be meted out to those who do not observe the distinctions between holy and common, clean and unclean: extirpation of lineage or death.[4] Though the distinctions are perhaps most frequently at issue in the Holiness Source, the Priestly Writing, and the Book of Ezekiel, there is much extant evidence that the preservation of holiness (for example, of the sanctuary, of holy offerings, of sanctified items) by the avoidance of profanation and pollution are concerns of other, sometimes earlier sources as well. In 1 Sam 21:2–10 (Eng., 1–9), an encounter takes place between David and Ahimelek, the priest of the sanctuary at Nob.[5] David and his men are hungry, and David requests food from the priest. Ahimelek replies that he has no "common bread" (leḥem ḥōl) in his possession, only the "holy bread" (leḥem qōdeš) displayed in the sanctuary before Yhwh. Because David's men are clean, they are permitted to eat holy bread.[6] Other examples from various sources suggest both the antiquity and importance of the distinctions holy/common and clean/unclean.[7]

It is no accident that texts such as Lev 10:11 and Ezek 22:26; 44:23 show such an intense concern that the priesthood and the rest of Israel should distinguish consistently and reliably between what is holy and what is common, and what is clean and unclean. Maintaining each of these distinctions is necessary for the very existence of a sanctuary and cultic service to the deity; without them, the continued presence of Yhwh in Israel's midst would be threatened. The locus of cult, the sanctuary, whether represented as tent shrine or tabernacle, temple complex or high place, is, in essence, holy space. Set apart from common territory, the sanctuary, however described, is the dwelling place on earth of the deity, who is himself quintessentially holy. The implements of the sanctuary, including its altar for burnt offerings, are likewise sanctified, as are the priests who oversee the sanctuary's operation and many of the offerings that Israelites bring to it. According to some materials apart from the Priestly Writing, the Holiness Source, and Ezekiel, worshipers, too, must be sanctified or must sanctify themselves (hitqaddēš) before coming into contact with holy space or holy things.[8] The holiness of the sanctuary may be threatened with either profanation or pollution. Profanation, the transformation of what is holy into what is common, means, in the case of the sanctuary, the transformation of Yhwh's holy abode into common territory, and, therefore, space no longer set apart for the deity's dwelling and his worship. Pollution of the sanctuary, through the introduction of a defiled person or thing into its space, would render the sanctuary utterly unfit for the deity's dwelling or service and would require elaborate rites of purification to return the sanctuary to its previous clean and holy status. It is a major duty of cultic servants to prevent the entry of uncleanness into the sanctuary sphere and likewise to prevent the occurrence of any illegitimate profanation. Thus, we see the concern witnessed in biblical texts to maintain the distinctions holy/common and clean/unclean, to keep what is holy from illegitimate profanation and to guard it from contact with polluting persons and things. These distinctions make Yhwh's presence possible in the cult; they allow him to dwell with Israel and accept his rightful due as Israel's national god and suzerain.

The holy/common contrast is my point of departure, for all other binary pairings related to the cult, including the opposition clean/unclean, presuppose it.[9] With the contrast between the holy and the common, sanctification is possible: cultic space is set apart for the deity's dwelling, and cultic items and personages are set apart for his service. Biblical texts suggest that pollution would pose no threat whatsoever were it not for the holy space, the holy items, and the holy deity requiring protection from it. In other words, in biblical representation, the notion of uncleanness has no meaning apart from the notion of holiness; pollution is only a consideration vis-à-vis the holy.[10] The contrast between holy and common establishes the limits of the sanctification of space, items, and foods; it determines the extent to which Yhwh's essential quality is distributed spatially and otherwise. The contrast between clean and unclean establishes who or what will qualify for admission to sanctified space or who might, given other necessary qualifications (for example, priestly lineage), gain access to holy items or foods. Thus, the opposition of clean to unclean pertains to persons, animals, and other items, distinguishing the admissible from the excluded. In contrast, the opposition of holy to common divides the divine and associated space, persons, animals, and other items from what is not divine or not associated with the divine through sanctification.[11] The holy/common distinction establishes a boundary around the sanctuary; the unclean/clean distinction determines who or what may cross it. In this chapter, I will explore the various dimensions of the contrast holy/common and will take up the opposition clean/unclean in the following chapter.[12]

I begin with an exploration of the uses of the term "holy."[13] What is holy according to biblical texts? First and foremost, the deity and his attributes are so designated. God's quintessential characteristic is holiness, and it imbues all aspects of his being and presence. His name is holy, as is his arm, his word, and his spirit.[14] He swears oaths by his holiness (Amos 4:2; Ps 89:36 [Eng., 35]). In Isa 6:3, angelic Seraphs praise Yhwh, who is enthroned in his temple: "Holy, holy, holy is Yhwh of hosts, the whole earth is full of his glory." In an archaic poem celebrating Yhwh's victory over Egypt at the Sea of Reeds, the poet asks rhetorically: "Who is like you, Yhwh, among the gods, who is like you, majestic in holiness, awesome with respect to praises, a wonder worker?" (Exod 15:11). The Book of Isaiah refers to the deity frequently as "the holy one of Israel" (qĕdôš yiśrā'ēl).[15] There are many other texts that bear witness to this essential characteristic of Israel's god. Aside from Yhwh himself and his attributes, Yhwh's angelic retinue is also described as a group of holy beings in a number of texts.[16] The Sabbath, Yhwh's day of rest, is holy according to certain passages.[17] The Jubilee year is sanctified according to the Holiness Source (Lev 25:12), and the festivals, too, are called holy in the Priestly and Holiness materials of Leviticus 23 and Numbers 28–29.[18] In Dan 11:28, the covenant is described as sanctified. Space where the divine is said to be present is holy. The site of the burning bush at Horeb, where Yhwh first speaks to Moses, is described as "holy ground," and Moses is ordered by Yhwh not to approach, but to remove his shoes from upon his feet (Exod 3:5). Similarly, when Joshua encounters the angelic commander of Yhwh's divine army at Jericho, he instructs Joshua as follows: "Remove your shoes from upon your feet for the place upon which you are standing is holy" (Josh 5:15). Yhwh's holy mountain is bounded and sanctified by Yhwh's order in preparation for his appearance before the people of Israel (Exod 19:23). The Israelite wilderness camp is constructed as holy space according to certain sources. It contains the tabernacle/tent shrine where Yhwh dwells, and several texts speak of the expulsion of polluted persons from the camp.[19] Narratives describing the conventional military camp of the monarchic era suggest that that camp, too, was often consecrated because of the presence of Yhwh, fighting for the people.[20] Finally, the sanctuary, in its various forms, constitutes the most salient example of bounded, holy territory devoted to the deity's abode and his worship.

Texts suggest the presence of multiple sanctuaries throughout the land of Israel until the centralization of the cult in Jerusalem under Deuteronomistic influence. These are frequently called miqdāš or qōdeš, "holy place," in biblical narrative.[21] Out of bounds to those who are judged unclean, sanctuaries receive pilgrims who bring with them offerings, both obligatory and voluntary, for the deity and the sanctuary's attendants.[22] A number of sources bear witness to the sanctity of various offerings, many of which were intended for the sustenance of the priests and their dependents.[23] The biblical text contains any number of sanctuary descriptions, both detailed and cursory, but three sanctuaries stand out due to the detail of the texts describing them: the desert tabernacle, Solomon's temple in Jerusalem, and the visionary temple described in Ezekiel 40–48. A large complex of chapters from the Priestly Writing provide a detailed treatment of the layout, construction, and staffing of the desert tabernacle/tent (Exodus 25–30, 40).[24] The configuration and construction of the temple of Solomon in Jerusalem is described in detail in 1 Kings 6. This description is supplemented by many other texts in the Deuteronomistic History, various prophetic books, and Chronicles that mention or allude to characteristics of the Jerusalem temple. Besides materials on the tabernacle and temple, the biblical text also contains a series of chapters in the Book of Ezekiel describing in much detail the structure of a future, ideal temple in Jerusalem and its cult. In addition to the extant textual evidence concerning these three sanctuaries, archaeological excavation has brought to light material evidence of cultic life in ancient Israel.[25]

No consistent picture emerges from the details of the various texts describing sanctuary structure, geography, implements, and personnel, for not surprisingly, the various sources have different points of view on these issues and preserve different traditions concerning them. For example, with respect to the legitimate priesthood and its functions, there is much disagreement among the various sources. The Priestly Writing, the Holiness Source, Ezekiel, and Chronicles/Ezra-Nehemiah, among other texts, portray a priesthood open to all male descendants of Aaron—one

family of the tribe of Levi—though closed to others who may make claims
to priestly status (for example, Num 17:5 [Eng., 16:40]). Other male descendants of Levi form a secondary class of cultic functionaries called
"Levites" in the schema of these sources. In contrast, according to Deuteronomy and related materials, all males of the whole tribe of Levi are
priests and may function as such (for example, Deut 18:1–8). No secondary class of "Levites" who are inferior functionaries exists for Deuteronomy and related materials.[26] A third position, present in Ezekiel 40–
48, claims the priesthood only for the descendants of Zadok, Solomon's
high priest. Other Aaronids are, by implication, excluded from the priesthood and classed with the "Levites," the secondary class of cultic functionaries present also in texts of the Priestly Writing, the Holiness Source,
and Chronicles/Ezra-Nehemiah.[27] Differences are evident among textual
witnesses with respect to the slaughter and preparation of the sacrificed
animal. In most texts, including the Priestly Writing, slaughter and preparation are performed by the offerer of the sacrifice, as in Lev 1:5–6; the
priests manipulate the animal's blood on the altar and arrange the pre-
pared pieces of meat on the fire, as in Lev 1:5, 8. But according to Ezek
44:11, slaughter is to be performed by the Levites, not the worshiper
bringing the sacrifice. The construction of the altar for burnt offerings is
a third example of disagreement among biblical sources. According to the
early legal collection known as the Book of the Covenant, the altar was to
be made of unfinished stones (Exod 20:25) or earth (Exod 20:24). Deut
27:5–6, recasting Exod 20:25, speaks only of an altar made of unfinished
stones (see also Josh 8:31). Yet the altar of the Priestly Writing is made of
wood covered with bronze (Exod 27:1–2).

Though biblical materials are inconsistent with respect to many aspects of the cultic life they describe, common characteristics are nonetheless evident. Each sanctuary description presupposes the holiness of the
shrine in question, as well as its need for protection from defilement,
though sources might disagree on exactly what (or who) is holy, or on
gradations of holiness. Each sanctuary description assumes the necessity
of priestly functionaries of some kind who do the work of the cult, however that work is defined. Each sanctuary described has a set of basic
items in common with other sanctuaries described elsewhere: an altar for
burnt offerings, incense altars, and implements for slaughter and preparation of meat. The various sanctuaries share a similar sacred geography
(house or other marker of the deity's presence [for example, a standing
stone]; courtyard with altar of burnt offerings), though details of that
geography may differ from text to text. Archaeological finds have confirmed some aspects of this general configuration. For example, the altar
of burnt offerings at Arad stood in the courtyard in front of the temple
structure. It was made of a mixture of unfinished stones and earth. Two

stone incense altars stood within the temple building, at the entrance to
the holy of holies.[28]

The geography of the sanctuary is described in detail in three sets of
texts: those concerned with the desert tabernacle/tent, those concerned
with the temple of Solomon in Jerusalem, and those concerned with Ezekiel's future temple. The tabernacle/tent complex of the Priestly Writing
consists of the tabernacle, a portable structure constructed of a wood
framework and covered by curtains, which in turn is covered by a tent. It
is surrounded by a courtyard (ḥāṣēr). The tabernacle is divided into two
spaces: an inner and most holy section, containing the ark, and an outer
section in which is placed a table for the display of various items,[29] a
lampstand, and an incense altar in front of the pārōket, a curtain separating the inner section of the tabernacle from the outer section. At the entrance to the tabernacle/tent stands a screen. In the courtyard, before the
entrance, stands the altar of burnt offerings. The basin in which the
priests wash their hands and feet before approaching the altar or entering
the tent is placed between the altar and the outer section of the tabernacle/
tent. The courtyard itself is separated from common space on the outside
of the complex by a series of pillars and curtains, the latter made of linen.
The entryway into the complex is, like the entry into the tabernacle itself,
screened off. Various passages describe the holiness of the tabernacle
complex and its contents: holy anointing oil is used to consecrate the tent,
the ark, the table and all its vessels, the lampstand and its implements, the
incense altar, the altar of burnt offerings and its associated items, and the
wash basin and its base. All are described as "most holy" (Exod 30:26–
29). In addition, the priests themselves are anointed and become consecrated (30:30). They wear special, holy garments when they serve Yhwh
in the tent or when they approach the altar of burnt offerings (Exod
28:40–43), the two occasions when washing hands and feet are required
of them (Exod 40:30–32). Priests are forbidden to pass from the outer
section of the tabernacle into the inner section; the pārōket separates the
two sections of the tabernacle. Only the high priest is permitted to cross
this boundary, and he does so only once a year, on the Day of Atonement
(or, Purgation[30]).

Various texts describe aspects of the sacred geography of Solomon's
temple complex, and 1 Kings 6–7 provides the most detail concerning its
construction. The temple building itself, following a well-known west
Asian architectural pattern,[31] is divided into three sections: the holy of
holies (děbîr), the innermost room in which the Ark of the Covenant is
placed; the "house" (bayit) or "temple" (hêkāl), a large central room containing an incense altar, lampstands, and tables, among other ritual objects; and the porch ('ûlām), at the entry to the temple, at which are
placed two ornamental pillars of bronze, called Yakin and Boaz. The

innermost chamber is the most holy place,[32] separated from the central room by a set of doors (1 Kgs 6:31–32). The central room, for its part, is separated from the porch by its own set of doors (1 Kgs 6:33–34). The temple building is surrounded by a courtyard in which the altar for burnt offerings and other items such as lavers and the molten sea are found. The purpose of the last mentioned item is not clearly stated in 1 Kgs 7:23–26, where its construction is described, though later tradition says that it was used by the priests for washing, as was the laver of the tabernacle court.[33] Determining the configuration of the sacred area surrounding the temple building is not an easy task, though the cumulative impression given by surviving texts suggests an external area divided into two courtyards, an inner court and an outer court. This configuration is clear in later texts and may be present in the earlier descriptions of the external area surrounding the temple. The text of 1 Kgs 6:36 mentions that Solomon built an inner courtyard (ḥāṣēr happĕnîmît) of cut stone and cedar; 1 Kgs 7:12 mentions a "great court" (ḥāṣēr haggĕdôlâ) along with an "inner court of the house of Yhwh" (ḥăṣar bêt yhwh happĕnîmît). The texts 2 Kgs 21:5 and 23:12 state clearly that the temple complex had two courts.[34] In 2 Chr 4:9, part of a later narrative of the temple's construction that draws upon and recasts material from 1 Kings 6–7, the same impression is given using a different vocabulary: it mentions both a "court of the priests" (ḥăṣar hakkōhănîm) and a "great court" (ʿăzārâ haggĕdôlâ).[35] Though 1 Kings 6–7 does not provide any information concerning the division of the outermost perimeter of the temple complex from common space, or the possible division of court from court, other texts mention various gates leading into the complex, implying that some kind of wall must have surrounded it.[36] One text mentions the presence of chambers assigned to individuals near one of these gates.[37] Texts that speak clearly of an inner and outer court suggest that the inner court was separated from the outer court by a wall with gates (for example, Ezek 8:3, 7, 8). Holiness is another subject about which texts describing Solomon's temple say less than one might like. In contrast to the descriptions of the tabernacle, which speak at length about the relative holiness of each section of the sanctuary complex and its contents, texts describing Solomon's temple rarely speak of the holiness of any part or item except for the inner room in which the ark stood. This room is called the "most holy place" or "holy of holies" on several occasions.[38]

Ezekiel 40–48, a text of the sixth century, presents a vision of a future temple establishment that departs in a number of respects from the configurations of both the tabernacle and Solomon's temple. The text is composite in its final form, having experienced extensive expansion and supplementation.[39] I shall attempt nonetheless to reconstruct the configuration of the temple complex and its surrounding territory based on a reading of the final form of the text, though the text in its final form presents difficulties. The temple complex itself, a square measuring 500 cubits by 500 cubits, is surrounded by a large holy district divided into two sections. The first section, measuring 25,000 cubits by 10,000 cubits, is assigned to the priests; the temple complex as well as the priestly dwellings are located here.[40] The second section of the holy district, of the same proportions, is assigned to the Levites. A wall separates the temple complex itself from the space outside of it (40:5).[41] The wall has three gates, one each on the east, south, and north. Each gate complex is stepped, with chambers on each side of each gate (40:6–16, 20–27). The gate complexes lead into the temple's outer court (ḥāṣēr haḥîṣônâ), which itself has a number of chambers. The outer court is territory intended for worshipers and nonpriestly cultic servants, who may not enter the inner court (ḥāṣēr happĕnîmît; haqqōdeš). The people are assisted in the outer court by the Levites, nonpriestly functionaries[42] who are entrusted not only with gatekeeping but also with the slaughter of the burnt offerings and sacrifices of the people according to Ezek 44:11. In each corner of the outer court, there are cooking areas where the nonpriestly servants of the sanctuary process the people's sacrifices (46:21–24). Opposite each of the three outer gates is a corresponding inner gate separating the outer court from the inner court (40:23, 27). The burnt offering and other sacrifices are slaughtered and washed in and around the north inner gate complex (40:38–43). The inner court contains two chambers for the priests (40:44–46), the temple itself and the altar for burnt offerings, which stands before the temple (40:47). The priests' chambers in the inner court are sanctified places where the priests store, process, and eat the most holy offerings (42:13; 46:19–20). When in the inner court, the priests are required to wear their holy vestments; they remove them and change into "other garments" when they leave the inner court and go to the outer court where the people congregate (42:14; 44:17, 19). The holy garments are not to come into contact with the people, lest they sanctify the people (44:19); they are stored in a holy locus within the inner court. The temple building itself is described in Ezekiel 40–41. Like Solomon's temple, it is divided into three parts: the holy of holies,[43] the "temple" (hêkāl), and the porch (40:48–49; 41:1–3). Sets of doors separate the holy of holies from the central chamber and the central chamber from the porch (41:23). Unlike most descriptions of Solomon's temple, Ezekiel 40–48 speaks frequently of the holiness of the sanctuary complex and the territory surrounding it.

Each of the three descriptions of sanctuary space that I have examined speaks directly of gradations of holiness, or at least implies that they exist as a part of the sanctuary system being described.[44] Tabernacle descriptions distinguish subtly three gradations of holiness. The inner section of the tabernacle is holier than the outer section, and the "curtain" (pārōket) marks the boundary between them: "The curtain shall divide for you between the holy and the most holy" (Exod 26:31–33, esp. v. 33). Only the high priest may enter the area designated "most holy," and he enters only one time in the year to effect purgation there. He wears special garments at that time, which he removes after quitting the inner section of the tabernacle; these he leaves in the outer section (Lev 16:23). The outer section of the tabernacle and the altar of burnt offerings are treated as if they possessed a greater degree of sanctity than the rest of the tabernacle complex, with the exception of the tabernacle's inner section. The priests are required to wash their hands and feet before they approach the altar or the tabernacle, and they must wear their holy garments when they do so; to neglect either requirement would result in death.[45] According to the Priestly Writing, these are the only two circumstances when the priests are required to perform the rite of washing and wear their holy vestments. Neither washing nor special clothing are required when the priests do other work in the sanctuary, nor when they eat their sanctified portions of the offerings. The impression that emerges from the various tabernacle descriptions is of a sanctuary sphere with a most holy section within the tabernacle itself behind the pārōket; an area of secondary holiness in the outer section of the tabernacle and around the altar of burnt offerings; and an area of tertiary holiness throughout the rest of the sanctuary complex (the courtyard except for the area around the altar). Screens with curtains mark the transition points between most holy and holy within the tabernacle, between secondary holiness and tertiary holiness at the entry of the tabernacle, and between tertiary holiness and the common at the entry to the sanctuary complex.[46] The altar, which shares secondary holiness with the outer section of the tabernacle, is not screened. Gradations of holiness are also communicated by the materials used to construct and decorate various tabernacle items (for example, gold items in the tabernacle versus bronze items in the court).[47]

Descriptions of Solomon's temple also suggest gradations of holiness, though the evidence here is more difficult to sort out than it is for the tabernacle. Several texts suggest that the inner chamber of the temple (dĕbîr) is holier than the other sections. It is called the "holy of holies," and it is separated from the middle section of the temple building by a set of doors, much as the area behind the pārōket is separated from the outer area of the tabernacle and designated "most holy."[48] A second set of doors separates the middle chamber of the temple from the porch, suggesting its superior holiness to that of the porch area. The inner courtyard, containing the altar of burnt offerings, is very likely understood to be holier space than the outer court, though surviving texts are not explicit about this. A few texts, however, associate the inner courtyard with the priesthood and the outer courtyard with the populace that comes to worship, suggesting the superior holiness of the inner court.[49] It is not clear from extant evidence whether or not the worshiper is forbidden access to the inner court of the temple. Other aspects of the holiness of the temple remain unclear. Did the area around the altar possess the same degree of holiness as the middle room of the temple building, similar to the tabernacle's pattern? And what degree of holiness does the porch possess? A number of questions about the gradations of holiness of Solomon's temple complex remain unanswered, though it appears that there are at least three and very likely more gradations of holiness there.

Ezekiel 40–48 speaks liberally of the holiness of component parts of the sanctuary complex, as well as that of the sacred area surrounding it, though the impression one gets concerning degrees of holiness from this description is rather confused. The whole territory set apart for Yhwh, 25,000 cubits by 20,000 cubits, is holy according to Ezek 45:1. The priestly section of the sacred territory, within which the temple complex and priests' houses are located, is described as "most holy" (qōdeš qodāšîm) by Ezek 45:3, suggesting it is more holy than the section assigned to the Levites. The temple complex itself is separated from the outlying holy territory by a wall with gates leading into the outer court, suggesting another boundary between grades of holiness. The outer court is separated from the inner court by another series of gates. Within the inner court is the altar for burnt offerings as well as the temple itself, divided into three chambers, the innermost called the "holy of holies" (41:4). Though the description of the sanctuary and its surroundings in Ezekiel 40–48 speaks frequently of the sanctuary complex's holiness and that of its surroundings, it makes only a few direct observations about gradations of holiness. Much, however, is implied in the descriptions of the component parts. It is clear that the boundary between the outer court and the inner court is of the highest significance for the circles responsible for Ezekiel 40–48 in its final form. Only priests pass over this boundary; nonpriestly cultic servants and the public are permitted to enter the sanctuary sphere only to the point of the outer court or the gate of the inner court. Priests must wear their holy garments when present in the inner court. Nothing is said about the area around the altar having any greater degree of holiness than any other part of the inner court (43:13–27). Nor is much said directly about the relative sanctity of the temple building, with its tripartite division and doors separating chamber from chamber. The altar area may not possess a greater degree of holiness than the rest of the inner court, given that the whole inner court is off-limits to nonpriests and that priests must wear their holy garments always while in the inner court. By contrast, with the tabernacle, the altar area is said to possess a greater degree of holiness than the court surrounding it, but there is only one court surrounding the tabernacle, and the public may enter it. This may be the reason why the altar area is privileged in tabernacle descriptions but apparently not in Ezekiel 40–48: it functions as a quasi-inner court, where the temple of Ezekiel 40–48 has two separate courts. The temple building, with its chambers separated by doors, probably possesses the greatest sanctity according to the schema of Ezekiel 40–48, with the holy of holies possessing the highest grade of holiness, followed by the large central chamber. The holiness of the porch relative to other parts of the inner court remains unclear, however.

On the whole, questions remain about the holiness schema of Ezekiel 40–48, though the description of the temple complex and its surroundings there suggests at least five or six gradations of holiness, if not more. In ascending order, they are the outer territory assigned to the Levites; then that of the priests, within which the temple complex stands; then the outer court of the temple complex; then its inner court; then the central chamber of the temple (?); and, finally, the holy of holies (the position of the porch remains unclear, as does the position of the altar).[50] This vision of the temple complex and its surroundings presents a sanctuary that in many ways resembles Solomon's temple, with a tripartite house surrounded by two courts, the innermost containing the altar of burnt offerings. Yet it adds a huge holy territory surrounding the temple complex and is much clearer about entry restrictions to the inner court.

Profanation of holiness is a frequent theme in texts concerned with holiness and its preservation. Most cases of profanation mentioned in the biblical text are violations and result in fines or more severe punishment. Yet in contrast to pollution, which is always to be kept far from the sanctuary sphere, profanation can be legitimate in certain, circumscribed contexts.[51] Illegitimate profanation is mentioned in any number of biblical texts. The divine name, the altar, the Sabbath, the sanctuary, holy items (including holy foods), the priest, and the deity himself may be profaned through illegitimate activity, contact, use or behavior. The Sabbath is profaned by prohibited activities construed as labor (see Exod 31:14; Isa 56:2, 6); the altar stones by working them with a tool (Exod 20:25); the divine name by not performing the commandments, swearing falsely, or sacrificing children to the molek (?), among other violations.[52] The holy foods belonging to the priests and, by extension, their dependents are profaned when unqualified persons eat them (see Lev 22:14–16); the sanctuary by a blemished priest approaching the altar or pārōket (see Lev 21:23); a priest by his daughter if she plays the harlot (Lev 21:9). Accidental profanation of holy items off-limits to the common people is a theme in several texts. Lev 22:14–16 (H) concerns a man who is not a priest (or, presumably, a priest's dependent) "who eats a holy item in error." As a result of this violation, the man must return the holy item to the priest,

adding a fine of one-fifth of its value. Lev 5:14–16 (P) is similar, though
the process of rectification is more elaborate. This law concerns a situation in which a common person has committed a violation with respect to
Yhwh's holy things (no specific violation is mentioned). The violator of
this text is obligated not only to pay restitution for the holy item to the
priest but must also pay a fine of one-fifth of its value, and he must bring
a reparation offering ('āšām) of a ram without blemish with which the
priest effects expiation for him.[53] Several texts speak of the ability of cultic servants to violate holiness through illegitimate profanation. One such
text is Num 18:26–32, which concerns the tithes received by the Levites
as payment for their service in the sanctuary.[54] According to this text, the
Levites are obligated to give to Yhwh an offering of 10 percent of the
tithes they receive from Israel, designated the "fat" or most desirable portion of the tithes. This portion is holy (vv. 29, 32)[55] and subject to profanation if it is not handled appropriately by the Levites, who could die as
a result of its mishandling (v. 32).

Legitimate profanation is possible in certain, circumscribed contexts if
proper procedures are followed. These are spelled out in Lev 27:9–33.
Animals, houses, and fields vowed to Yhwh become holy, no longer the
property of the one who vowed them. If the person who has sanctified
them through vowing them wishes to redeem them, he must add one-fifth
to the value of the item being redeemed; then it becomes his once again
(see vv. 13, 15, 19). Part of the tithe of the land may be redeemed—
though it is not a vowed item—through adding one-fifth to its value. This
is not, however, a possibility with the tithe of animals (vv. 31, 33). Devoted items (ḥērem) may not be redeemed under any circumstances (vv.
28–29).[56] The only required offering that Leviticus 27 allows to be redeemed is the tithe of the land; all other required offerings are presumably
not subject to redemption and are therefore comparable to the tithe of
animals or items devoted to Yhwh (ḥērem). The redeemable items listed
in this text are, for the most part, nonrequired items sanctified by choice.
Legitimate profanation, according to Leviticus 27, is therefore mainly a
mechanism to undo a vow. In cases of redemption, the addition of one-
fifth to the value of the redeemed item is similar, as others have noted, to
the fine of an additional one-fifth imposed on those who profane holiness
through acts of violation, as in Lev 5:14–16; 22:14–16. In each case, the
payment functions to enrich the sanctuary and its attendants. It also
serves to remind the person sanctifying an item of the personal cost of
profaning a holy thing.

There is another, unusual example of legitimate profanation that is
obligatory for all worshipers according to a number of texts.[57] Yhwh
makes a claim on the firstborn of animals and humans, which are holy to

him. An example of this claim occurs in Exod 13:2: "Sanctify to me every firstborn (běkôr), that which opens any womb (peṭer kol reḥem) among the children of Israel, among humans and among animals; it belongs to me." Yet a number of biblical texts add an obligatory provision to redeem both the human firstborn and the firstborn of unclean animals.[58] Redemption is accomplished through substitution of a sacrificial animal or through payment of a valuation, depending on the text.[59] In an interesting twist, Num 8:16–18 assert that the Levites, as a group, serve to substitute for the firstborn of Israel: "For utterly given over to me are they from the midst of the children of Israel in place of that which opens any womb, the firstborn of all from the children of Israel; I have taken them for myself. For to me belong every firstborn among the children of Israel, among humans and animals; on the day I struck down every firstborn in the land of Egypt, I sanctified them for myself, and took the Levites in place of every firstborn among the children of Israel."[60] The firstborn who exceed the Levites in number are redeemed through a payment of five shekels to the sanctuary (Num 3:44–51; 18:16). Num 3:41 goes one step further, presenting the animals of the Levites as a substitute for the animal firstborn in Israel.[61]

Holiness and Privilege

The contrast between holy and common, and between holy and most holy, have distinct hierarchical dimensions, and these certainly have implications for the assignment of privilege and the conferring of honor to participants in cultic rites. I begin my examination of the relationship of holiness and status with the priest and his position vis-à-vis common Israelites and other cultic servants. Various traditions bear witness to the privileged position of the priest in the cultic life of Israel. Texts describing the pre-monarchic and early monarchic periods convey the impression that it was possible for any male Israelite to perform priestly functions. But at least one text suggests that it was better to have a member of the tribe of Levi perform them than to have any non-Levite do so (Judg 17:13).[62] Materials of the Priestly Writing, providing some of the most detailed surviving prescriptions for and descriptions of cultic practice, speak of the holiness of the Aaronid priesthood, and Ezekiel 40–48 says as much about the Zadokites. In addition, Numbers 16:1–17:5 (Eng., 16:1–40)[63] and Ezekiel 44 bear witness to the separation of priests not only from common Israelites but from the Levites as well.[64] According to these texts, only priests of cultic servants are holy; they alone are privileged to wear holy garments, eat holy foods, and approach the deity to offer the fat and manipulate the blood.[65] Several texts suggest that the Levites have themselves been separated from the common people, though they are not sanctified (Num 16:8–10; cp. 8:5–22).[66] They have been brought near by Yhwh to serve in the sanctuary in various, nonpriestly capacities (for example, as gatekeepers), though not as near as the priests. Their lack of holiness in this cultic schema highlights the boundary between them and the priests and communicates their inferior status to that of the priests, as do texts that emphasize priestly control of the Levites (Num 3:5–10; 8:19).[67] The congregation possesses less status than the Levites, as they are not separated or brought near at all. Chronicles, in contrast, bears witness to an alternative ideology of holiness and its distribution. In Chronicles, the Levites are said to be holy (2 Chr 23:6; 35:3). The Aaronid priests, however, are most holy according to 1 Chr 23:13.[68] Though Chronicles restricts holiness less rigorously than do the Priestly Writing and Ezekiel 40–48, its schema is nonetheless hierarchical, with the priests possessing a greater degree of holiness than do the Levites, at least according to 1 Chr 23:13.[69]

What of the status of the people with respect to holiness? Like a variety of texts apart from the Priestly Writing, the Holiness Source, and Ezekiel, 2 Chr 30:17–18 speaks of common individuals who must sanctify themselves before cultic participation.[70] Though the exact meaning of this sanctification is not entirely clear, it probably suggests not much more than the acquisition of a temporary state of holiness necessary to participate in cultic rites according to these texts.[71] If this interpretation is correct, then Chronicles and the other texts mentioning the requirement that worshipers sanctify themselves stand in marked contrast to materials in the Priestly Writing and Ezekiel 40–48. These sources restrict holiness among persons to the priesthood alone and go to great lengths to keep what is holy (for example, priestly garments) out of the reach of those who are not, for fear that holiness will be communicated to the congregation (see Ezek 44:19).[72]

Two texts in particular illustrate well the status distinctions separating priest from Levite, and Levite from Israelite, and the hierarchical ramifications of these distinctions according to what one might call the "restricted holiness" schema of the Priestly Writing and Ezekiel 40–48.[73] Num 16:1–17:5 (Eng., 16:1–40) describes an attempted rebellion of Levites led by Qorah against what is presented as the God-given order of cultic service, an order that privileges Aaronid priests over all other cultic servants and over the congregation. The conflict focuses on who does or does not possess holiness and, consequently, in whose midst Yhwh is or is not present. Qorah and his followers claim that the quality of holiness does not reside exclusively with the Aaronid priests; in so doing, they themselves are understood by the text to make a claim to the priesthood

(v. 10).[74] Moses replies that Yhwh will himself demonstrate who is holy and who is privileged to approach him. This is accomplished by means of a ritual contest in which the Levites and Aaron take up censers to burn incense, a priestly prerogative forbidden to nonpriests according to this text. Levitic words pose a challenge to the superior rank of the Aaronids, but it is only through successfully performing the rite of offering incense that the Levites will realize priestly status themselves. Yhwh, however, supports Aaronid hegemony in this piece of Aaronid propaganda. He destroys Qorah and his party, thereby demonstrating to all Israel that only Aaronids are holy and privileged to be priests. The Qorahite censers are beaten into a covering for the altar; they are intended to serve as a sign to the Israelites of the exclusive claim on the priesthood held by the Aaronids (Num 17:5 [Eng., 16:40]). After the challenge of Qorah but before the ritual contest begins, Moses lectures the Levites on their proper station: "Is it a small thing to you that the god of Israel separated (hibdîl) you from the assembly of Israel to bring you near to him to do the service of the tabernacle of Yhwh and to stand before the assembly to serve them? He brought you near (wayyaqrēb ʾōtĕkā), and all your brethren the sons of Levi with you, yet you would seek also the priesthood?" (Num 16:9–10).

The assumption of this text is this: Aaronids possess holiness, in contrast to Levites, and are consequently closer to Yhwh than are the Levites. Thus, they possess a privileged status. But the text acknowledges that the Levites, too, occupy a privileged position, though one that is inferior to that of the Aaronids. Two distinct idioms of cultic privilege are used to describe the position of the Levites vis-à-vis the rest of the congregation: Yhwh separated them (hibdîl)[75] and brought them near (wayyaqrēb) to himself. These idioms recall expressions used in other texts concerning the privileged position of the priesthood.[76] I believe that they are used here in such a way as to indicate that the Levites occupy an intermediate status between that of the priests and the rest of the congregation. The elevated status of the Levites is clearly marked by the use of these idioms of cultic privilege. Yet the claim to high status communicated by the idioms is tempered in the narrative by the assertion that Levitic privilege is less than that of Aaronid priests: the Levites have been brought near, but may not approach with incense; they have been separated, but are not holy.[77] The Priestly narrative concerning the rebellion of Qorah and the Levites assumes that there are three basic status gradations in the cultic life of Israel: (1) preeminent status, assigned to the Aaronid priests and symbolized by their holiness and their proximity to Yhwh (for example, they *alone* approach him to burn incense [Num 17:5 (Eng., 16:40)]; (2) secondary status, possessed by the Levites, who have been separated and brought near to Yhwh, though not as near as the priests, and without the attribution of holiness; (3) tertiary status, possessed by the congregation, though little is said about this in the Qorah pericope.

Ezek 44:10–14, 15–31 also deal directly with priestly and Levitic status distinctions. In these passages, only the descendants of Zadok are priests; all others of the tribe of Levi, including non-Zadokite Aaronids, are classed as Levites.[78] The Zadokite priests, loyal to Yhwh when the people rebelled against him, are privileged: " 'They shall approach me (yiqrĕbû 'ēlay) to serve me, and they shall stand before me to bring near to me (lĕhaqrîb lî) fat and blood,' oracle of the Lord Yhwh. 'They shall enter my sanctuary and they shall approach (yiqrĕbû) my table to serve me' " (vv. 15–16). They alone enter the inner court of the temple[79]; they must wear their linen garments when present there and remove them when exiting, so as not to communicate holiness to the people (vv. 17–19).[80] In contrast, the Levites, though they perform a number of important functions in the sanctuary including gatekeeping and even slaughter,[81] may not approach Yhwh to perform as priest for him, nor may they approach the holy foods reserved for the priesthood and their dependents (v. 13).[82] The restrictions on the Levites are presented as punishment for their disloyalty to Yhwh when Israel went astray after idols.[83] The language of cultic function used in this text is interesting. The focus of priestly privilege is the presentation of the fat and the blood rather than offering incense, the focus of Num 16:1–17:5 (Eng., 16:1–40). Priestly privilege is also represented, as in a number of other texts, by exclusive access to the holy foods. Levites slaughter and control access to the sanctuary sphere,[84] among other functions. But they may not approach holy foods, nor may they offer to Yhwh the fat and the blood, the most privileged elements of animal sacrifice that in all cases belong exclusively to Yhwh (unlike meat, which is often eaten by priests and worshipers).[85] The language of approaching and bringing near shapes this discourse of priestly and Levitic status difference as it does the discourse of Num 16:1–17:5 (Eng., 16:1–40), though these idioms are not used at all of Levitic activity in the cult in Ezekiel 44, in contrast to their use in Num 16:9–10.[86]

The exclusive priestly claim to the presentation of blood and fat, the manipulation of blood on the altar, and the offering of incense to Yhwh secures for the priest his preeminent place in the life of the cult according to biblical representations. Access to the holy foods represents yet another way in which priestly privilege is both realized and communicated in biblical texts. Aspects of the holy foods are dealt with in some detail in two passages from the Holiness Source (Num 18:8–19; Lev 22:1–16) and a passage from the Priestly Writing (Lev 10:12–20).[87] The holy foods are the priesthood's portion of the offerings brought to Yhwh and are intended for the support and sustenance of the priests and their dependents. The holy foods are enumerated in Numbers 18 and, to a lesser degree, in Leviticus 10. They include the "most holy things" (qōdeš qodāšîm), to be eaten in a "most holy" locus only by clean males of priestly lineage: the cereal offering (minḥâ), the purification offering (ḥaṭṭā'ṭ), and the reparation offering ('āšām).[88] In addition, there are offerings reserved for both males and females, presumably of a lower grade of holiness than the "most holy" things: the "raised" offerings (tĕnûpōṭ)[89]; the best of oil, wine, and grain; the first fruits of agriculture; every devoted thing (ḥērem); and the firstborn of clean animals. All members of priestly households may eat these offerings as long as they are clean. Their consumption is not restricted to a holy place; only a clean locus is required.[90]

Yet which individuals are classed as members of the priestly household? This question is explored in Lev 22:10–13. The pericope begins and ends with a warning that the holy foods may not be eaten by an "outsider" (zār). This terminology, when used elsewhere in the Holiness Source and the Priestly Writing, can refer to one who is outside the lineage of priestly males.[91] Here, however, the term refers to anyone, male or female, who stands outside a priestly household. The boundaries of the priestly household are stated explicitly in the verses that fall between the formulaic prohibition in v. 10 and its repetition in a slightly variant form in v. 13. The household includes males of priestly lineage; wives of priests; never-married daughters; daughters who are divorced or widowed, have returned home, and have no children; and slaves of foreign origin acquired for money or born in the household. Excluded from the priestly household are daughters who are married to an "outsider"; widowed or divorced daughters with progeny[92]; widowed or divorced daughters who have not returned to their father's household; and hired laborers. Whether a daughter is included or excluded from the priestly household and the privilege of eating holy foods depends on both her locus (priestly household or elsewhere) and her primary male bond (to an "outsider" husband or to her father).[93] Though hired laborers possess too casual a relationship to the priest to eat the holy foods, slaves of foreign origin are treated differently, for they have been assimilated into the priestly household.[94]

Status distinctions clearly play a role in determining who eats which of the offerings intended exclusively for the priests and their households. At first glance, access to the most holy offerings appears to be conditioned by gender: males of priestly lineage may eat them; women of priestly households may not. But where do the male slaves fit? Lev 22:11 is not specific about which holy foods the slave of the priest may eat, and other texts concerned with the holy offerings do not mention slaves of priestly households. Nonetheless, it is evident that male slaves were not privileged to eat the most holy offerings; these were reserved exclusively for males of priestly lineage. Lev 10:13 and Num 18:9 suggest this interpretation, as do Lev 6:11, 22 (Eng., 18, 29); 7:6. Lev 10:13 and Num 18:9 state that the most holy offerings are for the priests and their sons. Num 18:10 says, ambiguously, that they are for "every male," though Lev 6:11, 22; 7:6 use the unambiguous "every male among the priests/sons of Aaron." Num 18:11 refers to "raised" offerings, intended for both sons and daughters; the same verse states that these offerings are available to "everyone who is clean in your household." Thus, it seems that the mention of priests and their sons is intended to indicate that the offering in question is to be consumed only by males of the priestly line ("every male" of Num 18:10 would then refer to every male of priestly lineage). The mention of sons and daughters, as in Num 18:11, is intended to indicate that the offering in question there is available to the whole priestly household, as the rest of that verse makes clear ("everyone who is clean in your household").[95] Therefore, the distinction between those who have access to the most holy offerings and those who do not is a distinction between males of priestly lineage and all others in the priest's household, male and female. Priests enjoy a primary status that grants them access to the most holy offerings; this status cannot be lost unless a priest were to become polluted.[96] Other members of priestly households enjoy a secondary and contingent status that allows them to eat the other offerings reserved for the priests and their households if they are clean. They acquire this secondary status only because of their primary bond of dependency to the priest who heads their household. When the bond is broken, as in the case of a priest's daughter who marries an "outsider," the privilege is lost. Presumably, a priest's wife who is divorced by the priest and a priest's slave who is sold to a nonpriest would likewise lose their access to holy foods, since it is completely contingent on their association with the priest. The priest's special holiness is, in a symbolic sense, extended to his dependents—with the exception of his sons who possess it in their own right—to allow them to partake of holy foods, since they need to eat and the holy foods are what the priests receive as their due.[97] Nonetheless, the status of priestly dependents (other than sons) is clearly distinguished from that of priests in that they do not have access to the most holy offerings nor to the holy locus where these are consumed.

The Levites of the Holiness Source have no access whatsoever to the holy foods, but they are assigned the tithe for their support.[98] Nonetheless, they are required to tithe the tithe that they receive from the people. That portion, referred to as the "fat part" (ḥēleb) of the people's tithe, is holy, and must be turned over to the Aaronid priests, who will consume it (Num 18:28–29). The reception of the tithe from the people and the giving of a tithe from the tithe to the priesthood functions to confer on the Levites an intermediate status between priest and populace. Their superiority to the populace is evident in their reception of the tithe; their inferiority to the priests results from their having to give to the priests the holy portion, or "fat part," of the tithe. The status of the priesthood is enhanced through the symbolism inherent in their reception of the "fat part" of the tithe. Just as Yhwh alone receives the fat of sacrificial animals (Lev 7:23), so the priests receive the "fat part" of the ingathering of agriculture and horticulture (cp. Num 18:12). It is unlikely that this symmetry is accidental.

Within the priesthood itself distinctions of rank are evident. The high priest of the Priestly Writing and the Holiness Source enjoys a position of preeminence among priests, and his privileged position is articulated in a number of ways. He alone has access to the holiest area of the sanctuary, which he enters once a year on the Day of Atonement (or, Purgation[99]). While there, he performs rites of blood manipulation intended to purge the holy of holies of the pollution of the people of Israel. He does the same for the tent and the altar.[100] He performs these crucial ritual acts not only for himself, but also for his whole priestly house and the people of Israel (Lev 16:17). Some Priestly and Holiness texts seem to suggest that only the high priest is anointed with holy oil.[101] The high priest wears special, distinct garments.[102] He is assigned control of the Urim and Tumim (oracular devices) and the Ephod, among other special items of his ritual repertoire.[103] In contrast to other priests, he cannot bury next of kin (Lev 21:11; cp. 21:1–4). Though other priests may marry a widow, according to the Holiness Source the high priest may marry only an Israelite virgin.[104] Each of these restrictions is intended to protect the holiness of the sanctuary and that of the high priest himself, given his greater access to what is most holy. All of these distinctions, whether of dress and appearance, responsibility, access to what is most holy, or restriction, communicate the high priest's higher status and greater privilege vis-à-vis the rest of the priesthood.

A relationship among holiness, status, and honor, implicit in the various texts that restrict access to holiness, holy territory, and holy things, is articulated explicitly in a number of texts concerned with offerings to Yhwh.[105] The deity, preeminent in holiness and foremost in the hierarchy of status, is also first in honor and expects to be treated in a manner befitting his station. Yhwh is honored by appropriate sacrifices (see Isa 43:23); he is dishonored by inappropriate offerings or by the withholding of what he is due.[106] Mal 1:6–7 illustrates well the offense taken by Yhwh when he is given inferior offerings. In this passage, the binary contrasts father/son and master/slave serve as models for Israel's relationship to its suzerain, Yhwh:

> "A son honors his father, a slave his master.
> If I am a father, where is my honor?[107]
> And if I am a master, where is my reverence?"
> says Yhwh of hosts to you,
> the priests who despise my name.[108]
> And you say, "How have we despised your name?"
> "(You) offer on my altar polluted food . . ."[109]

When offerings are withheld, Yhwh's reaction is similar. In Mal 3:8–10, Yhwh accuses the people of robbing him of the tithes and offerings to which he is entitled and demands that they be brought to him. If they are brought, he will bless the people. Just as Yhwh is appropriately honored when he receives his holy entitlement, so are the priests when they receive their allotted portion of the holy foods and likewise the Levites when they receive their due from the worshiper. Problems arise, however, when people take what is not theirs; in so doing, they dishonor or despise whoever is entitled, challenging his status position. Just as "outsiders" must not approach the holy foods reserved for the priesthood, so priests (and others) must not take what belongs to Yhwh. Just as the priests defend their privileged position (and thus, their honor) from challenges mounted by "outsiders" (see Num 16:1–17:5 [Eng., 16:1–40]), so Yhwh defends his position at the top of the status hierarchy from usurpation by priests.

Just such a scenario is described in 1 Sam 2:12–17, 27–30. Though some of the text of v. 29 is poorly preserved, we nonetheless get the impression that Eli the priest and his sons[110] have taken from Yhwh what does not belong to them.[111] The priests have their assigned portions (v. 28), which establish their status, yet they have taken what is Yhwh's (v. 29). By allowing this, Eli has given his sons precedence in honor over Yhwh: "You have honored your sons more than me" (v. 29). Yhwh responds as follows: "Those who honor me I will honor, and as for those who despise me, they will be diminished" (v. 30).[112] Yhwh then promises to end Eli's priestly line. Clearly, to take what is Yhwh's by right dishonors him and challenges implicitly his claim to superior holiness and preeminent rank. Yhwh responds to this dishonor with severity: Eli's priestly house will experience decline to the point of extinction. Honor here is reciprocal, though unequal: the honor bestowed upon one of lower rank is fitting for that individual; likewise, the honor rendered to someone of higher rank is apt for him. To repay honor is the appropriate response to one who bestows honor; likewise, to return humiliation is the goal of one who is diminished or despised.[113]

A second dimension to the priestly affront against Yhwh is added in 1 Sam 2:12–17. In vv. 15–16, we learn that it was the custom of Eli's sons to have their minions take meat from the worshiper before the fat belonging to Yhwh had been burned, though the worshiper would object to this modification of ritual practice. (Verses 13–14 also imply that the priests would take more than their share of meat from the typical worshiper.) In effect, the sons of Eli have usurped Yhwh's position of precedence through inversion of the order of ritual action. The text assumes that burning the fat, Yhwh's portion, properly precedes the taking of any priestly portion from the worshiper. Eli's sons reverse the proper order of the rites, thereby giving themselves precedence in honor over Yhwh. Verse 17 describes this act as a transgression—"exceedingly great in the eyes of Yhwh"—that treats Yhwh's offering contemptuously.[114] Thus, Yhwh is "despised" by the priests in two ways according to 1 Sam 2:12–17, 27–30: in vv. 27–30, the priests seize what is by right Yhwh's; in vv. 12–17, they take what is theirs (and more!) before Yhwh receives his due. Each ritual act is an affront to Yhwh and a challenge to his status, holiness, and honor; to both he responds severely, in self-defense, thereby restoring himself to his position of preeminence.[115]

Conclusion

The rhetoric of holy and common, of separation, of being brought near or encroaching,[116] so central to biblical texts describing the function and organization of the cult, is a rhetoric charged with social significance. Like the ritual action it describes, cultic rhetoric contributes to the realization and communication of status differences of both individuals and groups. Elites such as the priests and Levites are separated from the rest of the community, set apart to perform the tasks of the sanctuary and oversee its operation. They are brought near to Yhwh by Yhwh to serve him in his sanctuary, in contrast to others who are not brought near; these others, often called "outsiders," must not violate the boundaries that separate cultic functionaries from the populace, or they risk severe punishment, even execution (see Num 18:3–4). To be separated and brought near is to be privileged, to be elevated in rank, as the Levites are according to Num 16:9. In the texts that speak of separating cultic servants and bringing them near, the physical location of a group with respect to holiest space or items (such as the altar) says much about their status vis-à-vis other groups present in the cultic sphere.

Among the ranks of the cultic elite, distinctions of status are evident and are often expressed through the idiom of holiness. Some texts attribute holiness only to the priesthood among cultic functionaries (for example, the Priestly Writing); other materials speak of the Levites as holy and priests as most holy (for example, Chronicles). Among texts that attribute holiness only to the priesthood, the possession of holiness distinguishes the priests both from other cultic servants and from those who do not serve in the cult, giving them a unique standing in the community. Among texts that attribute holiness to both priests and Levites, degree of holiness distinguishes one holy group from the other, and both are distinguished from the rest of the community, who do not possess holiness. In both cases, the holy/common polarity is a powerful tool that generates distinction among groups, conferring on the possessor of holiness a status superior to that of those lacking it. Among the holy, the contrast most holy/holy functions similarly. The opposition most holy/holy is used in texts such as those I have examined to generate distinctions among persons with access to what is sanctified (cultic areas, items; holy foods). Thus, further hierarchical distinctions are made possible among the holy or those who have access to holy things.

In a sanctuary sphere of varying degrees of holiness, the greater an area's or an object's sanctity, the more highly guarded it is and fewer are the persons who may approach it legitimately. The extent of an individual's entry into sanctified territory establishes and communicates that individual's status. The complex series of gates and courts in the temple of Ezekiel 40–48 illustrates well the notion of gradations of holiness and its implications for status differences. The status of the temporal ruler ("the prince") envisioned in Ezekiel 40–48 is realized and communicated eloquently by his ability to enter the sanctuary only to the point of the threshold of the inner court's gate (Ezek 46:2); beyond this point, only priests may go. The people of the land may not even enter to the point of the threshold; they prostrate themselves at the opening of the gate, in the outer court (Ezek 46:3). Thus a hierarchy of status emerges clearly from the degree to which an individual may penetrate the sanctuary complex. Similar observations might be made about the high priest, priest, Levite, and common Israelite in descriptions of the tabernacle.

Sanctification confers concrete privileges that others lack on sanctified elites: they enter certain circumscribed areas of holy territory in the sanctuary; they perform elite ritual acts; they have access to the holy foods. It is not surprising that these privileges, through which the elevated status of sanctified elites is both realized and communicated, are jealously guarded, and texts of priestly provenance (such as the Priestly Writing, the Holiness Source, and Ezekiel) use the threat of fines, extirpation, and execution to discourage usurpation of any sort.[117] The holy foods are an example. Only males of priestly lineage may eat the most holy foods. Holy foods may be eaten by others in their households (wives, daughters, male and female slaves) who are clean, but they are off-limits to "outsiders," who are fined even if they take a holy offering for themselves accidentally (see Lev 22:14–16). Nonetheless, challenges to priestly privilege are narrated in several texts. Qorah and his Levitic allies challenge the priestly claim to exclusive holiness when they take up censers to burn incense, a rite that is reserved for the priests alone. They are destroyed by Yhwh for their attempt to usurp a priestly prerogative by attempting to perform a priestly rite (Num 16:1–17:5 [Eng., 16:1–40]). A second example is the case of the Elide priesthood in 1 Sam 2:12–17, 27–30. Yhwh's position of privilege in the cult is challenged by the Elides, who satisfy themselves before Yhwh receives his due and are said even to seize portions of Yhwh's offering. Their punishment for usurping Yhwh's position of privilege is the decline and eventual extinction of their priestly lineage.

2

Admission or Exclusion:
The Binary Pairing Unclean/Clean

THE opposition of unclean and clean (ṭāmēʾ/ṭāhôr), like holy and common, is ubiquitous among biblical materials concerned with cultic matters.[1] Present both explicitly[2] and implicitly in texts of varying provenance and date, the contrast between what is clean and what is unclean determines who or what gains admission to the sanctuary. It determines who, among those who are privileged, may have contact with holy items or foods. It establishes who may participate in quasi-cultic rites such as those of the Passover. All persons who are classed as clean may enter holy precincts, and appropriate clean animals and items may be brought in as well. Likewise, those who are not defiled may participate in quasi-cultic rites. In contrast, all persons and things classed as unclean are banned from the sanctuary sphere, from contact with holy items, and from quasi-cultic rites requiring purity. With respect to the sanctuary, polluted persons may not enter for the period of their defilement and unclean items are subject to purification before they may be brought in (see Num 31:20, 22–23); unclean animals or birds are, in contrast, entirely proscribed. Participation in quasi-cultic rites is forbidden to all who are impure.[3]

The concern to keep impurity out of the sanctuary sphere and other ritual contexts requiring purity is attested in several early texts. The Elohist's story of the pilgrimage of Jacob to Bethel to erect an altar there begins with Jacob's order to his household to remove alien gods from their midst, purify themselves, and change their clothes (Gen 35:2).[4] The Yahwist's narrative in Exod 19:10–15 tells of the people's preparations to meet Yhwh at Sinai, including their purification[5] and Moses' insistence that they avoid further defilement. In 1 Sam 20:24–26, feasting at the royal court at the New Moon is described, at which only the clean may be present. Though early materials attest to purity concerns, biblical notions of purity are most extensively documented in the Priestly Writing, the Holiness Source, and Ezekiel, with significant material in Deuteronomy and the Deuteronomistic History as well.[6]

Like holiness, pollution, at least as it affects humans, is measured in gradations; the degree of uncleanness determines how long a person is excluded and how difficult it is to regain admission to ritual contexts requiring purity. There is, however, no extant vocabulary of degree comparable to the contrast holy/most holy. The gradations of pollution are implicit, reflected in the amount of time spent unclean, the content and time investment of the rites required to achieve purification, and the expense of purification in terms of the offerings required. According to surviving texts, unclean persons may be excluded for a day, a week, or a longer period of time, depending on the source of the pollution affecting them. Rites of purification vary depending on the source of the defilement in question. In contrast, an unclean animal is simply unclean and subject to exclusion; its uncleanness cannot be purged through the passage of time or by means of rites of purification, though purification of certain unclean objects is possible.[7] The rabbis, elaborating on biblical impurity legislation, developed a vocabulary of degree missing from the biblical text, thereby making explicit what is only implicit in biblical materials.[8]

Some biblical texts entrust to the Levites what was surely one of the fundamental activities in Israel's cultic life: admission of the clean and exclusion of the unclean from the sanctuary.[9] Several other texts oblige the priests to teach purity distinctions to the populace.[10] This concern to distinguish unclean from clean has as its purpose the protection of sanctified space, objects, items, and persons. Biblical sources understand pollution to be the ultimate threat to what is holy; its presence can even force Yhwh to abandon the place where he resides on earth. Several examples of this understanding occur in materials concerned with the camp or the temple. In Num 5:3, a text of the Holiness Source, three types of polluters are ordered expelled from the wilderness camp "that they not defile their camp where I dwell in their midst." Deut 23:15 (Eng., 14) states explicitly that the holiness of the military camp must be preserved, or else Yhwh might abandon it: "For Yhwh your god walks in the midst of your camp to deliver you and to set your enemies before you. Your camp will (therefore) be holy, that he not see among you any untoward thing and turn away from you." In Ezek 43:7–9, Yhwh promises to dwell in Israel's midst forever as long as pollution is kept away from his dwelling place.[11] The ramifications of a polluted, abandoned sanctuary are many: an end to pilgrimage and feasting, to the offerings that support priests and other cultic functionaries, to the fulfillment of vows, to the purgation of sin, and to Yhwh's blessing of the land and its people.[12] In a word, a polluted, abandoned sanctuary would mean the loss of the context of worship, the necessary basis for forging and maintaining a relationship with Yhwh. Therefore, it is no wonder that many prescriptive texts concern themselves with preserving the holiness of the sanctuary and that many narratives find reason to mention purity concerns. Rather than being of interest only to the priestly elite, as is often assumed, distinguishing between the clean and the unclean was very likely a matter of some concern to common Israelites as well. After all, they frequently found themselves in a sanctuary context slaughtering meat, fulfilling a vow, or petitioning the deity, if surviving texts are any indication. Certainly many biblical texts other than the Priestly Writing, the Holiness Source, and Ezekiel bear witness to such an interest in purity.[13]

Agents causing impurity vary. They are associated with death, with sex and reproduction, with disease, with particular animals, birds, insects, and aquatic creatures, and with things alien (for example, alien lands, "idols," behaviors). They include some—though not all—bodily emissions.[14] Biblical sources hint at no single underlying organizing principle that might explain what each of these sources of defilement shares in common with the rest and why some are understood to be more severe than others. Modern scholars have proffered explanations, though none of these is completely convincing.[15] Extant evidence suggests that there were a variety of purity constructions in ancient Israel, not one alone; these differ somewhat with respect to which agents cause defilement, the purification procedures required for its removal, and the locus of the polluted individual before purity is restored.[16] Among the polluting agents witnessed in biblical texts are unclean animals and all animal carcasses; human corpses, bones, or graves; venereal discharges; emissions of semen; the blood of menstruation or parturition; skin disease (ṣāraʿat, inaccurately but commonly translated "leprosy"); excrement; and "idols." Proscribed sexual relations and exile to an unclean land are also mentioned in some texts as causes of pollution. The alien male's foreskin appears to be understood as a defiling agent in several texts; aliens themselves are polluters according to materials in Ezra-Nehemiah.

Sources of Impurity

A variety of animals, birds, insects, and aquatic creatures are unclean according to biblical texts concerned with the diet, and their impurity may be communicated to persons under certain circumstances.[17] Earlier biblical materials bear witness to the dietary dimension of purity. The Yahwist's flood narrative distinguishes clean quadrupeds from those that are not clean and ends with Noah's sacrifice of clean quadrupeds and clean birds (Gen 7:2, 8; 8:20). In Judg 13:7, 14, Samson's mother is enjoined from eating unclean foods since she is to bear a lifelong Nazirite. The classical articulation of dietary restrictions occurs in both Lev 11:1–47 and Deut 14:3–21.[18] Certain creatures are deemed polluting; others are clean and acceptable to eat. Among quadrupeds, those that split the hoof and chew the cud are clean (for example, sheep, goats, cattle, gazelles); all others are unclean and may not be eaten. Among water creatures, those with scales and fins are clean; all others are unclean and forbidden as food. Among insects, only those that have four legs and leap are clean (for example, the locust). The clean birds are not mentioned in Leviticus 11, though Deut 14:11 states that all clean birds may be eaten. All land creatures that swarm are unclean and may not be eaten. The carcasses of unclean creatures are polluting. Persons touching such carcasses are unclean until evening; at evening, they regain their purity. Persons carrying carcasses are polluted until evening and must wash their clothes in order to become clean again. According to Lev 11:39–40, persons who touch the carcass of a clean creature are defiled until evening; those who eat or carry any portion of such a carcass are unclean until evening and must wash their clothes.[19] A number of texts aside from Leviticus 11 and Deuteronomy 14 either forbid the eating of animal carcasses outright (Exod 22:30) or suggest that they pollute those who eat them (for example, Lev 17:15).[20]

Human corpses, bones, and tombs are a second source of pollution known from biblical texts. Though not mentioned in earlier materials, defilement from contact with corpses, bones, and tombs is a major issue in the Priestly Writing and the Holiness Source and is attested in Deuteronomistic materials and occasionally elsewhere.[21] Priestly and Holiness texts provide by far the most detailed information on this type of pollution and prescribe rites of purification necessary for cleansing. Any contact with bones, corpses, or tombs results in impurity for seven days, as does proximity to the locus of a death (Num 19:11, 14, 16). On the third and seventh days of their defilement, polluted persons must purify themselves (Num 19:12, 19; 31:19).[22] The Priestly Writers detail a series of purification rites in Num 19:17–19. Some of the ashes of the red cow, whose processing as an agent of purification was described in vv. 1–10a, are taken and mixed with "living water" (mayim ḥayyim)[23] in a container; then hyssop is dipped in the water by a clean man, who sprinkles the unclean with the purifying mixture on the third and seventh days of their impurity. On the seventh day, persons undergoing purification wash their garments and bathe; at evening, they are clean once again. The sprinkling rite is mandated not only for polluted persons, but also for polluted houses and items. The Holiness Source threatens defiled persons who do not follow the prescribed purification procedures with extirpation of lineage (vv. 13, 20), for by remaining unclean, they have in effect polluted the sanctuary. Num 31:19–24 describes required purification procedures for those in the army returning to the camp after battle. All soldiers who slew persons or had contact with corpses are unclean and must remain outside of the camp seven days. The text mandates purification rites on the third and seventh days, as in Numbers 19, though few details are mentioned (only washing clothes on the seventh day). An apparent gloss at the end of v. 19 includes captives among those who must purify themselves in this manner. Num 5:2–4 (H) also bears witness to the requirement that persons having contact with a corpse are excluded from the camp. Several texts seek to minimize priestly contact with the dead out of concern for the priest's purity and holiness. Holiness materials allow priests contact only with the corpses of close kin (mother, father, son, daughter, unmarried sister); all others, including wives, are out of bounds (Lev 21:1–4). Ezek 44:25–27 takes the same position but adds that the priest defiled by contact with a corpse must bring a purification offering to the temple when he is once again clean. The high priest, according to the Holiness Source, may not have contact with any corpse (Lev 21:11). The person bound by a Nazirite vow is similarly restricted (Num 6:6–7 [P]).[24] These limitations on priestly and Nazirite contact with corpses are no surprise, given the sanctity of the priest or Nazirite according to the texts that describe their respective death-related restrictions.

Genital discharges unconnected to seminal emission, menstruation, and parturition form a third class of impurities. The male with a discharge (zāb) is mentioned in one early text, David's curse of his nephew Joab and Joab's lineage: "Let there not be missing from the house of Joab a man with a discharge (zāb), who has skin disease (mĕṣōrāʿ), who grasps the spindle, who falls by the sword, and who lacks food" (2 Sam 3:29).[25] Num 5:2, a text of the Holiness School, excludes three classes of polluted persons from the wilderness camp: those who have skin disease, those who are afflicted with a discharge, and those who have had contact with a human corpse. Their exclusion is intended to protect the camp, Yhwh's dwelling place, from pollution. Discharges receive detailed treatment in the Priestly Writing's extended discourse on impurities. Lev 15:2–15 concerns the pollution and the purification rites of the man who has a discharge; Lev 15:25–30 treats the woman so affected in a somewhat abbreviated manner. Persons with a discharge are unclean for the period of the discharge and for seven additional days after the discharge has stopped. Any beds or furniture upon which affected persons lie or sit are polluted, as are inanimate objects touched by them. Lev 15:11 states that affected persons cease to communicate defilement by touch as long as they wash their hands (before touching?). Pollution is communicated secondarily when clean individuals touch persons with a discharge, are spit upon by such persons, or touch/sit upon polluted beds or furniture. Once a discharge has ceased, the affected individual remains unclean for a period of seven days, during which rites of purification are required (washing clothes, bathing).[26] On the eighth day, the person seeking to become clean brings two birds to the priest, one as a burnt offering and the other as a purification offering. The priest then effects purgation on behalf of the person because of the polluting discharge.

Emissions of semen are a source of defilement attested in a number of sources of varying provenance, including early materials.[27] In 1 Sam 21:2–10 (Eng., 1–9), Ahimelek, priest of the Nob sanctuary, allows David's men to eat holy bread as long as they have kept themselves from women. This restriction on contact with women, witnessed also in the Yahwist's Sinai narrative in Exod 19:14–15, is apparently a reference to the pollution caused by an emission of semen during sexual congress. David goes on to explain to the priest that women are always forbidden to his men, whether they are on a "common journey" or, by implication, a holy one (v. 6 [Eng., 5]). Thus, the men in David's war camp are always clean, whether or not the camp is sanctified. The war camp's potential for holiness also probably lies behind the adamant refusal of David's officer Uriah to visit his wife Bathsheba and have sexual relations with her while away from the war camp (2 Sam 11:9, 11). The presence of a man in the war camp who is polluted because of a seminal emission is at issue in Deut 23:10–12 (Eng., 9–11). This text requires the removal from the war camp of any man who is unclean due to an emission of semen. "At the coming of evening," says the text, "he shall wash in water, and when the sun has set, he may come into the midst of the camp." The Priestly Writers' teaching on impurities includes a section that concerns seminal emissions and the rites of purification mandated for persons defiled by them. Lev 15:16–18 states that a man who experiences an emission of semen is unclean until evening; likewise a woman who has had sexual relations with him and any garment or skin that semen has touched. The mandated rites of purification are the same for the man, woman, or object affected: washing in water and waiting until evening to become clean again. Finally, the seminal emission is among the sources of defilement listed by the Holiness Source that disqualify a priest from contact with holy foods. He, like others whose defilement lasts for only a day, must wash himself in water; when the sun sets, he is clean once again and may eat holy foods (Lev 22:4–7).

Menstruation and parturition are represented as severely polluting in biblical texts, as they are in many cultures past and present.[28] In 2 Sam 11:4, Bathsheba's process of purification from menstrual defilement is given passing reference.[29] The Priestly Writers' treatment of menstrual impurity (niddâ), found in Lev 15:19–24, is somewhat detailed, and not unlike their discourse on the man and woman with a genital discharge. The menstruant, according to this text, is unclean seven days, and all who touch her are polluted until evening.[30] Like the man or woman with a discharge, everything the menstruant sits on or lies on becomes polluted; all who make physical contact with such items are unclean until evening and must wash their clothes and bathe to regain their purity. Intercourse with the menstruant communicates her primary (and severe) impurity to

her sexual partner: "Her menstrual impurity will be upon him" (v. 24).
He becomes unclean seven days, and like the menstruant herself, he has
the power to communicate defilement to others: "Any bed on which he
lies is unclean." As with the woman with a discharge, the text says nothing explicit about the menstruant's rites of purification. I assume that the
text requires these implicitly, given that washing clothes and bathing are
mandated explicitly for persons who become unclean indirectly—and in
a much less severe way—through contact with items polluted by the menstruant.[31] The Holiness Source treats the menstruant in passing in Lev
18:19 and 20:18 from the perspective of sexual relations. Intercourse
with her is forbidden in Lev 18:19, and 20:18 penalizes such activity with
extirpation. The Priestly Writing mentions no such penalty in its treatment of sexual relations with the menstruant. Aside from the menstruant's partner taking on her pollution, no penalty as such is mandated by
the Priestly Writers.

The parturient is treated in Lev 12:1–8, a Priestly text. If she bears a
boy, she is unclean seven days, and the text compares her impurity to the
defilement of menstruation. Thirty-three additional days of purification
are required of her, during which she may not have contact with holy
items or enter holy space. If the parturient gives birth to a girl, she is
unclean fourteen days in the manner of her menstrual impurity and must
spend sixty-six days purifying herself. Nothing is said about rites of purification required of the mother, though the text does state that when
clean, she must bring a bird and a lamb to the priest as purification offering and burnt offering, no matter what the sex of the child. It is not clear
why the birth of a girl doubles the time period of the mother's uncleanness and that of her purification, nor is it evident why the same offerings
are required at the end of each purification process, given the asymmetry
of the processes in terms of time. The lengthy period of time mandated for
the parturient's purification even in the case of a male child may have
something to do with the continued loss of lochial fluids that can occur
for weeks after a woman gives birth; the text seems in fact to allude to
this.[32] The termination of the mother's initial period of pollution at the
seventh day in the case of a boy, the day before the boy's circumcision,
may not be accidental, though I am hard-pressed to explain its significance.[33] Nothing is said in this text about the parturient's potential to
transmit defilement to others, though the analogy made to the menstruant's pollution may be intended to imply something about transmission
potential as well.[34] Finally, the text says nothing about the child's purity
or lack thereof.[35] Though the treatment of the parturient raises a number
of difficult questions, it is clear that birth is represented as severely polluting, at least for the mother, and probably for others who have contact
with her.

Skin disease, known in the Hebrew Bible as ṣāraʿat, is a major polluter in biblical purity constructions. Frequently mistranslated "leprosy," ṣāraʿat is witnessed in texts both early and late.[36] It is one of two defiling conditions mentioned in David's curse of Joab's lineage (2 Sam 3:29), and it is also the focus of Elisha's execration of his servant Gehazi (2 Kgs 5:27). Among early materials concerned with skin disease, Num 12:2–15 stands alone in its richness of detail. In v. 2, the Elohist tells of Miriam and Aaron's challenging Moses' exclusive claim to prophesy.[37] Miriam is punished by Yhwh, who gives her skin disease, a condition whose color is compared to that of snow in v. 10. Aaron begs Moses to intercede on Miriam's behalf. His words to Moses are most revealing with respect to how the text views skin disease: "Let her not be like one who is dead, whose flesh is half consumed when he comes forth from his mother's womb" (v. 12). As long as Miriam has the condition, she is "like one who is dead." The comparison of Miriam to a newborn's diseased corpse suggests that the writer views skin disease as a form of symbolic death.[38] The narrative ends with Miriam's expulsion from the camp for seven days. It is not clear whether Miriam has been healed of the condition at the time of her removal, though this seems possible. The alternative is to assume that Yhwh did not heal her until the seventh day, at which time she was readmitted to the camp. In either case, the text bears witness to both the physical separation of the afflicted individual from the community and her symbolic association with the dead.

Later materials bear witness to a serious concern with skin disease. Deut 24:8–9 urges Israel to obey priestly teachings concerning skin disease and to remember what Yhwh did to Miriam (alluding to Numbers 12 or at least the tradition preserved there). Num 5:2, a Holiness text, mandates removal from the camp of all who are afflicted with skin disease and discharges, as well as those who have had contact with corpses. The Priestly narrative in Leviticus 13–14 is by far the most detailed biblical description of skin disease and contains a complex series of rites that the Priestly Writers require of the afflicted individual in order to regain purity. The text describes the various manifestations of skin disease and how a diagnosis of it is to be made by the priest. Once firmly established, the diseased individual is declared polluted and separated from the community: "As for the person afflicted with skin disease, his garments shall be torn, his hair shall hang loose, and he shall cover (his) upper lip; 'unclean, unclean' he shall call out. All of the days during which he is afflicted he shall be unclean. He is defiled: alone he shall dwell; outside of the camp shall be his residence" (Lev 13:45–46). Tearing clothes and allowing the hair to hang loose are mourning gestures known from other texts, as is covering the upper lip.[39] These ritual actions, like Aaron's comparison of Miriam to a corpse in Num 12:12, suggest a symbolic association of skin disease with death and afflicted individuals with the dead. Long-term physical isolation from the community, mandated here for the diseased person, may also have similar symbolic significance.

What of the suspected case of skin disease, which is not yet proven? A person who manifests suspicious symptoms is "shut up" (sgr [Hiphil]) for an interval of seven days (13:4, 5, 11, 21, 26, 31). If the diagnosis remains uncertain, that individual is "shut up" again for another seven-day period. If found to be unaffected at the end of one or another seven-day interval, the formerly suspect person is declared clean. The washing of clothes is mandated for the person who has been "shut up" more than once (vv. 6 and 34).[40] The locus of the individual who is "shut up" is not indicated by the text, nor is the exact nature of this action. Does "shutting up" in Leviticus 13 mean physical removal from the camp? Num 12:14–15 suggests that it does. This passage uses the same verb to describe Miriam's expulsion from the camp after she is afflicted with skin disease.[41] The washing of clothes mandated for the person who might have had skin disease but does not is quite striking, as it is a purification procedure. Why require a purification rite for one who was never unclean? Perhaps the clothes washing should be viewed as a prophylactic rite, required because the suspect person's condition resembles defiling skin disease enough to warrant protective measures such as washing clothes. After all, the text does conceive of the possibility that the suspect individual could, even after being declared clean by the priest, still manifest symptoms of defiling skin disease (Lev 13:7, 35). The alternative, which I find unlikely, is to assume that the text actually sees the suspect individual as unclean while suspect.[42]

The purification rites mandated for the individual healed of polluting skin disease are presented in some detail in Leviticus 14. They are among the most complex rites of transition described in any biblical text, and the meaning of a number of the individual components of these rites is not always evident. On the day of the afflicted individual's healing, the priest examines him outside of the camp. If the disease is indeed healed, the priest orders the rites of purification to begin. Two clean birds, cedar wood, crimson thread, and hyssop are required for the first stage of the healed person's transition back to purity and back to the community from which he has been separated. One of the two clean birds is slaughtered, and its blood is collected in a clay vessel over "living waters"; the cedar wood, thread, hyssop, and living bird are then dipped into the blood. The priest then sprinkles blood seven times on the body of the individual being purified, and after this, the living bird is released.[43] The text seems to suggest that the sprinkling itself effects purification (v. 7), though it continues to refer to the individual as "the one being purified" (hammiṭṭahēr) and speaks of the result of each further stage in the ritual process the same way. After the blood has been sprinkled and the bird released, the individual being purified washes his garments, shaves all of his hair, bathes, and, in the words of v. 8, "is clean." He may enter the camp at this point, though he is required to dwell outside of his tent for seven days. On the seventh day, he repeats the series of rites described: he shaves all of his hair, including that of his head, beard, and eyebrows, washes his garments, bathes, and "is clean" (v. 9). On the eighth day, the individual being purified brings offerings to the sanctuary. Two male lambs, a one-year-old ewe, a grain offering mixed with oil, and a measure of oil are brought to the priest. One of the lambs is slaughtered and offered as a reparation offering ('āšām), and some of its blood is placed by the priest on the right ear lobe, the right thumb, and the right great toe of the individual being purified. The priest pours some of the oil into his own left hand. Some of this oil is sprinkled by the priest seven times before Yhwh with his right finger, and some is placed over the blood on the ear lobe, thumb, and toe of the individual being purified. The rest of the oil in the priest's hand is put on the head of the formerly polluted individual. One of the other animals is then sacrificed as a purification offering. The recovered individual thus reaches the end of his purification rites. The description of the purification rites of this person speaks clearly of stages in the transition from pollution and separation from the community to purity and aggregation.[44] Each stage in the ritual process is marked by a series of mandated rites that contribute to the individual's purification and bring the individual one step closer to rejoining the community. At the end of the first series of rites, the person being purified may enter the camp, though he must remain outside of his dwelling. After a week, shaving, washing clothes, and bathing are repeated, followed by offerings and other unusual rites of blood and oil manipulation on the eighth day. The completion of these rites results in the individual's complete purification and aggregation. The time, effort, and expense required for the formerly afflicted individual to become clean once again and to rejoin the community communicate the extreme degree of his defilement.

Proscribed sexual relations are constructed as polluting in several texts of varying provenance.[45] Deut 24:4 forbids the return of a twice-divorced woman to her first husband "for she is," says the text, "defiled."[46] The reason for her defilement and its parameters are unclear, though it may relate only to her first husband.[47] Whether or not her defilement is communicable is also unclear, though if it is to serve as an effective deterrent to remarriage, it presumably is. The twice-divorced woman's pollution is described as if it were a permanent condition. The Priestly text Num 5:11–31 describes in detail the ordeal that a woman suspected of adultery by her husband must endure. On a number of occasions in that narrative, the woman, if guilty, is said to be defiled; if innocent, she is described either as "not defiled" or "clean" (v. 28). This is not unlike Lev 18:20, a Holiness text in which adultery pollutes (cp. 18:23, where the same thing is said about sexual relations between a man and an animal). In the larger context of Leviticus 18, the editorial framework of the chapter asserts that all violations enumerated there are polluting and result in the defilement of the land: "You shall not defile yourselves in any of these (ways) for through all of these, the nations whom I am driving out before you defiled themselves, and the land was defiled" (18:24–25).[48]

A variety of texts associate things alien with defilement. Foreign lands, the iconic representations of gods other than Yhwh ("idols"), and behaviors alleged to be characteristic of foreigners defile according to a number of texts. Several other passages of varying provenance seem to suggest that the alien male's foreskin is an agent of pollution, and certain texts in Ezra-Nehemiah go so far as to suggest that all aliens are polluters. Alien lands are associated with defilement in such texts as Amos 7:17; Hos 9:3–4; and Ezek 4:13. In Amos 7:17, the prophet Amos, speaking of Israel's impending doom, reports Yhwh's words to Amaziah, the priest of Bethel: Amaziah's children will die by the sword, his land will be taken over by others, and he "will die in an unclean land." Similarly, Hos 9:3–4, speaking of exile as Israel's future punishment, appears to draw upon this association of alien lands and uncleanness, specifically with respect to food: "They shall not dwell in the land of Yhwh. Ephraim will return to Egypt, and in Assyria they will eat what is unclean." Ezek 4:13 is similar. The priest-prophet Ezekiel, who has always avoided polluting foods, is ordered to defile himself as a public, symbolic act, by eating food polluted through cooking on human excrement. He is to do so in order that the people might know that "they will eat their food unclean among the nations where [Yhwh] will drive them."[49] Ps 137:4, "How can we sing a song of Yhwh in an alien land?" may allude not only to the pre-exilic tradition restricting Yhwh's worship to his land, but also to the uncleanness of the land where the exiles find themselves, and therefore the impossibility of cult there.[50]

"Idols" are polluting in a number of texts, including material of a relatively early date. In Gen 35:2, a text of the Elohist, Jacob orders his household to rid themselves of iconic representations of alien gods and to purify themselves before going to Bethel, where Jacob will erect an altar to Yhwh: "Turn aside the alien gods that are in your midst, and purify yourselves and change your clothes." Later texts bear abundant witness to the notion that "idols" pollute. In Ezek 36:18, Yhwh explains his reasons for destroying Judah: "I poured out my wrath upon them, because of the blood that they poured out upon the land, and because of their idols (with which) they polluted it."[51]

Behaviors allegedly characteristic of certain alien groups are defiling according to the Holiness Source's framing materials of Leviticus 18 and

20 and to several of the laws in that collection (for example, Lev 18:20, 23). Actions such as incest, adultery, sexual intercourse between males, human-animal sexual relations, and child sacrifice are described as polluting "abominations," characteristic behaviors of the Canaanites (Lev 18:24–30; 20:22–23) or of the Canaanites and the Egyptians (Lev 18:2–5). These actions, according to the framing materials of Leviticus 18 and 20, resulted in the expulsion of the previous dwellers of Canaan from the land. Should Israel do any of these "abominations," it too will be cast out. A number of texts can be read to suggest that the alien male's foreskin is an agent of pollution. In the Yahwist's ancestral narrative of Genesis 34, Shechem the Hivvite is said to have "polluted" Jacob's daughter Dinah when he raped her (vv. 5, 13, 27). This pollution is described as if it were a long-term condition rather than the temporary defilement caused by an effusion of semen. It may well be the result of Dinah's contact with Shechem's foreskin.[52] Isa 52:1, a text of the third quarter of the sixth century, envisions a future when the holy city, Jerusalem, will not again be invaded by aliens who are uncircumcised and unclean. The text can be read to suggest that the uncleanness of these alien invaders is due to their lack of circumcision.[53] Finally, Ezek 44:7 banishes uncircumcised alien males from the future temple envisioned in Ezekiel 40–48. This passage, too, may be understood to suggest that the aliens in question are agents of defilement. The verb ḥll is used of the aliens in v. 7. A term most frequently attested in the Holiness Source and Ezekiel, it usually means "to profane," though a number of passages demonstrate that it is also used by the Holiness Source, Ezekiel, and other texts with the meaning "to pollute" (as if it were the equivalent of lĕṭammēʾ).[54] The notion that all aliens are polluters is found in Ezra-Nehemiah. Here, circumcision and the worship of other gods are not issues; defiling aliens include women, children, and circumcised men who worship Yhwh. Marriage with aliens is understood to produce pollution of the bloodline.[55]

Excremental defilement is not mentioned in the Priestly Writing or the Holiness Source, though it is known from a number of other texts. Deut 23:13–15 (Eng., 12–14) seems to suggest that excrement is defiling, as does 2 Kgs 10:27. But two sixth-century narratives make the connection between excrement and defilement unambiguously. Ezek 4:9–15 narrates one of a series of symbolic acts that Yhwh orders the priest-prophet Ezekiel to perform. Ezekiel's symbolic acts dramatize and elaborate upon different aspects of the coming doom of Judah and Jerusalem, including siege, starvation, and exile.[56] In 4:9–15, Yhwh tells Ezekiel to make bread from a mixture of various grains, beans, and lentils and eat it during the extended time he is lying on his side to symbolize the years of punishment Yhwh will mete out to Israel and Judah. The bread, itself a symbol of coming shortages that portend starvation, will be baked in the sight of the people upon human dung, to symbolize the defilement of exile. Ezekiel objects immediately to this command; as a priest, he suggests, he has never defiled himself, from his youth to the present. Yhwh relents somewhat and allows him to use (apparently less-polluting) animal dung instead.[57] By polluting himself publicly, Ezekiel sends a clear and ominous message to those who are watching him: Judah and Jerusalem will go into exile, and cult will cease as a result.

A second text that suggests the polluting nature of excrement is Zech 3:1–10. Here, the high priest Joshua is on trial in heaven, and the text begins with Yhwh's rebuking the heavenly prosecutor (the Satan) and clearing Joshua of the unstated charges against him. Joshua, we are told, is standing before the court in garments covered in excrement. When Yhwh clears him, he orders the removal of these defiled garments and their replacement with festal attire. This act, according to Yhwh, symbolizes the removal of Joshua's iniquity. Zechariah the prophet, witnessing these proceedings, then suggests that a clean turban be placed on Joshua's head. Thus is Joshua cleansed. The Angel of Yhwh then promises Joshua a restoration of the temple and the cult if he walks in Yhwh's ways. Where Ezek 4:9–15 concerns the inevitable pollution of the priesthood that will result from exile to an unclean land, Zech 3:1–10 restores the high priest's purity through changing his clothes and promises a restoration of the cult. In both texts, excrement is used as a symbol of defilement.[58]

Degrees of Pollution and the Requirements of Purification

Degrees of pollution, comparable to gradations of holiness, are evident in extant biblical materials concerned with issues of defilement and purity, though no formal vocabulary of degree survives that might be compared to "holy" and "most holy." The notion of gradation or degree is, however, implicit in many texts describing polluting agents and the purification procedures mandated for those who are defiled by them.[59] Each type of defilement has its own purification requirements, and these frequently differ from the requirements mandated for other sources of pollution. Purification in every case requires the passage of a set period of time and may also demand the performance of specific rites; the locus of the individual during the period of pollution and the process of purification may require change as well. Some polluted individuals must wait one day before they can be clean again; others are required to wait a week or longer. Some polluted persons must bathe and/or wash their garments before they are purified; others, with more serious forms of defilement, might also be required to undergo additional purification rites[60] and bring offerings to the sanctuary. The value of the offerings imposed by prescriptive

texts differs depending on the source of pollution. Some offerings represent a minimal investment on the part of the individual seeking purification; others represent a considerable expense. According to certain texts,
some polluted persons are permitted to remain in the camp/community;
others are expelled for the duration of their defilement. It is in these distinctions that gradations of defilement may be discerned. Stages of purification, like gradations of defilement, are also evidenced in surviving
materials. Each purifying rite in a series of such rites brings the person
being cleansed a step closer to participation once again in the cultic life of
Israel. Here, some formal vocabulary of degree does survive in certain
texts.[61]

All forms of pollution result in the separation of the polluted individual
from cultic and quasi-cultic settings and from holy items. But some polluting agents render an individual unclean only "until evening," the minimum period of time that any polluted person can be unclean.[62] I will refer
to such defilement as "simple" impurity, to be distinguished from
"grave" or "serious" impurities that pollute an individual for seven days
or longer. The man who has experienced a seminal emission is one example of an individual who has become unclean because of a simple impurity. According to Lev 15:16–18, a text of the Priestly Writing, he is unclean until evening, as is his sexual partner and anything that his semen
has touched. That text requires the man to bathe sometime before evening: "He shall wash all of his flesh in water, and be unclean until evening." His partner must also bathe, and any garment or skin that the
semen has touched must be washed. There is no indication in the text that
persons polluted by an emission of semen must change locus for the period of their defilement and purification. Lev 15:16–18 seems to assume
only that such persons avoid the sanctuary and all things holy. Deut
23:11–12 (Eng., 10–11) also concerns seminal defilement, but presents a
somewhat different perspective from Lev 15:16–18. In this text, in contrast to Lev 15:16–18, the man polluted by an effusion of semen must
leave the camp (v. 11 [Eng., 10]), and he may not reenter it until the sun
has set and he has completed his purification procedure. The reason for
Deuteronomy's exclusion of the polluted individual from the camp is
given in 23:15 (Eng., 14): "Your camp shall be holy." In contrast, the
Priestly Writers allow most polluted persons to remain in the camp because the camp itself is not constructed as holy, only the tabernacle.[63] The
rite of bathing imposed by Lev 15:16–18 is also required in Deut 23:12
(Eng., 11), but the latter text is specific about when the rite occurs: "At
the coming of evening."[64] In contrast, Lev 15:16 says only that it must
occur sometime before evening.

Aside from those defiled by contact with semen, there are other persons
polluted for only one day. These include individuals who have had con-

tact with serious impurity spread by someone such as the man or woman
with a discharge or the menstruant.[65] Contact might be direct or indirect;
it includes touching the serious polluter or touching items defiled by the
serious polluter (such as a bed, chair, or saddle); the serious polluter
might also transmit impurity by spitting on clean persons. Individuals
defiled by direct or indirect contact with a serious polluter must bathe and
wash their garments, and they remain unclean until evening. It is interesting that it makes no difference whether contact with the serious polluter
is direct or indirect: the purification requirements are the same. To bathe
and to wash garments is a more demanding requirement than the bathing
required of persons having contact with semen. This suggests that seminal pollution is constructed as less severe than defilement through even
indirect contact with a serious polluter. Thus, gradations of pollution
may be discerned even among those who are unclean for only one day.

Persons with serious impurities are polluted for at least seven days,
some for longer periods of time. Though some texts treating serious impurities say little or nothing about the rites required of the individual
being purified, others present elaborate processes of purification. The
menstruant is defiled seven days according to Lev 15:19, but the text
makes no mention whatsoever of required purification procedures.[66] Persons having contact with a corpse are unclean seven days, with purification rites mandated for the third and seventh days according to both the
Priestly Writing and the Holiness Source.[67] The purification rites of the
individual polluted by corpse contact include bathing, washing clothes,
and being sprinkled with a special purifying solution.[68] Purity is achieved
at evening on the seventh day. The man or woman with a discharge is
unclean for the period of the discharge and for an additional seven days
of purification after it stops. Only the passage concerning the man with a
discharge specifies rites of purification (bathing and washing clothes), and
nothing is said about when these are to take place. On the eighth day,
offerings are mandated for both the man and the woman (Lev 15:13–14,
28–29). The individual with skin disease is, like the person afflicted with
a genital discharge, unclean for the period of the affliction. When the
disease has been healed, the individual who has recovered undergoes an
initial, elaborate series of purification rites: sprinkling with blood from a
clean bird, shaving the body, bathing, washing garments. These culmi-
nate in his freedom to enter the camp. He must, however, spend seven
days outside of his tent. On the seventh day, the person being purified
undertakes a second, less elaborate series of purification rites, and on the
eighth day, he offers sacrifices. The parturient is unclean seven days if the
child is male, fourteen days if female. An additional, lengthy period of
purification is prescribed for the mother, thirty-three days if she has borne
a boy, sixty-six if a girl. During this additional period of purification, the

parturient must not have contact with holy items and she must avoid the sanctuary. At the end of her period of purification, she is required to bring offerings to the sanctuary (Lev 12:1–8). As with the menstruant and the woman with a discharge, nothing is said explicitly about mandatory purification rites such as bathing and washing garments, though the text suggests subtly and indirectly that such rites are required of these women, just as they are of all serious polluters, including the man with a discharge.[69]

Gradations are discernible even among the serious impurities. These might be expressed in terms of the locus of the polluter before purification is completed; the number, extent, and repetition of the rites required for purification; and the offerings owed by the polluter once all impurity has been removed. The Priestly Writers, for example, distinguish between the person afflicted with skin disease and all others who are defiled, both by serious and simple impurities, by removing that individual from the camp but allowing all others to remain there (Lev 13:46; 14:3). The Holiness School may also recognize degrees of serious pollution when it requires the expulsion of the person who has had contact with a corpse, the person with a discharge, and the person afflicted with skin disease, but makes no mention of removing the menstruant or parturient.[70] The Deuteronomists, in contrast, appear to exclude all polluters from the camp without exception.[71] Thus, the Deuteronomists do not use locus to differentiate degrees of impurity, since all who are unclean are removed. The complexity and number of required purification rites, and the number of times rites are repeated, is a second way in which texts might distinguish degrees of serious impurity. Where the man with a discharge is required only to bathe and wash his clothes once before becoming clean, the person who has had contact with a corpse must perform these rites twice and must also be sprinkled with a special, purifying solution. Failure to perform all of these rites, the text states, will result in continued pollution and severe punishment (Num 19:12–13, 20). Finally, gradations of serious impurity might also be communicated by the value of the offerings required of the purified individual. The woman formerly afflicted with a discharge is required to bring two birds to the priest to complete her process of purification. In contrast, the parturient must offer a lamb and a bird, and the person who has recovered from skin disease three sheep, a measure of oil, and a grain offering. The difference in value among the offerings of these three individuals hardly needs to be pointed out. The expense of purification is greater for the parturient than for the woman or man who has recovered from a discharge, and it is greater still for the individual who formerly had a skin affliction.

Distinct stages of purification are evident from several extant texts. The best example is Leviticus 14. On the day that the person formerly afflicted with skin disease is healed, that individual undergoes an elaborate series of purification rites: blood sprinkling, release of a live bird, washing garments, shaving the body, and bathing. When these rites are completed, the person being purified enters a second stage of the purification process during which access to the camp is permitted but access to the domicile is still forbidden. This stage of the purification process lasts seven days. On the seventh day, three of the purification rites performed on the initial day of cleansing are repeated: shaving, washing garments, and bathing. Though burdensome, these rites are less elaborate than those of the first day of purification, suggesting that the severity of the impurity has been reduced both by the initial series of rites and by the passage of time. Once the second series of rites is completed, the person formerly afflicted with skin disease enters a third and final stage in the purification process, during which offerings are brought to the tent of meeting. At this stage, all impurity has been removed, allowing the formerly diseased person access to the sanctuary. But it is not until the fulfillment of the obligations of the eighth day (offerings, blood and oil manipulation by the priest) that the individual who has recovered from skin disease is truly cleansed and once again fully joined to the community.[72]

Stages of the purifying process may also be discerned in other materials, though these lack the richness of detail characteristic of Leviticus 14. The description of parturient's purification is one example (Lev 12:1–8). After either seven or fourteen days of impurity, the new mother enters a stage of purification lasting thirty-three or sixty-six days. During this time, she is forbidden to enter the sanctuary sphere or have contact with holy items. Though the text clearly distinguishes this stage from the seven or fourteen days of impurity, it informs the reader only that the parturient is still unclean. Nothing is said about specific purification rites, nor does the text tell the reader what the parturient is permitted to do at this stage that she was forbidden to do during the initial week to two weeks of defilement. Once the thirty-three or sixty-six days have been completed, the new mother reaches the final stage in her process of purification, when she brings offerings to the priest at the tent of meeting.

The Hierarchical Dimensions of Unclean/Clean

Like the opposition between the holy and the common, the contrast between what is clean and what is unclean has distinct hierarchical dimensions. Given the various sources of pollution mentioned in biblical texts, virtually all persons, female and male, would, at certain points in their lives, be subject to defilement. Persons who are unclean are at minimum separated from the sanctuary and from quasi-cultic ritual contexts (for example, the Passover meal in the home). Some texts even mandate exclusion from the community for some or all polluted individuals. Separation lasting at least a day is the common fate of all those who are polluted, but exclusion resulting from defilement differs in terms of its duration and the amount of effort and expense required for the polluted person to return to a state of purity. The length of a person's exclusion depends on the source of her pollution, as do the purification rites necessary for the defiled individual to regain purity. Thus, the contrast between unclean and clean has a hierarchical dimension rooted in the distinctions discernible between those who are pure and those who are defiled, on the one hand, and among persons who are polluted on the other.

Separation from the community has obvious personal and economic disadvantages, no matter what the cultural context. One cannot earn a living or maintain a network of social relations if one is spatially separated from the loci of communal life (home, workplace, public space). But exclusion from cultic and quasi-cultic contexts, which may seem a less severe form of marginalization to us, would also have had a profound effect on the ancient's life. Sacrificial contexts are represented as the primary loci for the slaughter, processing, and distribution of meat[73]; as such, they serve as a major site for the realization of hierarchy and its externalization. For the majority of the populace, those who lacked access to local, regional, and national administrative and diplomatic contexts, sacrifice and feasting probably would have been the primary ritual context and the preeminent public locus for the shaping of social relations. Texts suggest that sacrifice routinely brought together lineages and clans[74]; an even broader cross-section of the population would presumably have had occasion to meet at regional or national shrines, or at army sacrifices before battle. Rites of slaughter, processing, cooking, blood manipulation, and distribution of meat and other offerings determine the relative social status of participants, thus continually generating and regenerating the social order. In addition, the sanctuary is where worshipers prostrate themselves before Yhwh, where Yhwh is praised and petitioned, and where vows are fulfilled, transgressions made right. Quasi-cultic contexts such as the Passover meal are represented in various texts as central events in the ritual life of family and nation. To lose access—even for a relatively short period of time—to cultic and quasi-cultic contexts would surely have been viewed as a hardship, given the value and attractiveness attributed to meat, the desirability of participation in sacrificial rites, and the fact that such participation is enjoined in a variety of texts.[75] To be excluded for longer periods of time would have been more burdensome still and resulted in an even greater degree of marginalization for the individual in question. Because participation in cultic and quasi-cultic rites is central to establishing and communicating status, ex-

clusion from such rites effectively denies the excluded individual a place
in the social order.

It is therefore not surprising that impurities are often treated as much
more than simply an inconvenience to the bearer and to his familial relations. Several texts bear witness to the place of grave impurities in punishment and execration. In 2 Kgs 5:27, Elisha punishes his servant Gehazi by
cursing him and his descendants with skin disease perpetually. In 2 Sam
3:29, David's curse of his nephew Joab and his lineage includes mention
of both the person with a discharge and the individual afflicted with skin
disease. Ps 89:45 (Eng., 44) speaks of the punishment of a ruler whose
purity is removed and whose throne is cast down.[76] In 2 Chr 26:16–20,
elaborating on the narrative in 2 Kgs 15:4–5, the Judean king Uzziah's
skin disease is presented unambiguously as a punishment from Yhwh for
his arrogant attempt to usurp priestly control of the incense offering.
There is evidence that seriously polluted individuals with skin afflictions
were likened to the dead for the period of their defilement (Lev 13:45–46;
Num 12:12). This may have been true of other polluters excluded from
the community as well, though surviving literary materials are silent in
this regard. Many biblical texts speak of the separation of the dead from
Yhwh and from the living. According to Psalm 88, the dead cannot worship Yhwh, nor does he even remember them: "Do you do wonders for
the dead? Do the shades stand and praise you? Is your covenant loyalty
spoken of in the grave? Your faithfulness in the place of perishing?" For
the psalmist, the answer is obviously "no" (Ps 88:11–12 [Eng., 10–11]).
These actions and others denied to the dead are properly the province of
the living: "The living (person), the living (person), he is the one who
praises you, like me today," says King Hezekiah of Judah according to Isa
38:19.[77] Like the dead, those bearing a serious impurity are in a sense cut
off from Yhwh: they are unable to approach him with offerings for an
extended period; they cannot praise him in a cultic setting. When physically separated from the community, they are cut off from other persons
as well. Perhaps the shared social fate of the seriously polluted and the
dead explains the tendency of certain texts to compare the two groups.
For it would not be too much to say that those who have been removed
from the camp are, for all intents and purposes, symbolically dead, cut off
from both community and cult. Though the Priestly Writing mandates
the removal only of persons afflicted with skin disease, the Holiness
Source demands the separation of others, and Deuteronomy excludes
even the individual polluted by a seminal emission. The exclusions enjoined by texts such as Deuteronomy and the Holiness Source, if they
reflect actual community practice, would have generated a rather large
group of the symbolically dead at the margins of Israelite society.

The burden of exclusion from cultic and quasi-cultic settings because of impurity was not borne equally, according to surviving texts. Although some impurities theoretically affect all persons equally,[78] others are associated with particular classes of persons, differentiating them from others and functioning to disadvantage and even marginalize them. Individuals with skin disease and genital discharges are among the most socially marginalized in biblical texts. To have a genital discharge or skin disease is to be cursed according to 2 Sam 3:29 (cp. 2 Kgs 5:27). The pollution of individuals with skin disease or genital discharges, unlike that of any other class of persons, has the potential to be permanent if the conditions do not heal. Many texts speak of the exclusion of the person afflicted with skin disease from the community, and a number enjoin or imply such exclusion for those with genital discharges. It is no wonder then that the passages that explicitly liken the polluted with the dead are those describing persons afflicted with skin disease (for example, Lev 13:45–46; Num 12:12). After all, such individuals could potentially be cut off from cult and community for much or most of their lives.

Aside from persons with particular diseases, women experienced a number of the most burdensome impurities. The contrast between the effects of unavoidable pollution produced by men without disease and those produced by comparable women is quite striking. Where surviving texts agree that a male emission of semen causes defilement for one day, childbirth and menstruation result in the separation of the parturient and menstruant from feasting and sacrifice for much longer (Lev 12:1–8; 15:19–24). The male purifying himself from seminal pollution owes nothing to the cult, but the parturient must bring offerings of no small value. A man who ejaculates in a sexual situation pollutes his partner for only one day. In contrast, the menstruant engaging in sexual relations communicates her serious impurity to her partner, who remains unclean for seven days (Lev 15:24). If these rules reflect actual practice at some point in some Israelite communities, women subject to them would have spent a substantial amount of time cut off from cultic and quasi-cultic settings in comparison to men. Even if menstruation occurred less frequently among ancient Israelites than it does among contemporary Westerners,[79] frequent pregnancy would still result in forty or eighty days of pollution per birth according to Lev 12:1–8.[80] And then there are the negative cultural associations of menstruation and menstrual blood evident in biblical texts. Jerusalem's profound diminishment in status after her conquest by the Babylonians is illustrated in Lamentations 1 by a number of images, including that of the menstruating woman. Lam 1:8–9 associates menstruation both with transgression and with diminished status and shame, while 1:17 seems to tie menstruation to an image of abandonment by Yhwh. Male ejaculation, in contrast, has no comparable associations in extant literature. Thus, the opposition of clean and unclean in biblical texts differentiates men from women, and it disadvantages women in a number of respects. These include the amount of time women spend polluted by feminine impurities (and therefore separated from cultic and quasi-cultic settings); the expense of the offerings sometimes required of women to regain purity; and the negative cultural associations of an unavoidable feminine impurity such as menstruation.

Gender alone, however, does not determine the extent to which feminine impurities marginalize women, and so it would be a mistake to conclude that all women are equally disadvantaged. Life stage, as much as gender, determines who will be excluded from cultic and quasi-cultic rites and who will participate, since the pollution of menstruation and parturition is restricted to women of childbearing age. In the world of the text, preadolescent girls and postmenopausal women would not be directly affected by these gendered impurities; they would present no barrier to their participation in the ritual action requiring purity. If anything, women beyond their childbearing years and girls before puberty would be less subject to defilement than men who ejaculate. On this basis, is one then to conclude that women and girls who are not of childbearing age are somehow advantaged by biblical purity constructions? Though they do not experience directly the pollution of women during their childbearing years, I do not imagine that older women and young girls could escape completely from the cultural stigma of a distinctly feminine impurity such as menstruation. After all, girls eventually become menstruating women and older women have this characteristic in their past. Only by being a man, I would venture, could one avoid in all respects the tendency of biblical texts to disadvantage and marginalize women. Among persons in their reproductive years, the purity constructions represented in biblical texts clearly privilege men over women. They do so by means of their hierarchy of gendered impurities, constructing the male seminal emission as a simple impurity causing uncleanness only until evening and menstruation and parturition as serious impurities causing significantly longer-lasting pollution.

Other cultures with purity concerns similarly place women during their childbearing years at a disadvantage by treating menstruation and parturition as more highly polluting than other impurities. The "Sambia" and the Hua of highland New Guinea are two such contemporary cultures whose practices have been documented by social anthropologists.[81] G. Herdt, who did extensive fieldwork with the "Sambia," correlates male dominance of all aspects of "Sambia" life with extreme negativity toward women, toward their vaginas, and toward feminine impurities, all of which function to marginalize women of childbearing age. Can biblical purity constructions that place women of childbearing age at a social and cultic disadvantage be correlated with a similar pattern of male dom-

inance? Biblical marriage, lineage, and inheritance practices, the division
of labor, and the construction of public and private domains (including
the political and cultic spheres) all bestow great advantage on males,
though male social and religious dominance in biblical representation is
apparently not as thoroughgoing as the dominance of "Sambia" males in
Herdt's analysis. "Sambia" women are cut off from all elite activities. In
contrast, biblical women, though excluded from the priesthood, have access—at least theoretically—to other prestigious professions, such as
prophecy, and to the elite Nazirite vow, by means of which votaries become sanctified and must maintain a consistent commitment to purity
comparable to that of the high priest.[82] Even with these exceptions, a
correlation between the way in which biblical impurities are constructed
and male social, political, and religious dominance seems likely. Biblical
practices of pollution and purification, like marriage, lineage, and inheritance patterns, serve to perpetuate male dominance in various spheres of
life.

Aside from the way in which biblical purity constructions differentiate
certain diseased persons and women of childbearing years from others,
how else does the opposition clean/unclean function to produce social
difference? The contrast between purity and pollution is used in a number
of texts as a tool to reinforce sexual norms, distinguishing the violator
from those who conform to expected practice or placing the object of a
potential violator's interest off-limits. The use of the unclean/clean contrast to buttress sexual boundaries is especially well developed in the Holiness Source, though it is not a phenomenon exclusive to that source. In
Num 5:11–31, a text of the Priestly Writing, the woman who commits
adultery is said to be polluted; the innocent woman under suspicion is, as
might be expected, "not polluted" or "clean." Lev 18:20, a Holiness text,
also associates adultery with defilement. Similarly, Lev 18:23 claims that
pollution is the result of a human-animal coupling, and the framing materials of Lev 18:24–25 associate all sexual violations listed in the chapter
with pollution and warn that defilement by such behaviors will result in
expulsion from the land. According to Deut 24:4, the twice-divorced
woman cannot be taken back by her first husband because she is unclean.[83] Each of these texts uses the threat of defilement as a tool to reinforce sexual norms. The pollution described appears in each case to be of
a long-term nature, unlike the impurity caused by a simple seminal emission. In each instance, the potential violator is warned of the consequences of flouting what the text presents as normative sexual expectations. The first husband of Deut 24:4 presumably risks acquiring the
twice-divorced woman's uncleanness if he has intercourse with her. More
important, such an act is called by the text an "abomination" and will
bring sin upon the land. Persons involved in adultery become polluted

and risk defiling the land and being expelled from it, according to the members of the Holiness School responsible for Lev 18:24–25. Thus, by constructing non-normative sexual couplings as polluting and by suggesting that they will have serious negative consequences, these texts employ the clean/unclean opposition as a tool to discourage sexual boundary violations.

In Ezra-Nehemiah, struggle over defining the boundaries of the people itself leads to the employment of the rhetoric of impurity to justify exclusion from the community of all individuals classed as alien. Foreign wives and their issue are expelled from community and cult (Neh 13:1–3, 23–27), along with alien males who worship the god of Israel (Neh 13:4–9). The rhetoric of holiness, pollution, and purification is used explicitly in several contexts to provide a rationale for this exclusionary program (for example, Neh 13:4–9, 28–30; Ezra 9:1–2). The program itself is innovative, in that early texts do not speak of alien blood as defiling to Israel's lineage, nor do they bear witness to the notion of a "holy seed" (Ezra 9:2) requiring protection from pollution through intermarriage and the production of children of mixed heritage. I will have much more to say about the alien constructed as a polluter in chapter 3.

Distinctions among common persons, priests, and the high priest with respect to purity behavior represents another way in which differentiation between classes of persons emerges out of the contrast between what is clean and what is unclean. All persons participating in sanctuary rites must be clean, but priests must maintain their purity more rigorously and more consistently than others because of their characteristic locus in the sanctuary, their labor (bringing near offerings), and, presumably, their special sanctification. The high priest must be more rigorous still. Priests are more restricted than the common people with respect to the circumstances in which they may legitimately become defiled, and the high priest is even more restricted than the priests. Although the common person may become defiled through contact with any corpse, Lev 21:1–4 states that the priests may not become polluted in this way except for close kin, defined in the text as mother, father, son, daughter, brother, or unmarried sister. In contrast, the priest may not defile himself as a husband. Lev 21:10–11 suggests that the high priest's purity must be guarded even more vigorously and consistently. He may not pollute himself through corpse contact even for his father or his mother. Ezekiel's protest to Yhwh in Ezek 4:14 suggests poignantly the degree to which the priest might labor to keep himself from all avoidable defilement throughout his life. The degree of restriction of legitimate defilement therefore distinguishes the priest from the common person, and the high priest from the priest. It, like the attribution of holiness, both realizes and communicates the superior status of priests to common persons, and the superior status of the high priest to priests.[84] Contact with impurities correlates well with access to holy space, items, and foods. The less access to what is sanctified, the more contact with impurities that is permitted; the more access to the holy, the fewer the instances of sanctioned defilement.

The institution of the Nazirite, as described by the Priestly Writing in Num 6:1–21, allows the temporary sanctification[85] of a nonpriest of either gender. This temporary sanctification is established in exchange for a series of lifestyle restrictions (including rigorous purity behavior) that are in several respects as or more demanding than restrictions applicable to the high priest.[86] These restrictions, which include the avoidance of all corpse contact and all products of viticulture, must be observed for the period of the Nazirite vow. Num 6:1–21 describes an institution by means of which men or women can thus become holy for a set period of time, practice publicly a degree of self-abnegation that is not unlike that enjoined for the high priest, and thereby enhance their status.[87] In this way, the Priestly Writers would provide ambitious individuals with an opportunity to differentiate themselves from the rest of the nonpriestly population, if only temporarily, and experience something akin to the heightened status of priests. Why would the Priestly Writers, a circle concerned elsewhere to secure the boundaries separating holy from common, provide such an opportunity for the nonpriestly populace? Perhaps it is because the Nazirite's sanctification is temporary and inseparable from her vow; it is not of the same order as the sanctification of the priesthood and therefore not a threat to priestly status and prerogatives. If anything, the contrast between Nazirite holiness and that of priest and high priest only serves to reinforce and underscore the difference between the priestly class and all others in the Priestly schema, including Nazirites. The very presence of the Nazirite is a reminder that even the elite among nonpriests, those willing to embrace restrictive lifestyle modifications, have no enduring claim to holiness as do priests.

Conclusion

The contrast between clean and unclean determines who may participate in the rites of the sanctuary or quasi-cultic rites, and among priests and their dependents, who may have access to holy foods. Those who are classified as unclean are kept apart from holy space, sanctified foods, and all rites requiring purity. But polluted persons who must remain apart from cultic and quasi-cultic contexts do not form a homogeneous class. Gradations of uncleanness, implicit in texts describing cultic rites, differentiate among those subject to impurities just as degrees of holiness produce distinctions among those who are classed as holy. Differences among the polluted in the length of their impurity, the rites necessary to become clean, the locus of pollution and purification, and the expense of purification distinguish one defiled individual from another, creating distinct classes of polluted persons. Therefore, the hierarchical dimensions of the opposition of unclean to clean emerge out of the differentiations made between those who are clean and those who are unclean, and among polluted individuals. Persons excluded for a day from cultic and quasi-cultic settings have much less at stake than others whose periods of separation are much longer. To be cut off from the sanctuary means to lose access to the primary context of meat consumption, the major locus for the shaping of social relations, the place of prostration and prayer, where vows are fulfilled, and where transgressions are expiated. To lose access to quasi-cultic contexts such as the Passover means exclusion from rites that rehearse formative events in the life of the people of Israel. And the marginalizing effects of separation from cultic and quasi-cultic settings are intensified the longer the separation lasts, to the point where some texts cast persons suffering from skin disease as symbolically dead because of their separation from sanctuary and community. Therefore, it is striking to note the classes of persons surviving texts exclude for long periods of time: individuals with certain diseases and women of child-bearing age, suggesting that considerations of disease, gender, and life stage all play a part in determining patterns of exclusion.

The clean/unclean dyad produces social distinctions in other ways as well. A number of texts use purity distinctions as a tool to reinforce normative sexual boundaries, threatening potential violators with what appears to be long-term pollution. Texts in Ezra-Nehemiah employ the opposition clean/unclean to serve an innovative program intended to recast the external boundaries of Israel by excluding alien wives, their children, and alien males who worship Yhwh from the community and cult. Differences in purity behavior within the community produce distinctions between classes of persons. Priests must avoid pollution far more rigorously than common people and the high priest most rigorously of all. A common person may, in the schema of the Priestly Writing, take on more rigorous purity behaviors and other forms of self-abnegation while holy during the period of a Nazirite vow. Rigorous purity behavior and other characteristics of the votary bestow enhanced status vis-à-vis other common individuals.

3

Generating "Self" and "Other":
The Polarity Israelite/Alien

THERE are few subjects in contemporary academic discourse as current as the problem of self and other. In one field after another, scholars have turned their attention increasingly to issues of self-definition and difference and an ever-burgeoning literature bears witness to this fact.[1] Self and other have emerged in contemporary discussion as inseparable, socially constructed categories subject continuously to challenge and revision.[2] Thus, self-definition and its counterpart, the constitution of the other, are continuous, interlinked "projects" without a terminus, "projects" that all groups pursue in an ongoing fashion.[3] Through defining the other, a group determines what it is not; in short, it establishes its boundaries. The other is, therefore, an essential component of any group's project of self-definition.[4] The other may be constituted in any number of ways. Gender, lineage, religion, nationality, ethnicity, race, sexuality, or some combination of these may be privileged when a group seeks to define itself and its other.[5] Whether constituted as physically external to a group or present within its midst, the other is also potentially problematic, even threatening to the social order, for the other may challenge the self-definition of the group in question by transgressing its boundaries in some way and thereby calling them into question.[6] Therefore, a group may take action to exclude, marginalize, or restrict that which it constructs as other. Once removed or contained, the other no longer poses an immediate threat to a group's self-definition.

Biblical texts are replete with representations of the other, especially the other as foreigner. Aliens live both in Israel's midst as well as at her borders. Texts mention free male resident outsiders (gērîm), female and male slaves of alien origin, foreign mercenaries and their dependents, and the foreign wives of Israelite men among the populace of Israel. It is no surprise, therefore, that in much of biblical discourse, Israelite/alien is a commonplace binary contrast. Like the pairings holy/common and unclean/clean, the polarity Israelite/alien is a highly effective strategic device used by authors of biblical texts to construct difference, contributing significantly to the realization and communication of hierarchical social relations in biblical cultic settings. Yet foreign status per se does not necessarily result in exclusion of an individual from participation in the ritual action of the cult, or even in that individual's social marginalization through participation in cultic action. It could be grounds for exclusion or at least prove to be an impediment to that individual's participation, but not necessarily. In some biblical texts, exclusion or marginalization depends entirely on a combination of characteristics that might include the individual alien's gender, ethnic origin, status as either resident or nonresident, generation after immigration (where relevant), status as either slave or free, and, among males, status as either circumcised or uncircumcised. In other texts, exclusion of all persons constructed as alien is the rule. Among texts that allow for the incorporation of certain aliens into the political-ritual body of Israel, such incorporation does not necessarily suggest that the incorporated alien has achieved any kind of status advantage. To the contrary, as I will show, routes to incorporation, as represented in biblical texts, may bestow upon the alien an inferior status as a dependent of an Israelite patron. Thus the Israelite/alien polarity, in contrast to a binary pairing such as clean/unclean, is anything but a straightforward tool for making distinctions among individuals and groups. In addition to foreignness, other considerations may play a significant part in determining the way in which texts represent both the extent of the alien's participation in Israel's cultic life and the participating alien's social status.

Forms and Functions of the Polarity Israelite/Alien

In order to explore profitably the dyad Israelite/alien and the hierarchical differentiations it produces, I begin by noting that this particular binary pairing has a variety of forms in biblical texts. Each of these draws a distinction between the Israelite and those classed as other, but with different emphases and sometimes for different purposes. There are three forms of the polarity that I will examine in this chapter: (1) circumcised/uncircumcised (mûl/ʿārēl),[7] which occurs in texts both antedating and postdating 587 BCE; (2) Israelite or native/(foreign) resident outsider (běnê yiśrāʾēl or ʾezrāḥ/gēr), which is common especially in texts of the Holiness and Deuteronomistic Schools; and (3) "exile" community (haggôlâ)/peoples of the land(s), which is found frequently in Ezra-Nehemiah in descriptions of the interactions of the returnees from Babylon with others around them.[8] In short, what I am calling the Israelite/alien binary pairing really describes a set of related oppositions.

Circumcised/Uncircumcised

The first form of the Israelite/alien polarity that I shall examine is the relatively common pairing circumcised/uncircumcised. It occurs, implicitly or explicitly, in biblical materials from various periods, including early texts such as David's Lament over Saul and Jonathan (2 Sam 1:19–27) and the pre-Deuteronomistic narrative material in 1 Samuel. It also occurs in texts of the sixth century, including Holiness Source materials such as Exod 12:43–49, Holiness-related Ezek 44:7, 9, and in Isa 52:1.[9] In several passages, including Ezek 44:7, 9, circumcision is privileged as the requirement par excellence for entry into the sanctuary sphere.

A variety of pre-exilic texts construct a firm boundary separating those who are uncircumcised from Israel. Circumcision is required of alien males who wish to intermarry with Israel according to the Yahwist's ancestral narrative in Genesis 34.[10] After the rape of Dinah by Shechem the Hivvite, Shechem proposes to marry Dinah. Dinah's brothers, the sons of Jacob, respond by informing Shechem and his father Hamor that marriage is impossible: "We are not able to do this thing, to give our sister to a man with a foreskin, for it (hî') is a disgraceful thing (ḥerpâ) to us" (Gen 34:14). Whether the brothers are speaking of the foreskin itself as the "disgraceful thing" or the act of giving their sister to a man who possesses one,[11] it is clear that the presence of the foreskin is the impediment to marriage.[12] The puzzling, repeated claim of Dinah's brothers that Shechem the Hivvite had defiled (ṭimmē') their sister when he forced her to have intercourse with him, as if this were a permanent or long-term condition,[13] may suggest that the foreskin was constructed as an agent of defilement by the circles that produced this narrative.[14] Alternatively, because certain other biblical texts understand proscribed sexual activity to result in a woman's pollution,[15] Genesis 34 may simply describe another case of defilement resulting from an illicit sexual union. A third possibility is that the pollution of Dinah could have something to do with the forced nature of Shechem's sexual act, though this seems much less likely to me than the other two alternatives. There are many examples elsewhere in the Hebrew Bible of the verb 'innâ used, as it is in Genesis 34, to describe what we would call rape, yet none associates the act with a long-term state of pollution. Gen 34:7 states that Shechem "had committed an outrage (nĕbālâ) in Israel by sleeping with Jacob's daughter," but this verse does not help us decide between these options. The verses in Genesis 34 that associate Shechem's act with long-term pollution probably suggest that the foreskin itself—most likely the "disgraceful thing" of verse 14—is understood to be a profoundly polluting agent, though it is possible that the pollution is simply the result of illicit sexual activity. In any case, Genesis 34 views the male foreskin as a marker of the alien and an impediment to entering the Israelite community from the outside.

In 2 Sam 1:19–27 and the pre-Deuteronomistic prose narratives of Judges and 1 Samuel, much attention is focused on the uncircumcision of the Philistine enemy.[16] In fact, they ascribe so much significance to Philistine foreskins that the term "uncircumcised (person)" ('ārēl) is sometimes used in these texts simply as another way of saying "Philistine."[17] The narratives suggest that uncircumcision was an unusual state of affairs for men of the region, and later texts such as Jer 9:24–25 (Eng., 25–26) do not contradict this impression.[18] As outsiders who did not practice circumcision, the Philistines apparently stood out.[19] The attention that the writers of these texts devote to Philistine uncircumcision gives way to what can only be called grotesque fetishizing of the foreskin of the alien other in the narrative of Saul's bride-price challenge to David in 1 Sam 18:17–27. Saul wants David to marry his daughter, but David is hesitant, fearing that he cannot afford to do so.[20] Saul, through his servants, responds directly to David's reluctance: "The king has no delight in a bride price (mōhar) except[21] one hundred foreskins of the Philistines, in order to be avenged against the enemies of the king" (1 Sam 18:25). David meets the challenge and marries Saul's daughter Michal. The foreskin in this text, like the scalp in some early modern North American settings, is treated synecdochically as a body part representing the whole person. To choose it over some other form of proof of slaughter suggests the extent of the culture's fascination with this particular emblem of otherness.

Clearly, to be uncircumcised in early texts such as Genesis 34 and 1 Samuel 18 is to be emblematically alien. Though no early texts speak of controlling admission into cultic settings, one might be tempted argue on the basis of the texts discussed that uncircumcised male aliens were likely forbidden from participating in cultic activities. After all, 1 Samuel 18 bears witness to the privileging of the foreskin as an emblem of otherness, and Genesis 34 associates uncircumcision with disgrace and may even ascribe to it the power to pollute. Though suggestive, this evidence is not sufficient to allow for confident assertions regarding the status of uncircumcised male aliens vis-à-vis the Israelite cult in early contexts. On their status one can only speculate, and there are other sources of data that may suggest indirectly that such foreigners were admitted to cultic and quasi-cultic settings early on.[22] Perhaps it is best, given the limitations of surviving evidence and what it can tell us of actual cultic practice, to offer two possible alternatives: the ban on uncircumcised male aliens in Yhwh's sanctuaries and in quasi-cultic settings such as the Passover celebration either has a long history in Israel, implicit in early texts and stated explicitly later, or it is a development evidenced in certain circles (for example, the Holiness School, Ezekiel) by the sixth century. If it is a later development, it may be no coincidence that explicit exclusion of uncircumcised male aliens from Israelite cultic contexts is attested in the same Holiness Source materials as the innovative sixth-century notion that circumcision is a "sign of the covenant" between Yhwh and Israel.[23] The circle that increases circumcision's significance as an identity marker of the Israelite people also sharpens the boundaries of cult with respect to uncircumcised alien males.

Later texts are clearer than earlier texts with respect to the status of the uncircumcised male alien vis-à-vis the sanctuary sphere and its analogues. Exod 12:43–49, a text to be attributed to the Holiness School,[24] states that uncircumcised alien males are forbidden to "eat the Passover (sacrifice)," a required observance in the home for all Israelites according to this text.[25] One class of foreigner, the resident outsider (gēr), may "make the Passover," in contrast to other classes of aliens mentioned—the "(nonresident) alien," (ben nēkār) and the "(foreign) wage laborer" (tôšāb wĕśākîr)—but he and all his dependent males must be circumcised first in order to do so.[26] Like Genesis 34, this text conceives of the possibility of a male alien's entry into the Israelite community and (in this case) its ritual life by means of circumcision. Once circumcised, the resident outsider of foreign origin "will be like the native of the land" with respect to the privilege of "making the Passover." The power of circumcision to change status is emphasized in the ideology of this text.

Other materials of the sixth and fifth centuries proscribe the entry of uncircumcised alien males into the sanctuary sphere. Ezek 44:4–9 may be understood to speak of the polluting power (hll)[27] of uncircumcised aliens who enter Yhwh's sanctuary, whatever role they might have there.[28] The passage describes the presence of aliens in the sanctuary as an "abomination" (vv. 6–7) and states that its legislation applies to "every alien (who resides) in the midst of the children of Israel" (v. 9), apparently a reference not to visitors but to resident outsiders of alien background.[29] Isa 52:1, a text of the third quarter of the sixth century, forbids the entry of "(the) uncircumcised (person who is) unclean" or "(the) uncircumcised (person) and (the) unclean (person)" ('ārēl wĕṭāmē') into Jerusalem, which is described here as "the holy city." In the ideology of the writer of this text, the holiness of the sanctuary sphere has been extended to the whole of Jerusalem, and those who are uncircumcised are banned from entry.[30] If we translate 'ārēl wĕṭāmē' "(the) uncircumcised (person who is) unclean," we have here an association of uncircumcision with the power to pollute, as we may have in Ezek 44:7 and Genesis 34. This translation as a hendiadys construction is the best way of understanding the expression 'ārēl wĕṭāmē', as the verbal forms governed by it are in the singular.[31]

Though Israelites were not alone among the peoples of their geographic area in practicing circumcision of males,[32] the texts discussed here privilege circumcision as a boundary marker between Israel and the other. What are the implications of this? First, circumcision is a marker of difference whose potential effectiveness as a regulator of entry into community and cult is limited, since near neighbors such as Ammon, Moab, and Edom, and even an important far neighbor, Egypt, are understood by the tradition to practice circumcision.[33] Furthermore, the opposition circumcised/uncircumcised is a gendered marker of self and other, since it pertains only to males. The entry of alien women into Israel's polity and cult remains unaffected by this physical but culturally produced distinction. Finally, it is a marker not normally visible in the public sphere.[34] Nevertheless, for all its limitations as a bearer of ethnic distinction, circumcision plays a central part in distinguishing the alien from the Israelite in a number of biblical sources.

Texts both early and late bear witness to the importance of the opposition circumcised/uncircumcised. The male body, specifically the male sexual organ, becomes the locus of discourse in this particular strategy of differentiation. Uncircumcision, represented as a bar to entry into Israel's political-ritual community for uncircumcised foreign men, is not by definition a permanent impediment. Several texts mention or allude to the option of circumcision for the uncircumcised alien male who wishes to join the community's cultic life. The foreskin, to which elements of the culture attributed polluting power by the sixth century, and possibly much earlier, could be removed, rendering the alien male resident fit for full participation in the cultic life of the community according to texts such as Exod 12:48.

Israelite or Native/(Foreign) Resident Outsider

The second form of the Israelite/alien polarity that I will explore is the pairing native/(foreign) resident outsider ('ezrāḥ/gēr) or Israelite/(foreign) resident outsider (běnê yiśrā'ēl/gēr).[35] The distinction occurs with some frequency in the Holiness Source, and Deuteronomistic materials also bear witness to it. I avoid the more common translation "resident alien" for gēr because not all persons assigned to this class are foreigners; some are displaced Israelites.[36] I prefer the English "outsider" to "alien" because "alien" in American usage suggests foreignness, where "outsider" suggests only that the person so described is not a local. Thus, I distinguish between resident outsiders who are foreigners and resident outsiders who are Israelites; the term gēr is used for both in the biblical text. My focus, of course, is the resident outsider of alien background. In the texts I shall discuss, I understand the gēr to be a long-term,[37] foreign, male[38] resident in Israel who is by definition outside of the lineage-patrimony system[39] and therefore potentially[40] in a position of dependency on an Israelite patron.[41] A number of texts suggest that status as a resident outsider is inherited from generation to generation, so that the newcomer's children and their descendants are also classed as resident outsiders.[42] Some materials allude to the resident outsider's having a household with his own male dependents, some of whom could presumably be slaves.[43] Though the resident outsider's condition is sometimes described as needy and vulnerable, the possibility of his prospering is raised in several texts (for example, Lev 25:47; Deut 28:43). Perhaps Lev 25:23 defines the condition of the resident outsider most succinctly in its metaphorical application of the term to Israel vis-à-vis Yhwh: "As for the land, it shall not be sold in perpetuity, for the land belongs to me. For resident outsiders (gērîm wĕtôšābîm) are you *with me*." Here, the defining characteristics of a resident outsider are a lack of a property holding and residence with and dependence upon a patron who holds property and who allows some of it to be used by the resident outsider. This is why the term gēr can be used both for foreigners and for displaced Israelite males who have left the locus of their patrimony. In either case, the displaced man is potentially a dependent (client) of a landholding patron, in whose vicinity he resides.

How is it possible to know whether a text is speaking of a resident outsider of foreign origin or a displaced Israelite? Texts of the Holiness School are on the whole less ambiguous in this regard than are texts of the Deuteronomistic School. The Holiness Source's frequent use of the binary opposition native/resident outsider suggests that the resident outsider in question is a foreigner rather than an Israelite. The use of the term "native" ('ezrāḥ) elsewhere in Holiness texts makes this clear: "In booths shall you dwell seven days; every native in Israel shall dwell in booths in order that your generations know that in booths I made the Israelites dwell when I brought them out from the land of Egypt" (Lev 23:42–43). "Native" here is surely a reference to all those understood to be Israelites, including those who are displaced; it is unlikely that it refers simply to locals. Israelites—both locals and those who are displaced—observe the feast by imitating the dwelling style of their ancestors.[44] In contrast to Holiness materials, those of Deuteronomistic provenance are more complex. In some Deuteronomistic texts, it is evident that the foreign resident outsider is intended, while in others, it is more difficult to determine to whom the term gēr refers. Thus, I am forced to be more cautious in drawing conclusions about the Deuteronomistic School's treatment of the resident outsider of alien background.

In Holiness materials, the binary pairing native/(foreign) resident outsider is used frequently as a rhetorical device indicating the totality of the community subject to covenant stipulations. Every male who is counted as a member of the community fits into either the native category or the (foreign) resident outsider category. Though the main agenda of the texts employing the opposition is to argue for the inclusion of the resident outsider of foreign heritage in the community, the distinction between native and resident outsider is nonetheless maintained by the binary strategy of the text. A prime example of the use of this opposition in an inclusive way is Exod 12:43–49. Verse 48 speaks of the resident outsider of foreign origin who wishes to "make the Passover." In order to do so, he must circumcise himself and his male dependents, and then he may "approach to make it." The text goes on to say that "he will be like the native of the land" after his circumcision. Verse 49 elaborates on this assertion: "One teaching (tôrâ) will there be for the native and for the resident outsider who resides in your midst." In this text, it is clear that the hypothetical resident outsider in question is a foreigner and not a displaced Israelite, for he is uncircumcised. The technical term gēr is used for the alien both before he is circumcised (v. 48), and after (v. 49), when he follows the same "teaching" as the native. The rhetoric of "one teaching" cannot apply to the uncircumcised resident outsider since the text explicitly states that he is forbidden to eat the Passover sacrifice and therefore subject to a different "teaching" from that of the native on the one hand and the circumcised resident outsider on the other. Circumcision—and by implication, participation in at least this sacrificial aspect of the ritual life of the community—is clearly optional for the uncircumcised resident outsider in Exod 12:43–49. According to the text, the circumcised resident outsider stands within the community rather than outside of it, though as an entity distinct from the native. The binary pairing native/resident outsider functions to communicate totality rather than to exclude: each male who is counted among members of the community fits either one category or the other. The uncircumcised resident outsider, however, stands outside of the covenant community, along with the various classes of nonresident foreigners.

In many other Holiness texts, the resident outsider is obligated to conform to covenant stipulations in the same manner as the native: he must avoid leaven during Unleavened Bread (Exod 12:19)[45]; afflict himself on Yom Kippur (Lev 16:29)[46]; sacrifice correctly (Lev 17:8; 22:18–19); not eat blood (Lev 17:10, 12, 13); not eat animal carcasses or torn beasts (Lev 17:15); and avoid "abominations," including child sacrifice (Lev 18:26; 20:2). His penalty for cursing Yhwh is the same as that of the native: death by stoning (Lev 24:16, 22). He and his own household share also in the privileges of the covenant: the ritual of pardon for involuntary transgressions is open to the resident outsider of foreign background (Num 15:26, 29, 30),[47] as is the ritual of processing the red heifer to create purifying waters (Num 19:10b).[48] Editorial refrains such as "one teaching for the native and the resident outsider" and "the resident outsider and native alike" occur in many of these texts of the Holiness Source that speak of the resident outsider's obligations and privileges.[49] Are these texts concerned only with the circumcised resident outsider of alien origin? Did the uncircumcised gēr have any obligations or privileges? The other cultic and quasi-cultic Holiness texts that mention the resident outsider are not explicit about requiring circumcision, as Exod 12:48 is, but one of them, Num 15:14–16, is constructed in much the same way as Exod 12:43–49. Num 15:14–16 concerns offerings to Yhwh. According to this text, as in Exod 12:48, it is optional for the resident outsider to offer the offerings in question, but should he do so, he is to offer them in the same manner as the native (v. 14). The text emphasizes that he has the same standing as the native before Yhwh (v. 15). No mention is made of circumcision in this text. Circumcision is also not mentioned directly in Num 9:14, which is very similar to Exod 12:48; it, too, concerns the Passover and gives the resident outsider of foreign background the option of participating as long as he conforms to the "statute of the Passover and its ordinance" (kĕḥuqqat happesaḥ ûkĕmišpāṭô). This somewhat opaque expression may include circumcision as it is treated in Exod 12:48, though this is unclear.

There are several ways one might approach the questions raised by these texts, but one solution stands out as most likely. It is possible that the Holiness Source proscribes certain behaviors offensive to Yhwh (such as eating blood or carcasses, child sacrifice, eating leaven during Unleavened Bread, avoiding self-affliction on Yom Kippur) for all residents of the land, whether circumcised or not, while reserving ritual privileges such as the Passover and other sacrifices only for circumcised resident outsiders of foreign background and for natives. Only the texts that describe sacrifice (Exod 12:48; Num 9:14; 15:14–16) speak at all of the foreign resident outsider having the option to participate; the proscriptive texts offer no choice. I suspect that other texts that speak of cultic privileges, texts such as Num 19:10, which describes the production of purifying waters and seems to imply potential participation by resident outsiders of alien background in the process, probably also refer to the circumcised resident outsider. If we do not understand the Holiness Source to advocate a two-tiered system of incorporation for the resident outsider of foreign origin, we are forced to embrace a second possibility: In all cases where H speaks inclusively of the resident outsider, only the circumcised resident outsider is meant. This seems highly unlikely, as it would imply that activities such as child sacrifice were permitted to uncircumcised resident outsiders in the thought of the Holiness School but forbidden to Israelites and circumcised resident outsiders. It is difficult to imagine Holiness circles sanctioning a practice such as child sacrifice by anyone in the land, given their understanding that such actions have the potential to pollute the land and result in Israel's expulsion from it: "You shall keep my statutes and ordinances, and not do any of these abomina-

tions—the native and the resident outsider who resides in your midst—
for all these abominations the people of the land who were before you
did, and the land became polluted. Let the land not vomit you out because
you polluted it, as it vomited out the nation which was before you" (Lev
18:26–28). It seems very likely that the Holiness School has set up a two-
tiered system of obligation and privilege, with the elite level of participation, the level required of the native, open to the resident outsider of foreign background who is willing to be circumcised. Other alien residents
must observe a basic set of proscriptions intended both to prevent Yhwh's
wrath and to protect the land from intolerable pollution, but they are not
required to sacrifice or participate in other cultic activities.

What is one to make of the frequently emphatic nature of the Holiness
texts that insist that covenant obligations and communal privilege belong
equally to the circumcised resident outsider of alien background and to
the native? Num 15:14–16 is an excellent example of such a text: "If there
resides with you a resident outsider or one who is in your midst for your
generations, and he would make an offering, a soothing odor, to Yhwh,
as you do so he shall do. As for the assembly, there is one statute for you
and for the resident outsider who resides with you[50]; it is an eternal statute for your generations; the resident outsider will be like you before
Yhwh. There will be one teaching and one law for you and for the resident outsider who resides with you." The emphatic nature of this text and
other Holiness passages suggests a state of affairs quite different in the
setting(s) in which they were produced. Perhaps the frequently repeated
refrains ought to be taken as an appeal for reform, a program of change
advanced by members of the Holiness School who are concerned to find
ways to integrate the resident outsider of foreign background more fully
into the Israelite community. Given the limitations of the evidence, I can
only speculate about the range of social and temporal settings of the Holiness School. Certainly Holiness circles were in existence by the late monarchy and probably continued into the early Persian period.[51] An early
post-exilic date for the Holiness materials advocating the integration of
the resident outsider is, therefore, a distinct possibility. The most probable context for this material is a time when Israel is in its own land, with
foreigners present as residents and temporary workers or visitors. The
context should also be a time of debate about the status of the foreigner
in Israel, particularly with respect to participation in the cult. A number
of texts from the sixth and fifth centuries attest to conflict in the community about the place of foreigners in Israel's polity and cult.[52] And at least
some of the Holiness material emphasizing the integration of the resident
outsider seems to be secondary to the texts in which it occurs, suggesting
a later date than the texts it glosses.[53] This evidence, while not decisive,
suggests that a date in the early Persian period would not be out of order

for the Holiness material advocating integration of the resident outsider into Israelite polity and cult.[54]

Holiness-related voices go even further than the Holiness Source with respect to the integration of the resident outsider. Ezek 47:13–48:35 describes the redivision of the land of Israel into patrimonial shares after the exile. Ezek 47:22–23 appears to be a gloss on the larger description of the land's redivision,[55] using language reminiscent of the Holiness materials advocating integration.[56] These verses state that resident outsiders who have fathered children in the land shall receive patrimonial shares of the land in the tribes in which they reside. The resident outsiders in question must be aliens, since they have no place in the kinship and patrimony system. Displaced Israelite outsiders would possess their own kin and patrimony in another part of Israel; there would be no reason to incorporate them into Israel for a second time.[57] The assignment of patrimonial shares to resident outsiders of foreign background is a radical departure from previous practice, which viewed the foreign resident outsider and his descendants as outside the lineage-patrimony structure of Israel. Even Holiness texts that insist on the equality of the native and the circumcised resident outsider in cultic and quasi-cultic settings do not propose to integrate the resident outsider in this radical way. To give the foreign resident outsider a share in the patrimony effectively eliminates all difference between him and the native, fully assimilating him into the lineage and inheritance structure of the society. Presumably, persons previously classified as alien would now be incorporated into the genealogical traditions of the people, which express kinship both by blood and by acquisition. In a word, this radical reform envisioned by Ezek 47:22–23 represents the granting of (fictive) kinship to the resident outsider; he becomes at last a brother rather than an other. It also represents a return to what was apparently an early practice in Israel: When emerging tribes fully incorporated alien groups, their incorporation was reflected in the genealogical idiom, and their alien origins were for all intents and purposes erased. The Judahite genealogical record provides the best example of this kind of radical assimilation of outsiders in early Israel. As early Judah grew, it absorbed a number of non-Israelite groups as well as the tribe of Simeon. Extant evidence suggests that Judahite groups such as the Jerahmeelites, Qenizzites, and even Zerah, Judah's second clan, were originally foreign and were absorbed into Judah's kin structure, with absorption expressed in Judah's genealogical record.[58] Ezek 47:22–23 may have been intended as a challenge to the limited integration program characteristic of late Holiness materials found in the Pentateuch. It appears to allude to this program in its use of the Holiness-like expression "they will be for you like the native among the children of Israel." Where the binary strategy of late Holiness material seeks to integrate the resident outsider to a large degree without casting aside the distinction between foreigner and Israelite, Ezek 47:22–23 effectively advocates the elimination of that distinction entirely.

There are a few Holiness texts that appear to contradict the many that insist on "one teaching" for the native and the resident outsider of foreign heritage. According to Lev 23:42, only the native is obligated to dwell in booths during the festival of Sukkot. In Lev 25:45, it is permissible to enslave the foreign resident outsider and his descendants permanently, though it is forbidden in this text to reduce a fellow Israelite to slave status even for a temporary period of time. One law concerns festival observance, the other social practice. I have shown that some Holiness texts insist on equal cultic and quasi-cultic obligations and privileges for the circumcised resident outsider (for example, the Passover sacrifice in Exod 12:48–49) and others speak of equal justice (for example, Lev 24:16); these texts are framed by Holiness clichés emphasizing a single "teaching." In neither Lev 23:42 nor 25:45 is a single "teaching" evident for both the native and the resident outsider of alien background. How does one explain the apparent contradiction between these two texts on the one hand and the other Holiness texts that insist on one "teaching"? It may be that, as I have mentioned, the Holiness circles responsible for the "one teaching" ideology, those who allow for the incorporation of the circumcised resident outsider in all cultic and quasi-cultic activities, are among the latest Holiness redactors.[59] They have glossed earlier texts addressed only to native Israelites to reflect their perspective, though they appear to have missed Lev 23:42. Lev 25:45, which at its core contradicts their viewpoint, could not be glossed to suit their program and was therefore left as they found it. These proposals, though they attempt to make sense of apparent contradictions, are at best speculative. At minimum, the Holiness corpus bears witness to more than one view on the status of the resident outsider of foreign origin, though the dominant viewpoint of the text in its final form is clearly the "one teaching" position.

The use of the term gēr is more difficult to unravel in Deuteronomistic materials than it is for materials of the Holiness Source. Where the binary rhetoric of the Holiness School frequently distinguishes the resident outsider of foreign origin from the native Israelite, Deuteronomists resort to such a rhetorical strategy less often, though binary and triadic approaches are certainly evident in some Deuteronomistic texts, as I will show.[60] When the term gēr occurs in Deuteronomistic materials, it is often in a nonbinary formulaic listing of the dependents of the Israelite head of household, as in Deut 5:14: "The seventh day is a cessation for Yhwh your god; you shall not do any labor—you, and your son, and your daughter, and your male slave, and your female slave, and your ox, and your ass, and all your animals, and your resident outsider who is in your towns." In this and similar dependent lists,[61] the resident outsider as well as a variety of other dependent persons—slaves, women, minors of both sexes, the Levite, the widow, the fatherless—are contrasted with the head of household or elder, who is addressed as "you" by the text.[62] Yet, such texts tell us nothing of the origin of the resident outsider. Is he a foreigner or a displaced Israelite? Neither would have a claim to a share in a local patrimony; both are potentially dependent on a local patron with property. The question is a crucial one since the resident outsider, who is so frequently listed among the dependents of the head of household, clearly has cultic obligations and a place in the Israelite assembly[63] in certain Deuteronomistic texts. To further complicate matters, a few other Deuteronomistic texts in which the resident outsider is clearly foreign exclude him from Israelite cultic obligations (Deut 14:21) or from the covenant itself (Deut 28:43–44).[64] These materials potentially contradict dependent lists in such texts as Deut 5:14; 16:11, 14; 26:11; 29:10; 31:12, which include the resident outsider among Israelites subject to covenant obligations, if the dependent lists are understood to refer to a foreign resident outsider rather than a displaced Israelite.

It seems best to begin with texts for which I can make a case that the resident outsider in question is a foreigner rather than a displaced Israelite. From these, it is possible to get a sense of how at least some currents in Deuteronomistic thought conceived of the place of the resident outsider of foreign extraction, and perhaps then we can come to some judgment concerning how to understand the resident outsider of the dependent lists. First, I will examine briefly a number of texts that advocate or allude to equal treatment of the resident outsider. In Deut 1:16, Moses speaks of commanding judges to hear cases and make judgments "between a man and his brother or his resident outsider." The man's "resident outsider," when contrasted with his "brother," is clearly of foreign background, since "brother" is an idiom for a fellow Israelite.[65] The resident outsider is, however, entitled to equal justice according to this text. A similar contrast between brother and resident outsider is present in Deut 24:14, which speaks of two possible origins of wage laborers: They may be drawn from either Israelites ("your brethren") or resident outsiders. Deut 10:19 orders Israelites to "love the resident outsider, for you were resident outsiders in the land of Egypt." The comparison with the Israelite tradition of residence in a foreign land may suggest that the resident outsider in question is an alien.[66] In any case, the resident outsider here, as elsewhere, is cited for special protection since he is viewed as vulnerable.[67] Finally, there is Josh 20:9. This text concerns the establishment of cities of refuge for persons guilty of manslaughter. The text states that the cities of refuge have been established "for all the children of Israel and for the resident outsider who resides in their midst." Though Josh

20:9 establishes a binary contrast between the resident outsider and the native Israelite, both have the privilege of fleeing to the cities of refuge should the need arise. What can be concluded from these four texts? Certainly nothing about the foreign resident outsider's place in the cult, since none of these passages refers to cultic matters. None speaks directly of his place in the Israelite community, though there is advocacy of equal treatment in judicial settings for the resident outsider who is a client of an Israelite and equal access to what the texts present as the standard mode of escape from the avenger of blood.[68] It would be odd to argue for equal justice and equal privilege (in the case of the cities of refuge) if the resident outsider of foreign origin had no standing in the community. These texts are suggestive of standing, but on them alone a convincing case for the foreign resident outsider's positive cultic and covenantal status in Israel cannot be made.

The resident outsider of the Deuteronomistic dependent lists—whether a foreigner or a displaced Israelite—is included in the Israelite community. Like other dependents, he has cultic obligations and privileges but inferior status to that of the household head. His inferior status is communicated by means of his appearance in lists of dependent persons. In Deut 16:11, 14, the resident outsider, along with the head of household, his children, his slaves, and associated local Levites, widows, and fatherless persons, are obligated to "rejoice" before Yhwh on pilgrimage to Yhwh's sanctuary.[69] Here, as in other Deuteronomistic contexts, the resident outsider is included in the list of the head of household's dependents. Deut 26:11 on the first fruits and 5:14 on Sabbath rest are similar, stating cultic obligations for the resident outsider, who is listed among the dependents of the household head.

Several texts speak explicitly of the resident outsider's place among the Israelite people. In Deut 31:11–12, the resident outsider is clearly counted among the people who gather to hear the "torah" recited in the seventh year at the festival of Sukkot: "You shall read this teaching (tôrâ) opposite all Israel in their hearing. Gather the people, the men, and the women, and the children, and your resident outsider who is in your towns, that they might hear and that they might learn and fear Yhwh your god, and that they shall be careful to do all the words of this teaching." The resident outsider, obligated to hear and obey, is by implication a part of "all Israel." Deut 29:9–11 (Eng., 10–12) is similar, but more explicit with respect to the resident outsider's dependent status. In this text, the elders and leaders are addressed: "You are stationed today, all of you, before Yhwh your god—the heads of your tribes,[70] your elders, and your rulers, all the men of Israel; your children, your wives, and your resident outsider who is in the midst of your camp, from hewer of your wood to drawer of your water—in order for you to pass into the covenant of Yhwh your god, and into his curse, which Yhwh your god is making with you today." The resident outsider, like women, children, and slaves, is not among "the men of Israel," the "you" addressed directly by the text. Yet he, like the other dependents, is a part of the covenant community; like the others, he embraces the covenant and its stipulations. His dependency is communicated not only by his placement in the list of dependents that follows the list of "all the men of Israel," but also by the use of the possessive pronoun "your": he is "your" (the head of household's) resident outsider.

Josh 8:33, 35 are the last of the dependent list texts that I shall take up. In these, the resident outsider is included in the assembly (qāhāl) of Israel among the various dependent classes (women, children, etc.), and what appears to be a Holiness School gloss occurs in v. 33, suggesting that at least some Holiness-related hand believed that the resident outsider of the Deuteronomistic dependent lists was a foreigner: "And all Israel and its elders, rulers and judges, were standing on one side of the ark and on the other, opposite the Levitical priests who bore the ark of the covenant of Yhwh, *resident outsider and native alike*,[71] half opposite Mt. Gerizim and half opposite Mt. Ebal."

A third group of Deuteronomistic texts views the resident outsider as someone who is not part of the Israelite assembly and does not have covenantal obligations. In these texts, it is clear that the resident outsider in question is an alien. Deut 14:21 treats the disposal of defiling carcasses: "You shall not eat any carcass; to the resident outsider who is in your towns you shall give it, and he will eat it, or sell it to the (nonresident) alien (nokrî), for a holy people are you to Yhwh your god." In contrast to Deuteronomistic texts discussed previously, this law distinguishes between Israelite and resident outsider, as well as between resident outsider and (presumably) nonresident foreigner. Unlike the similar law in the Holiness Source, which forbids the resident outsider as well as the Israelite to eat meat from a carcass (Lev 17:15–16), this law allows the foreigner and the resident outsider to eat such meat, though it is to be given to the resident outsider and sold to the foreigner. The resident outsider, like the nonresident foreigner, is not part of the "holy people" of Yhwh and therefore exempt from the restriction, but he may receive the forbidden meat as a gift, perhaps because he is poor and in need. The text uses a triadic construction to establish three distinct groupings, each of which are subject to particular treatment, but two of which share exemption from an obligation imposed on community members.

A second text of interest is Deut 28:43–44, which is part of a series of curses that will come to rest upon Israel should it break its covenant with Yhwh. It is intended to contrast with the blessing found in Deut 28:12–13. In that blessing, "you," the Israelite, will "lend to many nations, but will not borrow. Yhwh will make you the head and not the tail, and you will do nothing but ascend . . . for you obeyed the commandments of Yhwh your god." In the curse, the resident outsider "who is in your midst will ascend over you . . . he will lend to you but you will not lend to him. He will become the head and you will become the tail." Though not in the direct manner of Deut 14:21 and Josh 20:9, Deut 28:43–44 suggest nonetheless that the resident outsider in question is a foreigner. The blessing of Deut 28:12–13 foresees Israelites prospering economically and dominating "many nations." This dominance is expressed through the idiom of money lending. Proverbs 22:7 makes the point using similar language, except with respect to individuals: "A rich man rules over the poor, and a borrower is a slave to the man who lends." The curse of Deut 28:43–44 reverses the blessing in all respects: The Israelites who have broken the covenant will descend continually, will borrow and not lend, will become the dependents, to their shame. And the party that will prosper is the resident outsider, who takes the place of the "many nations" in the blessing. This parallel of the resident outsider of the curse with "many nations" of the blessing suggests both that the resident outsider is a foreigner and that he is not subject to the curse and therefore outside of the covenant. Where the resident outsider is frequently vulnerable and dependent in other Deuteronomistic texts, the Israelite plays that role here. What Israelites conceive as the norm—a vulnerable, dependent resident outsider of foreign lineage attached as a client to a prosperous Israelite—is here reversed. The notion that the resident outsider of alien origin stands outside of the covenant, lacking cultic obligations as a result, may or may not contradict the portrayal of the dependent lists—this depends completely on whether the resident outsider of the lists is viewed as a foreigner or a displaced Israelite.

Some evidence I have presented—Deut 1:16; Josh 20:9; the Holiness School's interpretation in Josh 8:33—certainly suggests the possibility that the resident outsider of the dependent lists is a foreigner, but these data are not a sufficient basis on which to fashion a compelling argument. In contrast, Deut 23:4–9 (Eng., 3–8) speaks clearly of foreign, long-term residents, though it does not use the technical term gēr to describe them. In this much-discussed text,[72] the Ammonite and the Moabite and their descendants are permanently forbidden from entering "the assembly of Yhwh"; historical reasons are given for their exclusion. In contrast, the descendants of the Edomite and the Egyptian may enter Yhwh's assembly in the third generation. Though the text does not use the term gēr, it speaks clearly of long-term alien residents of the land of Israel, the same class of persons referred to as "resident outsiders" (gērîm) in other texts. Deut 23:4–9 (Eng., 3–8) refer to those long-term residents using masculine singular gentilics: Ammonite, Moabite, Edomite, Egyptian. I believe that this text has in mind specifically male immigrants and their male descendants, since (1) Ammonite, Moabite, Edomite, and Egyptian are grammatically masculine and singular when listed as subjects governing the verb "to enter," and (2) descent is traced through the male in the surviving texts of this culture. The exact meaning of entering the assembly of Yhwh in this text is uncertain, though such entry probably means to join the covenant community, embracing cultic obligations and privileges. This interpretation is supported to some extent by the earliest interpreters of Deut 23:2–9 (Eng., 1–8), who understood entry into the assembly to mean entry into the sanctuary.[73]

What do the male members of these four groups share in common? Interestingly, each of these peoples is said to practice circumcision according to Jer 9:24–25 (Eng., 25–26), and three of the four (Ammonites, Moabites, and Edomites) are Canaanite-speaking contiguous neighbors of Israel. Deut 23:4–9 (Eng., 3–8) appears to be a text that seeks to restrict admission to the covenantal community on the basis not of the opposition circumcised/uncircumcised or foreign lineage, but of both membership in one of four particular foreign groups and gender. The text shows no intent to restrict the admission of *other* foreigners or female Ammonites, Moabites, Edomites, and Egyptians. Deut 23:4–9 (Eng., 3–8) does, however, allow for the admission of male resident outsiders of Edomite and Egyptian extraction after the passage of three generations. By implication, male resident outsiders of foreign heritage who do not belong to the four groups in question, and all foreign females, are unaffected by these restrictions. If my interpretation of Deut 23:4–9 (Eng., 3–8) and its implications is correct, then there is certainly solid ground on which to argue that the dependent lists, which place the resident outsider in the assembly, could refer to the foreign resident outsider. After all, the foreign resident outsider is—with a few exceptions—generally admissible to the assembly as implied in Deut 23:4–9 (Eng., 3–8). Though not decisive for interpreting the dependent lists, this text serves at least as an independent witness in Deuteronomy to the entry of aliens into the assembly.

The possibility that the resident outsider of the dependent lists is a foreigner is now established for Deuteronomistic materials. Therefore, I will now explore some of the implications of reading the dependent lists in this way as I assess the Deuteronomistic School's treatment of the resident outsider, particularly in light of the views of the Holiness School. Indicators of the dependency of the resident outsider are found throughout both Holiness and Deuteronomistic materials. In the Holiness Source, the resident outsider's dependency is suggested in many texts by his presence "with" an Israelite patron, who is addressed as "you" in the texts; this dependency is not, however, foregrounded. Concern in the Holiness Source focuses rather on circumcision as the requirement par excellence for full incorporation into the cultic life of Israel. Once circumcised, the resident outsider of foreign background has the option to embrace the same cultic obligations and privileges as the native Israelite, and this form of potential equality is emphasized repeatedly by the "one teaching" rhetoric common to Holiness materials. The resident outsider of the Holiness Source remains a distinct entity, however; the binary contrast between him and the native underscores the resident outsider's abiding difference. He is never absorbed into Israel and his full participation in Israel's cultic life is optional, unlike that of the native.

In contrast to the Holiness Source, which foregrounds circumcision as the route to full incorporation into the cultic community, Deuteronomistic materials—if I read them correctly—cast dependency as the route to integration in Israel. The resident outsider who participates in cultic life is always presented in Deuteronomistic texts as the client of an Israelite household head. He enters the sanctuary sphere not in his own right, but with his patron and his patron's other dependents. Socially, he is the inferior of the local, native adult male. His status in Deuteronomistic materials is comparable to that of women and minors, though he is neither. The social inferiority of the resident outsider is both realized and communicated in the very cultic settings that he enters as a dependent of his patron. If there is any historical resonance to this portrayal of the resident outsider as client, then the resident outsider's dependent status would probably have functioned to enhance his patron's honor in the community. Patrons would have been motivated to acquire clients in order to increase their own status vis-à-vis rivals, if Roman evidence is any indication.[74] Nonetheless, the resident outsider of the Deuteronomistic dependent lists, if he is a foreigner, is more fully integrated into the Israelite community than the foreign resident outsider of Holiness materials. He is part of the "people" (Deut 31:12); he enters the covenant (Deut 29:9–11 [Eng., 10–12]); he stands in the assembly (Josh 8:35). Even the term "Israel" sometimes includes him (Josh 8:35), as it never does in the Holiness Source, which always maintains a distinction between native or Israelite on the one hand, and resident outsider of foreign origin on the other. If I am correct to understand the resident outsider of the Deuteronomistic dependent lists as a foreigner, then, ironically, the Deuteronomistic School's incorporation by a strategy of subordination results in a greater degree of belonging than does the Holiness School's strategy of optional incorporation by means of circumcision, with an emphasis on equality. Yet even the Deuteronomistic School does not fully and permanently absorb the resident outsider of alien origin into the people Israel, since he is not incorporated into the lineage-patrimony system (contrast Ezek 47:22–23).

Both Holiness and Deuteronomistic materials struggle with how to position the resident outsider of foreign extraction vis-à-vis the people of

Israel. The foreign resident outsider is a problem: He is among Israelites for the long-term, even many generations, but he is not one of them. He is in a precarious position: He has no place in the lineage structure, with its advantages (such as redemption or blood vengeance); he has no claim to a part of the national patrimony. The place of a resident outsider in a community is always potentially open to challenge, as Gen 19:7–9 show. Difference makes him a potential target for xenophobes (Esth 3:8); his loyalty to the host people is always potentially suspect (Exod 1:8–10). The majority voices in both the Deuteronomistic and Holiness corpora opt for integration of the problematic resident outsider of alien heritage, the Deuteronomists by means of subordination, the Holiness School by means of circumcision. Minority voices in both sources opt for exclusion or marginalization. Debate within and between these sources underscores the problematic position of the alien who resides in the midst of a people not his own.

"Exile" Community/Peoples of the Land(s)

The third manifestation of the Israelite/alien dyad that I will examine is the opposition "exile" community/peoples of the land(s), which occurs frequently in Ezra-Nehemiah. Other ways of expressing the Israelite/alien contrast in Ezra-Nehemiah include holy seed (zeraʿ haqqōdeš)/peoples of the lands in Ezra 9:2; Israel/persons of mixed background (ʿēreb) in Neh 13:3; and seed of Israel (zeraʿ yiśrāʾēl)/aliens (běnê nēkār) in Neh 9:2. The setting for the narratives in which the opposition of Israelite and alien generates difference is Judah of the Persian period. The narratives describe a time of troubles during which both Ezra and Nehemiah are portrayed undertaking reforming missions from the eastern Empire to Jerusalem (Ezra 7; Nehemiah 2).[75] Where both the Holiness Source and Deuteronomistic texts find ways to integrate the resident outsider of foreign origin into what they represent as a majority Israel, the situation described by Ezra-Nehemiah is quite different. Ezra-Nehemiah constitutes "Israel" strictly as the returnees and their allies[76]; those who do not support the program of this "exile" community's leadership are excluded from the community's institutions and cultic life.[77] Ezra-Nehemiah's "Israel" is a much troubled entity in its own land; its leadership seeks to separate it socially from all persons classed as alien, for these are perceived as a threat to the people. It is not surprising that the integrated resident outsider of alien background is noticeably absent from the discourse of these books, since for them all persons and things understood as alien are unwelcome in Israel.[78] Even wives of foreign origin and their children are expelled from the community in these narratives; this is per-

haps their most striking characteristic. The exclusion of alien wives and
their issue, an innovative move, is portrayed in Ezra-Nehemiah as the
result of initiatives by the returnee leadership. It is accomplished through
the use of the opposition Israelite/alien, with alien constituted to include
foreign wives and their children. Exclusion is justified through exegetical
elaboration of earlier texts such as Lev 18:24–30, which urges Israel to
avoid the polluting acts ("abominations") of its Canaanite predecessors;
Deut 23:4–9 (Eng., 3–8), which restricts access to the assembly for males
of four groups of alien residents; and Deut 7:1–6 (esp. v. 3), which forbids
Israelites to intermarry with the Canaanites and other predecessors of
Israel in the land.[79]

The powerful discourse of purity explicitly informs several of the narratives that describe and justify the forced removal of persons classed as
alien. The notion that all things alien are polluting—including alien
blood—is not encountered in Deuteronomistic materials, the Holiness
Source, or any other earlier texts. An ideological innovation, it functions
in Ezra-Nehemiah to buttress the text's exclusionary program. Like all
innovations, the idea that all things alien defile has roots in earlier texts
and traditions. The opposition "exile" community/peoples of the land(s)
is an effective tool used in Ezra-Nehemiah to separate the "true" Israel
from all persons classed as alien. Unlike the polarity circumcised/uncir-
cumcised, this opposition is not gendered. Where the pairing circumcised/
uncircumcised applies to males only, "exile" community/peoples of the
land(s) applies to men, women, and children. Nor does this opposition
construct a permeable boundary around Israel, as the dyad circumcised/
uncircumcised does. An alien male can become circumcised and thus
qualify to participate in all aspects of cultic life according to the Holiness
Source; in contrast, there is simply no way to overcome classification as
an alien polluter in Ezra-Nehemiah.

The idea that aliens defile is suggested by a number of texts in Ezra-
Nehemiah.[80] Two texts in Nehemiah 13 are the clearest illustrations of
this notion, though other texts may also suggest the idea less directly.
Ezra-Nehemiah speaks frequently of the Israelites' separating themselves
from foreign wives and their children; the text also mentions removal
from the community of other aliens and of Israelites who will not divorce
their foreign wives. Neh 13:4–9 describes the removal of the belongings
of Tobiah the Ammonite, a Yhwh-worshiper, from the temple court. A
room of the temple complex that had been a storage place for offerings
had been given by a priest Elyashib to Tobiah, a rival governor of Nehemiah. At Nehemiah's order, Tobiah's belongings are thrown out, the
room is purified, and the offerings formerly stored in the room are restored. Purification of the room suggests that it was viewed as polluted,
and the source of the pollution, the text implies, is the presence of Tobiah

the Ammonite and his belongings. Notice that according to the purity ideology attributed by implication to the priest Elyashib, the alien Yahwist Tobiah could not have been an agent of pollution; if he were, he would not have been admitted to the temple sphere in the first place. But according to the innovative purity ideology of Ezra-Nehemiah, the very presence of the Ammonite Tobiah and his belongings is apparently polluting. Nehemiah's removal of Tobiah's belongings should probably be understood to suggest Tobiah's expulsion from the temple sphere, though the text says nothing explicitly about this. Neh 13:28–30 also understands aliens to have the power to pollute, in this case in the context of intermarriage within the priesthood. Verse 28 states that one of the sons of Yoyada the son of Elyashib the high priest[81] had married a daughter of Sanballat the Horonite, governor of Samaria. Nehemiah expels this grandson of Elyashib from his presence, and speaks in v. 30 of purifying a polluted priesthood "from everything alien" (wĕṭihartîm mikkol nēkār).[82] The priestly lineage, in this case, has become polluted as a result of intermarriage. Ezra 9:2 lends itself to a similar interpretation, though it only implies that intermarriage with aliens pollutes the bloodline; there is no explicit statement of this, as there is in Neh 13:28–30. Ezra 9:1–2 states that the people have intermarried with aliens, so that "the holy seed has been mixed (wĕhitʿārēbû zeraʿ haqqōdeš) with the peoples of the lands." The unusual expression "holy seed"[83] suggests a lineage constructed as subject to defilement and requiring vigilant protection from all sources of pollution[84]; all things holy require such protection, as texts describing the responsibilities of the priesthood illustrate. The idea of a "holy seed" is most likely an elaboration of an older notion of Israel as a holy people, a notion found prominently both in Deuteronomistic and Holiness materials (for example, Exod 19:6; Lev 20:26; Deut 14:2).[85] The idea that the "holy seed" has been "mixed" with alien nations suggests that it has been polluted by such mixing, just as any holy item, person, or locus may become polluted if it comes into contact with a polluting agent.

A few other texts in Ezra-Nehemiah may suggest that aliens are polluting, given the more explicit statements in passages such as Neh 13:4–9 and 13:28–30, but the texts themselves are not entirely clear in this regard. In Ezra 6:21, the returnees and their allies who had separated themselves "from the uncleanness of the nations of the land" make the Passover together. In Ezra 9:11, Canaan is described as "a land of defilement (niddâ) because of the defilement (niddâ) of the peoples of the lands (and) because of their abominations which have filled it from end to end with their uncleanness (ṭumʾātām)."[86] The source or sources of alien pollution are not entirely clear from these two texts. Ezra 6:21 says nothing about actions specifically and might refer to either actions or the aliens themselves. Ezra 9:11 mentions alien abominations, presumably an allusion to

Leviticus 18, where polluting actions of aliens are cataloged. But Ezra 9:11 also speaks of pollution in such a way that one can understand both alien actions and the aliens themselves to be polluting. Though "because of their abominations which have filled it from end to end with their uncleanness" refers to polluting actions, the phrase "because of the defilement (niddâ) of the peoples of the lands" is ambiguous and could refer to the peoples themselves, rather than their actions, as the source of pollution. Given the clearer examples of the notion of the polluting power of aliens in Neh 13:4–9 and 28–30, I am inclined also to see in Ezra 6:21; 9:2, 11 reference to the polluting power of aliens.

What are the origins of this idea that aliens defile? It was argued many decades ago that the pollution of alien worship was the source of the notion that aliens themselves pollute.[87] Certainly, "idols" are represented as polluting in a number of texts antedating Ezra-Nehemiah.[88] The idea that aliens pollute, however, has several antecedents. Some or all of them probably contributed to the development of the notion of alien pollution. Pinpointing a single source for the idea is impossible, since allusion is generally not made in the texts of Ezra-Nehemiah to earlier texts on which this notion is based. Therefore, the best that can be done is to point out several possible antecedents. Aside from the polluting power of "idols," there is a tradition witnessed in a number of biblical texts that alien lands are polluting.[89] A third antecedent for the idea that aliens pollute is the notion that some of their characteristic behaviors pollute. Holiness materials in Leviticus 18 and 20 represent the most extensive articulation of this idea in the biblical anthology. Leviticus 18 and 20, more extensively than any other biblical texts, associate aliens with polluting actions. But nowhere in these texts are aliens themselves said to be polluting. The framework in Lev 20:24–26 speaks of Yhwh's separating Israel from the nations: "You shall be holy to me, for I, Yhwh, am holy, and I have separated you from the nations to be mine" (Lev 20:26). Since so many alien behaviors are polluting according to this text, it would not be a surprising move by later exegetes to conclude that the aliens themselves are a source of pollution and worthy of removal from the community. The emphasis in Lev 20:24–26 on Yhwh's separation of Israel from the nations, and Israel's obligation to distinguish between what is clean and unclean, may have served as a further stimulus to this kind of exegesis. A fourth possible antecedent for the idea of alien pollution is the notion that uncircumcised male aliens are polluting. This idea, which may be present in Ezek 44:7, Isa 52:1, and Genesis 34, might have provided a basis for the generation of the notion of the defilement of all aliens. The idea that all aliens pollute may in fact be simply an elaboration of the notion that uncircumcised male aliens are agents of defilement. A reading of texts that associate pollution with alien lands and alien actions, in

conjunction with other texts such as Deut 23:4–9 (Eng., 3–8), which bans
certain alien groups from the assembly, might have provided the impetus
to associate the pollution caused by uncircumcised male aliens with all
aliens, including women. Expansive readings of earlier biblical texts such
as Leviticus 18 and 20 and Deut 23:4–9 (Eng., 3–8) are, after all, characteristic of Ezra-Nehemiah, as others have noted.[90]

The exclusion of all aliens, including foreign women and their children, from the Israelite community and cult is a monumental departure
from practices represented in earlier texts. In materials antedating Ezra-
Nehemiah, the ancestry of a child is traced through the father. If a child
has an Israelite father, the child is an Israelite. Even in the case of a concubine mother, texts give the impression that the child is counted as the son
or daughter of his or her father. A number of passages antedating Ezra-
Nehemiah bear witness to the Israelite lineage of a child born to an Israelite father and a non-Israelite mother. Gen 46:20 describes the origin of
Ephraim and Manasseh, the eponymous ancestors of two major tribes of
Israel: They are the sons of Joseph and his Egyptian wife Asenet, yet they
are Joseph's heirs and through them is his lineage traced. Another example from ancestral materials is Moses' son Gershom, whose mother is
Zipporah, daughter of the priest of Midian (Exod 2:21). Even so, Moses'
priestly line is traced through Gershom according to Judg 18:30.[91] Other
narratives claim that David's great-grandmother Ruth was a Moabite immigrant to Judah (Ruth 4:17). Absalom, David's son by his wife Maacah
of Geshur, would have been David's eldest surviving child and heir to the
throne had he not been killed during his rebellion (2 Sam 3:3). The Israelite lineage of each of these persons is not at issue in the texts that describe
them; each one of them inherits his claim to Israelite descent from his
father and genealogies record and underscore that claim.[92] Other evidence suggests that even a foreign concubine's son could be counted
among the sons of an Israelite father and could inherit with the sons of his
wives. An example of this is 1 Chr 7:14, a genealogical fragment of the
tribe of Manasseh from which we learn that Manasseh's Aramean concubine bore to him Asriel and Machir; the latter became the father of Gilead, the eponymous ancestor of an important Transjordanian Israelite
group.[93]

In contrast to this evidence concerning the lineage of children of an
Israelite father, Lev 24:10–16, 23 suggest that the child of an alien father
and an Israelite mother is an alien. The text concerns the punishment of
a man who curses Yhwh during a fight with another man. In it, the man
who curses Yhwh, who is the son of an Israelite woman and an Egyptian
man, is referred to as "the son of the Israelite woman" (Lev 24:10, 11),
while his rival is called "the Israelite man." Clearly, the man who curses
Yhwh is not regarded as an Israelite by this text, though his connection

with Israel is foregrounded through reference to his mother. What then is his status? In the final form of this Holiness text, emphasis is placed on the idea of equal punishment for the native and the resident outsider of foreign heritage who violate Yhwh's laws (vv. 16, 23). The Holiness redactors seem to understand the story to be about a foreign resident outsider who commits a capital crime and is justly executed for it. Thus, according to the text, it would seem that the son of an Israelite woman and a father who is a resident outsider of foreign origin is classed as an alien rather than a native Israelite.

Why was the ancestry of the father determinative of a child's ancestry? The answer lies in the residence and inheritance structure typical of Israelite village life according to recent reconstructions based on readings of archaeological and textual sources.[94] A father headed a multigenerational household referred to as a bêt 'āb, or "father's house," in biblical texts. Normally, sons remained in their "father's house" until they established a household of their own at their father's death. Fathers bequeathed to sons shares in the patrimonial land on which the family tomb was maintained.[95] A son kept his father's name alive in Israel through ancestral rites[96] and through his succession to the patrimony. Thus, archaeological and textual sources suggest that patrilocal residence and patrilineal inheritance of landed property were characteristic of the male experience in village life. Given these practices, it would be truly surprising if a male's lineage were not determined by his father's background. The father, after all, provides the son's link to his patrimony and to his primary kin group. The life experience of a daughter differed significantly from that of a son, though texts suggest that she, too, remained in her father's house until marriage and might return to it at divorce or widowhood.[97] Typically, a woman left her father's house at marriage and moved in with her husband's extended family, where she was incorporated into the family structure. This social structure, characterized by patrilocal residence and patrilineal inheritance for males and the movement of women in (wives) and out (daughters) at marriage, would have allowed for a relatively unproblematic absorption of foreign wives, since alien women, like Israelite women, were not lineage bearers themselves.[98] It is therefore unsurprising that no early laws proscribe or restrict intermarriage between Israelites and foreigners. The typical intermarriage, given the social structure and practices, would have involved a foreign woman and an Israelite man and would therefore not affect the lineage. Some foreign women might have found themselves as refugees in Israel, displaced because of famine or war[99]; others were no doubt brought to Israel as captives. Deut 21:10–14 prescribes a routine when an Israelite man wishes to marry a captured foreign woman. The law expresses no disapproval whatsoever of the practice, though it restricts the rights of the Israelite husband with respect to his captive wife should he wish to divorce her. On the whole, texts of the monarchic and exilic eras give the impression that the intermarriage of an Israelite man and an alien woman was not understood to be much different from the marriage of two Israelites, since the consequences for the children were basically the same: Israelite status.

There are a number of texts antedating the fifth century that seek to proscribe intermarriage, or at least express discomfort with it. Several texts in the ancestral narratives bear witness to the notion that marriage within the kin group is desirable and speak negatively of intermarriage with the inhabitants of the land of Canaan (Genesis 24; 27:46–28:2). Genesis 34 may be read to suggest that a lack of circumcision was an impediment to the marriage of an Israelite woman to an alien man; the text, however, implies that circumcision would, under normal circumstances, have addressed the problem sufficiently. Deuteronomy forbids intermarriage specifically with the Canaanites and other inhabitants of the land at the time of Israel's supposed conquest, though it is unclear what practical application such a proscription would have had during the period of the text's composition (that is, late monarchy or exile). The reason given for the proscription is the danger posed by alien worship to Yhwh's exclusive covenant claim on Israel (Deut 7:3–4). Alluding to Deut 7:3–4 and interpreting it in an expansive fashion to refer to aliens other than Canaanites, 1 Kgs 11:1–4, condemns Solomon for his many foreign wives, who seduce him into worshiping their gods. The Deuteronomists understand the successful secession of the northern tribes to have been the result of Solomon's disloyalty to Yhwh (1 Kgs 11:11).[100] In addition to these passages concerning intermarriage among Israelites, several texts specifically forbid priests to marry alien women.[101] In short, though intermarriage between an Israelite man and a foreign woman is viewed unproblematically by many biblical texts antedating the fifth century, the occasional text takes a negative position on it in certain specific contexts (Deut 7:3–4; Ezek 44:22) or more generally (1 Kgs 11:2–5). These texts bear witness to what appears to have been a minority position of certain circles in Israel.

How was it possible to defend a position favoring the expulsion of foreign women and their children from the Israelite community of the fifth century? Such a radical departure from past practice was justified by means of several exegetical innovations. Exegetes brought together a number of originally unrelated texts with negative views of alien groups, their actions, or intermarriage. Read each in light of the others, these texts were used to formulate an expansive exegesis that could support the exclusion of all aliens from the Israelite community.[102] A primary example of this expansive exegesis is Ezra 9:10–12, a polemic against intermarriage constructed as a prayer of Ezra to Yhwh:

> Now then, what shall we say O our God, after this, for we have forsaken your commandments which you commanded through your servants the prophets as follows: "The land which you are about to enter to inherit is a land of defilement because of the defilement of the peoples of the lands (and) because of their abominations which have filled it from end to end with their uncleanness.[103] Now then, your daughters you shall not give to their sons, and their daughters you shall not take for your sons; you shall not seek their welfare or their good ever, in order that you be strong and eat the good things of the land, and you give (it) to your children as an inheritance forever."

As M. Fishbane has pointed out, Ezra's prayer draws upon materials from Lev 18:26–30; Deut 7:3–4; and Deut 23:4–9 (Eng., 3–8).[104] The ban on intermarriage with the Canaanites in Deut 7:3 is recast here as a proscription of all intermarriages. Ezra 9 justifies the strict interdiction on all intermarriages by means of allusion to Lev 18:26–30, which associates defiling abominations with the Canaanites, and by means of quotation from Deut 23:7 (Eng., 6), which commands Israelites not to seek the welfare of the Moabite and the Ammonite, who are banned from the assembly of Yhwh.[105] In Ezra 9:11, the defiling abominations of the Canaanites in Lev 18:26–30 have become characteristic of aliens generally and are a justification for avoiding intermarriage. The text may also associate uncleanness with the aliens themselves, as I have noted ("because of the defilement of the peoples of the lands"). In 9:12, the command of Deut 23:7 (Eng., 6; "you shall not seek their welfare . . ."), uttered with respect specifically to Ammonite and Moabite males, has been recast to apply to all aliens in question.[106] Similar exegetical moves are evident in Neh 13:1–3, 23–27. Neh 13:1–3 describes a public reading of the Torah in the hearing of the people. After hearing of the permanent exclusion of the Ammonite and the Moabite in Deut 23:4–7 (Eng., 3–6), the people are said to separate "everyone of mixed background from Israel" (kol ʿēreb miyyiśrāʾēl).[107] Again, an expansive reading of Deut 23:4–7 (Eng., 3–6) results in the exclusion of far more persons than the law in Deuteronomy intended. "Everyone of mixed background" must refer to the children of intermarriages, children with Israelite fathers who would have been classed as Israelites in the past. Now, however, they are classed as aliens, set in rhetorical opposition to Israel and expelled from the Israelite community according to the text.[108] Neh 13:23–27 is similar. This text makes use of Deut 7:3 to justify Nehemiah's attack on Israelite men who have intermarried with Ashdodite, Ammonite, and Moabite women, though Deut 7:3 does not apply to any of these three groups in its original textual setting. In Neh 13:25, however, the verse is understood to refer to all alien groups, including Ashdodites, Ammonites, and Moabites. Neh 10:29–31 (Eng., 28–30) has a similar understanding of the meaning of Deut 7:3.

The circle responsible for these texts uses biblical exegesis as a tool to promote an innovative program of exclusion. Several biblical texts that antedate Ezra-Nehemiah, and express negative views of certain alien groups, their behavior, and intermarriage with them, are interpreted in Ezra-Nehemiah in an expansive manner that allows them to provide support for the exclusivist program of the leaders of the returnees. Deut 7:3–4, which proscribes intermarriage with the Canaanites because of a fear that intermarrying Israelites would worship other gods, is recast here as a general ban on intermarriage, even with non-Israelite Yhwh worshipers! Deut 23:4–9 (Eng., 3–8), which dealt only with males from four particular groups and had no explicit link to intermarriage in its original setting, is understood here to support a ban on marriage to aliens. Each of these texts is used in turn to support the exclusion of not only foreign wives but also their children. The introduction of the notion that aliens themselves are defiling buttresses this program of generalized exclusion based on the leadership's reading of several earlier texts. If aliens are defiling, their ability to pollute justifies their absolute exclusion from cult and community, both of which are constructed as holy.

There are interesting implications to the move in Ezra-Nehemiah to classify the children of Israelite fathers and foreign mothers as aliens. In Ezra-Nehemiah, ancestry is no longer traced exclusively through the father, though the books in their final form preserve conventional genealogical materials tracing lineage through males. In earlier texts, as I have argued, an alien mother did not affect a child's Israelite ancestry as long as the child's father was an Israelite. The lineage of children of mixed marriages depended on their father alone. The ideology of Ezra-Nehemiah represents a major innovation in the way in which a child's ancestry is determined. The mother is now understood as a lineage bearer like the father, and alien ancestry from any source results in a child's classification as an alien and, therefore, exclusion from the community. The different modes of determining ancestry in these texts illustrate nicely the way in which "alien" and "native" are malleable social constructions rather than static, transhistorical, and transcultural categories. They are the products of social processes that occur in particular historical contexts rather than simply givens. Where the child of an Israelite father was, before the fifth century, represented as a native, no matter what the ancestry of the mother, in Ezra-Nehemiah the native category belongs only to those whose parents are both classed as Israelites. "Alien," understood in texts antedating the fifth century to apply to persons of foreign birth or persons lacking an Israelite father, becomes in Ezra-Nehemiah a term applied to persons with any foreign blood.

What is the origin of the innovative program of alien exclusion characteristic of Ezra-Nehemiah? I believe the etiology of the notion of alien exclusion can be traced to the Holiness School's rhetoric of separation from the nations, avoidance of impurity, and Israel's holiness, which finds expression in Lev 20:24–26: "I am Yhwh, your god, who has separated you (hibdaltî 'etkem) from the peoples. You will distinguish (wĕhibdaltem) between clean beast and unclean, and between unclean fowl and clean. . . . You shall be holy to me, for I, Yhwh, am holy, and I have separated you (wā'abdîl 'etkem) from the nations to be mine."[109] For the Holiness School, Israel is called upon to be holy like its god.[110] Part of being holy is the avoidance of defilement, illustrated here by allusion to the dietary laws. Israel, according to Holiness circles, has been separated from the peoples to be Yhwh's. Through appropriate actions, Israel can be holy like Yhwh; maintaining holiness is a matter of avoiding what defiles.[111] The separation of Israel as holy in Holiness texts is modeled on the separation and holiness of the sanctuary and its servants.[112] The ideology of Ezra-Nehemiah co-opts and transforms the Holiness notion of a holy Israel separated from the peoples whose charge is to avoid defiling things in order to be holy like its god. The rhetoric of separation (bdl) from other peoples, intended in the Holiness Source simply to foreground Israel's special status as Yhwh's people and buttress the Holiness School's call for the avoidance of polluting actions and things, is concretized in Ezra-Nehemiah in the expulsion of those classed as alien from the community and in the separation from all persons and things understood to be defiling.[113] The holiness for which Israel is ordered to strive in the Holiness Source becomes in Ezra-Nehemiah a matter of lineage. Israel is the "holy seed"; it must be protected through separation from the nations (Ezra 9:1–2; cp. Neh 9:2).

Contesting Alien Exclusion from Israel and Its Cultic Life

Isa 56:3–7 presents what is perhaps the best extant example of resistance to the exclusion of the alien from cult and community. There has been much debate about the historical context that might have produced such a pericope; some commentators have argued for an early post-exilic date while others have insisted that the text ought to be read in light of the fifth-century reforms described in Ezra-Nehemiah.[114] The text reads as follows:

> Let the alien who has attached himself to Yhwh not say,
>   "Yhwh will surely separate me from his people."
>   And let the eunuch not say,

"I am a dried up tree."
For thus says Yhwh,
to the eunuchs who observe my Sabbaths,
and choose what I delight in,
and grasp onto my covenant:
I will give to them in my temple and within my walls
a monument and name
better than sons and daughters.
An everlasting name I will give to them,
which shall not be cut off.
And as for the aliens who have attached themselves to Yhwh,
to serve him and to love the name of Yhwh,
(and) to be his servants;
all who keep the Sabbath so as not to profane it,
and who grasp onto my covenant:
I will bring them to my holy mountain,
and I will cause them to rejoice in my house of prayer.
Their burnt offerings and their sacrifices
will be acceptable on my altar,
for my temple will be called a house of prayer for all nations.

This passage appears to allude to an expansive interpretation of Deut 23:2–9 (Eng., 1–8), not unlike the kind of exegesis witnessed in such texts as Ezra 9:12. In Deut 23:2–9 (Eng., 1–8), select alien males, males with damaged genitals, and the mamzēr (?)[115] are banned from entering "the assembly of Yhwh." The proscription of Ammonites, Moabites, men with damaged genitals, and the mamzēr is without limitation; the interdiction on Edomites and Egyptians is voided in the third generation. Isa 56:3–7 seems to be responding to an understanding of Deut 23:2–9 (Eng., 1–8) that would ban all aliens and eunuchs[116] from community and cult, including those aliens who are loyal to Yhwh's covenant. This expansive interpretation of the proscriptions of Deut 23:2–9 (Eng., 1–8) is here challenged: the alien "who has attached himself to Yhwh" has a place in Israelite cultic life and community, as does the eunuch who observes Yhwh's commandments. The language of the challenge is both interesting and potentially significant for any attempt to date this text. Verse 3 urges the alien not to say, "Yhwh will surely separate me (habdēl yabdîlanî yhwh) from his people." The language of separation from Yhwh's people in this verse recalls vividly the very distinct rhetoric of Ezra-Nehemiah, as has long been noted, and suggests that this text may indeed be responding to the exclusionary program of the returnee leadership described in those texts.[117] This understanding of Isa 56:3–7 finds support in the observation that the program of the text's opponents, as presented in Ezra-

Nehemiah, is indeed based on an expansive reading of Deut 23:4–9 (Eng., 3–8), which would ban all aliens from the community. Ezra 9:12 bears witness to just such a reading of Deut 23:4–9 (Eng., 3–8). Furthermore, the use of a particular expression for an alien, ben nēkār, recalls the usage of Neh 9:2: "They separated the seed of Israel from all aliens."[118] Thus, it is certainly plausible to see Isa 56:3–7, if not 56:1–8, as a composition of the fifth century, a response to the exclusionary program described in Ezra-Nehemiah.

If Isa 56:3–7 is responding to an exclusionary program not unlike that which is portrayed in Ezra-Nehemiah, how does it resist or subvert it? Yhwh speaks eloquently and authoritatively, through the medium of the prophet, in favor of the inclusion of the pious alien and eunuch in the ritual life of the cultic community. The text of Isa 56:3–7 boldly asserts that contrary to the view of its author's opponents, Yhwh will not separate (bdl) the alien "who has attached himself (lwh) to Yhwh" from the people of Israel. It goes on to spell out what it means to be so attached: serving Yhwh and loving his name; observing the Sabbath so as not to profane it; grasping onto Yhwh's covenant (v. 6). Some, because of the use of the particular verb "to serve" (šrt), have seen in the alien who does these things a cultic functionary of some kind, or at least someone who qualifies for such "service."[119] Though this is possible, such cultic service is not the focus of the passage. To love Yhwh's name, to observe the Sabbath, to be Yhwh's servant ('ebed), and to rejoice cultically in the sanctuary and offer acceptable sacrifices are not activities restricted to cultic personnel. On the contrary, they are activities common to all worshipers of Yhwh, and they are the focus of Isa 56:6–7. Once in the temple sphere, the alien is described as a worshiper offering acceptable sacrifices, not as a cultic functionary.[120]

The use of the verb lwh, "to attach," in Isa 56:3, 6 is not without interest. It is apparently used in this text as the antithesis of bdl, "to separate": the alien "who has attached himself to Yhwh" is precisely the person whom the opponents of alien inclusion would have Yhwh separate "from his people" and, by implication, his cult. The verb lwh is used elsewhere for the incorporation of both the resident outsider (gēr) and other nations into Israel in transformative prophetic visions such as Isa 14:1: "For Yhwh will have compassion on Jacob, and will choose Israel once again. He will set them in their land, and the resident outsider will be attached (wĕnilwâ) to them, and they will be joined (wĕnispĕḥû) to the House of Jacob." Zech 2:15 (Eng., 11) is similar: "Many nations will be attached (wĕnilwû) to Yhwh on that day, and will become my people."[121] Some texts use lwh as an idiom for entering into a covenant: "Come, let us attach ourselves (wĕnilwû) to Yhwh (in an) eternal covenant that will not be forgotten" (Jer 50:5).[122] The use of lwh in Isa 56:3, 6 recalls these other texts in which aliens are incorporated into the community. If I am correct to date Isa 56:3–7 to the fifth century, then texts such as Isa 14:1 and Zech 2:15 would be earlier, and thus Isa 56:3–7 might well be alluding to them as a strategy to buttress its inclusive position against the ideology of exclusion.[123] Just as the opponents of the group that produced Isa 56:3–7 drew upon earlier, authoritative texts to construct their position, so the circle responsible for Isa 56:3–7 might have had their own such texts as well.

Another way in which Isa 56:3–7 might resist exclusionary ideology is its treatment of the alien in relation to holiness. In Ezra-Nehemiah, the alien is constructed as a threat to holiness, a polluter whose presence in the sanctuary and whose connection by marriage or blood to Israelites must be terminated.[124] In contrast, the alien of Isa 56:3–7, "who has attached himself to Yhwh" will be brought by Yhwh himself to Yhwh's holy mountain and will be made to rejoice in Yhwh's temple, as Yhwh's other worshipers do. Yhwh will accept the alien's offerings because, the text suggests, Yhwh's temple is "a house of prayer for all nations." In contrast to the program of Ezra-Nehemiah, which seeks to separate all aliens from what is holy, Isa 56:3–7 has Yhwh promising to bring the alien who is committed to the covenant into contact with Yhwh's holy mountain and its temple, where his offerings will be accepted on Yhwh's altar. Contact with what is holy, according to this text, has been earned by the alien in question because of his commitment to the covenant. The alien is anything but an excluded polluter in Isa 56:3–7.

Cultural Mechanisms of Alien Incorporation into Israel

I have now completed my examination of three forms of the binary opposition Israelite/alien in the biblical text. These differentiate those classed as Israelites from others using somewhat different strategies, often for different purposes. Binary strategizing may produce either permeable or impermeable boundaries around Israel and its cult, depending on the context and goals of the group responsible for the texts in question. Where Ezra-Nehemiah uses a binary strategy of differentiation to create an absolutely impermeable boundary around Israel, other materials, such as the Holiness Source and Deuteronomistic texts, also use binary strategies, but these allow for the incorporation of the resident outsider of foreign extraction. In the texts in which the alien may be incorporated, how is this incorporation accomplished? I will now explore the textual evidence for mechanisms of alien incorporation into Israel.[125] Through ritual action, texts suggest that it is possible for certain aliens in certain contexts to find a place in the corporate entity Israel and in its cultic life.

Incorporation might require the alien to assume a new status (for example, as slave or client), or it might involve the erasure of the alien's previous identity, including the alien's foreignness. Rites of transition accomplish incorporation, moving the alien from an external locus to a place in the community and its ritual activity.[126] My examination will focus on three examples of individuals who become incorporated into the social and ritual body Israel: the male slave owned by an Israelite, the female war captive who becomes the wife or concubine of her Israelite captor, and the resident outsider of alien lineage who becomes a client of an Israelite patron. I focus on these three individuals because extant texts describe ritual processes by which they come to be incorporated into the Israelite community, or at least make allusion to such processes.

The Foreign Male Slave

Biblical narratives and legal texts speak from time to time of slaves of foreign origin. Unlike the Israelite enslaved because of debt, whose period of compulsory servitude was limited,[127] enslaved aliens could be made to serve for a lifetime.[128] Their progeny were also slaves, and both they and their children could be bequeathed as part of an inheritance from one generation to another.[129] Surviving texts suggest that enslaved foreigners captured in war or purchased from a seller for money were a common phenomenon on the west Asian cultural scene in various periods. Physically displaced and outside of local networks of kinship, the foreign slave was dependent to a very large degree on his master; he was "an extension of his master's power," "a social non-person" in the words of O. Patterson, author of a major synthetic, cross-cultural study of slavery. Patterson speaks insightfully of the "social death" and "natal alienation" of the slave: "[A]lienated from all 'rights' or claims of birth, he ceased to belong *in his own right* to any legitimate social order. . . . He was truly a genealogical isolate."[130] The "natally alienated" slave found a place in the master's society at its margins. Patterson shows how both the slave's "natal alienation" and his incorporation into the master's household as a marginal entity were accomplished through rites of transition common to many cultures. They include naming, donning of special clothing, distinct hairstyles, and body markings.[131] There must certainly have been rites of transition in Israel that brought into being both male and female slaves at the time they were bought or captured and functioned to incorporate them into the new community where they might spend the rest of their lives. Unfortunately, only one detailed description of such rites of transition survives in our texts: Deut 21:10–14, on the female war captive's transition and incorporation. No comparable description of the transition rites of the male slave is extant. There are, however, several texts that speak of the role of circumcision in the incorporation of a male slave into the community and its ritual life, as well as some other texts that may help us to imagine other components of the male slave's rites of transition. Exod 21:5–6 and Deut 15:17 are two examples of the latter. Both texts describe the voluntary ritual transformation of a Hebrew slave into a lifelong bondman through rites of oral confession and ear boring by the owner at a special locus. The Hebrew slave, obligated to serve only six years, may choose permanent servitude according to Exod 21:5–6: "If the slave says, 'I love my master, my wife, and my children; I will not go forth a freeman,' then his master shall bring him to God; he shall bring him to the door or the doorpost, and his master shall bore his ear with a boring instrument, and he shall serve him forever."[132] One aspect of the preceding scenario might represent a normal ritual means by which a foreigner was made into a slave in Israel. The rite of ear boring could well have been a central ritual component of this transformation. What was done to the Hebrew slave in the exceptional circumstance described by Exod 21:5–6 and Deut 15:17 might have been the norm for the newly acquired foreign slave, at least in some communities.[133]

Several texts portray circumcision as the central rite of the foreign male slave's process of incorporation into the community. Genesis 17:10–14, which conceives of circumcision as a sign of the covenant between Yhwh and Israel, requires the same circumcision rite for male slaves as for sons born to Israelite fathers. "Every male" circumcised on the eighth day includes slaves, both houseborn and those acquired for money; the "covenant in the flesh" is borne equally by the male slave and the free male Israelite. Exod 12:43–49, concerning the eating of the Passover sacrifice, requires circumcision of the foreign slave acquired for money (v. 44). The text suggests that the slave, like the free Israelite male, has no choice in the matter: "As for any male slave acquired for money, you shall circumcise him; then he shall eat it." In contrast, the resident outsider of foreign background has the option to be circumcised and eat the Passover sacrifice but is not required to do either according to this text (v. 48). The nonresident foreigner (ben nēkār) and the (foreign) wage laborer (tôšāb wĕśākîr) form a third category of persons in this text; they are forbidden to eat the Passover under any circumstances, as are all uncircumcised males (vv. 43, 48). In both Genesis 17:10–14 and Exod 12:43–49, the foreign male slave is treated like the free Israelite male rather than like any class of alien: he must be circumcised and eat the Passover. In Exod 12:43–49, the slave's treatment is explicitly contrasted with that of the resident outsider of alien origin, the nonresident foreigner, and the (foreign) wage laborer.

What is one to make of this apparent full incorporation of the slave into the Israelite cultic community? At first glance, these texts appear to privilege the foreign slave: Unlike nonresident foreigners and uncircum-

cised resident outsiders, he eats the Passover; like free Israelite males, and
in contrast to all women, bond or free, he bears the sign of the covenant
in his flesh. Upon closer scrutiny, however, it is evident that privileging of
the slave is not what these texts really suggest. On the basis of cross-
cultural evidence, Patterson argues that the "natally alienated" slave is "a
human surrogate" without "a socially recognized existence outside of his
master," a "quasi-person," with a "marginal," "vicarious" existence.[134]
Patterson's characterization helps us to understand the apparent privileging of the slave with respect to circumcision and the Passover sacrifice: He
is subject to the same ritual requirements as his master and has access to
ritual privileges, *but solely as an extension of his master's person*, not in
his own right. Paradoxically, the slave's apparent privilege at first blush
really stems from the extent of his debasement. He is his master's possession, with no independent place in the social order apart from his master.
Thus he is circumcised as the free Israelite male is circumcised and eats the
Passover as native Israelites eat it. His diminished status is realized and
underscored by the very ritual means that appeared at first glance to
produce and signal privilege: eating the Passover with his master's
household.

The absorption of the slave into his master's identity in effect erases his
foreignness. As a result of his circumcision, the slave makes the transition
from foreigner to blank slate on which a new identity and status are in-
scribed. The slave's new identity of dependency and debasement and his
lack of any independent place in the social order explain why a priest's
slaves eat the holy foods according to Lev 22:10–13, but any "outsider"
(zār) to the priesthood may not eat them and even the priest's daughter
may not eat them if she marries an "outsider": "Any outsider may not eat
holy (food). The priest's wage laborer[135] may not eat holy (food). As for
the priest, if he acquires a person as property (in exchange) for his money,
he may eat it [holy food] and his houseborn slaves[136] may eat his food. As
for the daughter of a priest, if she marries a man who is an outsider (zār),
she may not eat of the offering of holy foods. But if the priest's daughter
is a widow or divorced and has no progeny, and returns to her father's
house as in her youth, of the food of her father she may eat. But any
outsider (zār) shall not eat it." The slave, as an extension of his owner's
person and as his dependent, partakes of his owner's exclusive diet of
foods that may not be eaten even by common Israelites, let alone by any
aliens.[137] Only other members of the priest's family have the privilege of
eating "holy food," and his daughter who marries a nonpriest loses that
privilege, for her primary kinship link has shifted to her "outsider" husband and his family. In effect, the once-foreign slave is treated in this law
as if he were a quasi-family member of the priest, eating food the access
to which is otherwise controlled by one's primary links of kinship. The

slave's access to this privileged diet is sanctioned because he lacks an independent social existence apart from his master and because he is completely dependent on his master to provide for his dietary needs.[138] Once again, apparent ritual privilege really functions to produce and underscore the slave's debasement and his lack of an independent social existence.[139]

The Female War Captive

A second case of a foreigner incorporated by means of ritual action into the social body Israel is the female war captive, whose rites of transition are described in some detail in Deut 21:10–14: "You shall bring her into the midst of your house, and she shall shave her head, cut [?][140] her nails, and remove the garment of her captivity[141] from upon her. She shall dwell in your house and weep for her father and mother one month.[142] After this, you may come to her and become her husband, and she shall become your wife."[143] The text describes the process by which a foreign woman, taken by force to the home of her captor, makes the transition from alien captive to wife or concubine[144] of an Israelite male. A series of ritual actions are presented that are intended to begin that transition. The shaving of the hair of the head, the cutting of the nails, and the removal of the "garment of captivity" move the woman into a period of liminality during which she mourns her parents, whom she will never see again. It is probable that they have become "socially dead" to her, though they are not physically dead. These gestures are all to be understood as rites effecting the separation or alienation of the woman from her previous identity. As others have noted, hair, nails, and secretions of the body are easily manipulated, and they are sometimes treated in certain cultures "as symbolically equal to the person from whom they came."[145] To shave off the hair and cut the nails in combination with discarding the "garment of captivity" and mourning socially dead parents seem in this context to mean to cut off the captive from her past, erasing her old identity and making it possible for her to assume a new identity in Israel.[146] Nonetheless, some have argued that the shaving here ought to be understood as a mourning rite[147]; others, as a purification rite.[148] The pairing of shaving the head with cutting the nails suggests neither mourning nor purification, given what is known of the ritual requirements of each of these processes.[149] It seems as if the ritual combination of shaving, cutting nails, discarding the "garment of captivity," and mourning socially dead parents is best explained as a formula intended to erase the woman's past and set the stage for her incorporation into the Israelite community, accomplished through her marriage to her captor.[150] In contrast to the foreign male slave's rite of circumcision leading to his incorporation, this text mandates a series of rites necessary for the process of the woman's alienation from her old identity and her aggregation to her new one.

The Resident Outsider of Foreign Origin

The resident outsider of alien heritage is a third example of a foreign individual who can be incorporated into the community according to some texts. The Holiness Source and perhaps Deuteronomistic materials suggest the possibility of the foreign resident outsider's incorporation through his attachment to an Israelite patron, with the Deuteronomists foregrounding this form of subordination as a primary means of entry into the community. Though both Holiness and Deuteronomistic passages allude to clientship from time to time, neither source describes a foreign resident outsider's rites of attachment and subordination to a patron.[151] Nor do we have any descriptions of rites through which the resident outsider might honor his patron, confirming his subordination during the period of his clientship.[152] We do, however, have 1 Sam 20:5–7, 18–19a, 24–34, which describe Saul's irritation at David's absence from his table at the New Moon festival. This text portrays the festive occasion of the New Moon as a ritual context in which the king is honored at court by his retainers, who are honored in turn. Perhaps the local patron and his clients practiced reciprocal honoring in a similar way in the local patron's own home at regular intervals (for example, feasts). We have several texts that describe or allude to how a patron or suzerain might honor his clients or vassals—including resident outsiders of alien origin—by means of gift giving and feting, and in so doing draw distinctions among his subordinates with respect to honor, thereby creating a hierarchy of honor.[153] Unfortunately, little more can be said about the details of the patron-client relationship as it applies to the resident outsider of foreign extraction. We can, however, mention circumcision as a primary mechanism of the foreign resident outsider's incorporation. The Holiness Source requires circumcision of the uncircumcised resident outsider who wishes to "make the Passover" (Exod 12:48). The foreigner in question is described as residing "with" an Israelite, an indication of his status as a client. Exod 12:48 also alludes to the possibility of the uncircumcised foreigner's having dependents of his own ("every male belonging to him shall be circumcised"). This Holiness text, as I have discussed, suggests that it is optional for the resident outsider of alien lineage to acquire full cultic access and obligation by means of circumcision. This is in contrast to the uncircumcised foreign male slave, who, like free Israelites, is circumcised and eats the Passover sacrifice. Exod 12:48 seems to conceive of the possibility of a foreign resident outsider's clientage without his full cultic participation.[154] This is certainly odd, if I am correct that cultic rites are an important context in which patrons and clients honor one another and in which clients compete for honor from their patrons. Perhaps non-cultic contexts provided sufficient opportunity for uncircumcised foreign clients to honor their patrons and be honored in turn.

Conclusion

In any society, foreignness and its antitype, native status, are social constructs rather than givens, and the very characteristics that constitute the alien or the native may change over time. Some contemporary American and European examples illustrate these claims. According to current law, the children of foreigners who are born in the United States are American citizens; they have the same rights and obligations as any other American, even if their parents are illegal alien residents or foreign visitors. Legal immigrants to the United States may, after the passage of five years (three years in the case of legal immigrants who marry American citizens), apply for naturalization. The child of American parents who is born abroad is normally entitled to American citizenship if one parent has been a resident of the United States for not less than five years before the child's birth. Thus, status as an American is usually determined either by birth in the United States or by naturalization, though sometimes, as in the case of the child of Americans who is born in a foreign country, lineage plays a central part in determining nationality.[155] Contemporary Germany takes a rather different approach to defining who is and is not a German. According to German law, the children of Turks and other foreign residents who are born in the country are foreigners, as are their children and their children's children. Legal immigrants as well as their descendants have, until very recently, been routinely excluded from German citizenship, which may be extended, however, to outsiders who can prove German parentage or, in some cases, lineage. Thus, status as a German is typically dependent not on birth in Germany, or even naturalization, but on possession of what the law defines as German descent.[156] In both the case of the United States and the case of Germany, foreign status and citizenship are inseparable from the context in which they are at issue. Each society defines who is an alien and who is a native, and each determines just how porous the boundary between the native group and the other will be. It may be extremely porous, as in the case of the contemporary United States, where the naturalization of foreign legal immigrants occurs routinely. It may be far more rigid, as in the case of contemporary Germany, where there has been little opportunity for naturalization until very recently. Yet definitions of self and other within a particular society may also change over time, since such definitions are the products of historically situated social processes. In the case of American citizenship, lineage played a far greater role in the past than it does today and was at times constituted differently.[157] Earlier definitions of American citizenship excluded members of racial and ethnic minority groups wholesale (for example, blacks, American Indians, and Chinese immigrants and their American-born descendants).[158] The racial dimensions of American citizenship law in fact go back to the first congressional Naturalization Act (1790), which made white racial categorization as well as minor national and state residency requirements mandatory for the acquisition of American citizenship.[159]

Like the contemporary examples I have discussed, biblical constructions of the Israelite and the alien are products of historically molded social processes and subject to both resistance and change. Those who are defined as foreign in texts of one generation might not be so defined in earlier materials (for example, the children of Israelite fathers and foreign mothers in Ezra-Nehemiah). Likewise, those previously understood as alien may become fully incorporated into the political-ritual body, losing their foreign status entirely as in the program of Ezek 47:22–23. Movements to reconstitute self and other, to reconfigure or solidify the boundaries separating Israelites from aliens, were apparently (and not surprisingly) contested by those who stood to lose status or their place in the community and its ritual life. Some evidence of such resistance survives in texts such as Isa 56:3–7, which is probably a response to fifth-century attempts to narrow the definition of who is an Israelite and limit who has a role in Israel's cultic life.

The essential activity of differentiating between the Israelite and the foreigner is accomplished in biblical texts by means of the employment of several forms of the binary pairing Israelite/alien. A number of texts privilege circumcision as that which both constitutes and marks the boundary between the Israelite and the other. The opposition circumcised/uncircumcised occurs, both explicitly and implicitly, in texts from various time periods. It constitutes the alien other as an uncircumcised male subject to exclusion from cultic and quasi-cultic rites because of his foreskin, which may be constructed as polluting by a number of texts (Isa 52:1; Ezek 44:7; Genesis 34). Yet, as I have argued, circumcision is at best only a partially adequate way to fashion and mark difference: it is gendered, applying only to males; it is not readily visible; and it is a characteristic of a number of near neighbors as well. Also, the removable foreskin allows for boundary crossing if the uncircumcised alien is willing (or, in certain cases [for example, male slaves], obligated) to become circumcised.

Other texts, particularly those of the Holiness and the Deuteronomistic Schools, evidence a different form of the binary pairing Israelite/alien:

Israelite or native/(foreign) resident outsider. In Holiness texts, for example, the opposition native/(foreign) resident outsider is used frequently as a rhetorical device to indicate the totality of the covenant community, while maintaining the distinction between native and resident outsider of alien heritage. A third manifestation of the dyad Israelite/alien occurs in several forms in Ezra-Nehemiah. Here, the boundary defining who is an Israelite is reconstituted to exclude the foreign wives of Israelite men and the children of intermarriages. In earlier texts, the children of Israelite fathers would have been classed as Israelites and foreign wives themselves would have been easily assimilated into the political-ritual body of Israel through marriage to Israelite males. Yet this becomes impossible once Israel's lineage is constructed as sanctified and foreign descent is cast as polluting to it. The introduction of the binary contrast clean/unclean in this context of lineage creates a completely unporous boundary that is not subject to the influence of other factors such as slave or free status, gender, or circumcision.

This focus on lineage as determinative of group status is not at all novel to the ideology of Ezra-Nehemiah. Earlier constructions of native status privileged lineage over place of birth: Lev 25:45–46 and Deut 23:4–9 (Eng., 3–8) both speak of generations of aliens born in the land of Israel. In the ideology of Ezra-Nehemiah, native status remains lineage based, but the father's status is no longer automatically determinative of a child's status in the way that it is in many other texts that speak of marriages between Israelite males and foreign women. A mother's alien status in Ezra-Nehemiah in fact neutralizes the Israelite status of the father; it has become the primary determinant of the child's identity, much in contrast to the situation presented in earlier texts.

A number of biblical texts bear witness to a dread of the empowered resident outsider of foreign origin. The curse of Deut 28:43–44, perhaps the quintessential expression of this fear, envisions a shameful scenario in which the foreign resident outsider prospers continually at the expense of the Israelite, who experiences persistent decline, to the point where the Israelite becomes the economic dependent of the resident outsider while in his own land. This scenario is presented as the culmination of the other curses that will come upon covenant violators: infertility, famine, disease, military defeat, death. The potential domination of the foreign resident outsider, whether a realistic possibility or not, was clearly something to be feared and avoided, like the other curses, according to the circles responsible for this text. The foreign resident outsider, living among Israelites but not one of them, required containment. But how could he best be contained? What kinds of restriction were necessary to neutralize the threat he posed? The threat posed by the alien could be addressed through exclusion from the community of Israel and its cultic life or through incorporation into that community with inferior status. Ezra-

Nehemiah advocates a blanket exclusion of all persons constructed as alien. At the same time, various integrative strategies are evidenced in other surviving texts. Majority voices in the Holiness Source advocate incorporation with an emphasis on circumcision as the means to this end; a number of Deuteronomistic texts foreground integration through subordination to an Israelite patron. In cases where the boundary separating the alien from Israel is permeable, the degree of an alien's dependency affects the alien's ability to cross the boundary and the degree of his or her integration. The male slave and the female slave are the most dependent of dependents, having had their previous identity and lineage entirely erased; they are, not coincidentally, represented as the most thoroughly integrated of foreigners, having in effect lost their alien status altogether.[160] The foreign resident outsider, in contrast, is portrayed in Holiness and Deuteronomistic texts as more integrated than nonresident aliens, who are generally marginal to Israelite polity and cult, yet he retains his alien identity nonetheless.[161] Most texts that mention the resident outsider of alien background portray him as a dependent of an Israelite patron.

There are significant gender dimensions to biblical representations of foreignness. The privileging of the binary pairing circumcised/uncircumcised in many texts, an opposition relevant to males only, results in an androcentric focus of the discourse on the other in these texts. To be uncircumcised is an impediment only to foreign males; alien women are unaffected by a restriction on the uncircumcised and may pass over the boundary separating Israel from other nations with relative ease. The androcentric focus of texts privileging circumcision as an act constituting and marking the boundary between Israelites and the other is not at all surprising, given that male residence is represented as patrilocal, descent as patrilineal, and landed property as inherited from the father, normally by sons. Women are brought in from outside the lineage as wives and are integrated easily into the lineage they join through marriage; daughters leave their father's house at marriage to become wives of other men. Perhaps this is the reason why foreign resident women are mostly represented as less threatening than foreign resident men: It is routine to import wives from outside the lineage, and women are routinely integrated into the families into which they marry. Sons, for their part, inherit their status and property from their father. It makes little difference who their mother is, or where she came from. A foreign man, in contrast, is not so easily integrated. He is an anomaly, since he has moved from his land and his family. He might be uncircumcised. If he marries an Israelite woman, his children will have alien status.

4

The Qualified Body: The Dyad Whole/Blemished

THE opposition whole/blemished (tāmîm/possessing a mûm) is the last of the privileged polarities that I will consider in this investigation. Though much less frequently attested in extant materials than the oppositions holy/common, unclean/clean, and Israelite/alien, it is significant nonetheless for its role in generating distinctions of hierarchical import in texts describing the workings of the cult. The contrast between what is constructed as whole and what is constructed as blemished is applied in biblical texts to the bodies of sacrificial animals, priests, and worshipers. A blemish (mûm) may be defined as one of a number of adulterating somatic alterations. It may be the result of birth, disease, or injury (accidental or intentional).[1] Somatic alterations constructed as blemishes in biblical texts include blindness, lameness, genital damage, various other physical injuries or defects (for example, broken bones, overgrown limbs), skin afflictions (scabs, sores), and other abnormalities caused by disease (an eye defect).[2] Most, if not all, of these conditions are visible to the eye.[3] A number of them are clearly characterized by an unappealing somatic asymmetry of some kind (for example, limbs of uneven length). Some of these conditions are permanent; others may be temporary.[4] In all cases, a body with a blemish has lost its quality of wholeness and completeness.[5] The opposition of whole and blemished bodies is therefore analogous to the contrast between whole altar stones ('ăbānîm šĕlēmôt) and those that have been adulterated through cutting with a tool, thereby losing their holiness (Deut 27:5–6; cp. Exod 20:25).[6]

According to texts such as 2 Sam 14:25, Cant 4:7, and Dan 1:4, one characteristic of physical beauty is a lack of blemishes. David's son Absalom is described in 2 Sam 14:25 as the most beautiful man in Israel: "From the sole of his foot to the top of his head," says the verse, "there was no blemish in him." Cant 4:7 and Dan 1:4 are similar, directly associating physical beauty with a lack of defects. Texts such as these suggest indirectly that blemishes themselves are seen as ugly. Defects have explicitly negative associations in a number of texts. Blemish is the equivalent of "ruin" according to Lev 22:25, a text concerned with sacrificial animals; Mal 1:14 is similar, referring to a blemished animal as a "ruined thing."[7] Deut 17:1 refers to the sacrificial animal with a defect as an "abomination" (tôʿēbâ), and glosses on Deut 17:1 and 15:21 further underscore the negative associations of blemishes. In Deut 17:1, the defect

is defined as "any evil thing" (kol dābār rāʿ); in Deut 15:21, "evil" is used
to modify "blemish." Context suggests that "evil" (raʿ) in these glosses
has a physical sense and is perhaps best translated "disfiguring" or
"ugly."[8] Though a somewhat cryptic passage, 2 Sam 5:6–8a suggests
nonetheless that blindness and lameness in persons are stigmatizing conditions. Verse 8a refers, in fact, to the lame and blind as "those hated by
David's soul."[9] In short, biblical texts that mention physical defects tend
to attribute negative qualities to them.

Directly and indirectly, texts from a variety of sources assert that a
sacrificial animal with a blemish is disqualified from serving as an offering to Yhwh. Texts of the Priestly Writing, the Holiness Source, and the
Book of Ezekiel that prescribe sacrificial practice require that animals to
be offered for sacrifice to Yhwh must be "whole" (tāmîm).[10] "Whole" is
defined in some texts explicitly as meaning "without a blemish." Lev
22:17–25, a text of the Holiness School, provides the most detailed treatment of the physical defects of sacrificial animals in the biblical anthology
and lists various blemishes that render sacrificial animals unacceptable as
offerings to Yhwh. According to v. 21, all blemishes disqualify afflicted
animals from sacrificial use, even for the free-will offering or the vow.[11]
Deut 17:1 states the unacceptability of the blemished sacrificial animal
unequivocally: "You shall not sacrifice to Yhwh your god ox or sheep
that has in it a blemish—any disfiguring thing—for it is an abomination
to Yhwh your god." Deut 15:21–22, speaking of the required offering of
the firstborn of sacrificial animals, is similar: "And if it has a blemish—
lame or blind, any disfiguring blemish—you shall not sacrifice it to Yhwh
your god. In your towns you shall eat it, the unclean and the clean together, like the gazelle and hart."[12] According to Deut 15:21–22, the
blemished sacrificial animal is to be treated as the equivalent of nonsacrificial clean game animals. Like the gazelle and hart, it may be eaten
outside the sanctuary sphere by all, including those who cannot meet purity requirements. The text suggests that the blemished sacrificial animal
has lost its sanctity; the restrictions normally imposed on its use and consumption are lifted because it is inferior and unacceptable to Yhwh as a
sacrificial offering.[13] Still, it is a clean animal and suitable for consumption outside of a sacrificial context according to this text. Thus, the blemished sacrificial animal has not become the equal of the forbidden unclean
animal. Though Deut 17:1 refers to it as an "abomination," as Deut 14:3
refers to unclean animals, it may be eaten according to Deut 15:22, unlike
unclean animals. It has lost status and is now the equivalent of a clean
nonsacrificial animal, but it has not been reduced to the status of an unclean animal.

Malachi 1 appears to have a different perspective on blemished sacrifices. This fifth-century text[14] condemns the priesthood for offering such

animals to Yhwh: "When you bring near a blind (thing) for sacrifice, is it not evil? And when you bring near a lame or sick (thing), is it not evil?" (1:8).[15] Yhwh, through the prophet, makes clear the unacceptability of blemished offerings and goes so far as to curse the person who dares to present them (1:14). Yet Malachi 1 goes farther than any other biblical text concerned with blemished sacrificial animals. Unlike other materials, it associates such animals with impurity. In Mal 1:7, the priests are condemned for offering "polluted food" (lehem měgō'āl) on Yhwh's altar. It is clear from the text that this "polluted food" is made up of the blemished sacrifices mentioned in the very next verse. The defective offerings of Israel are contrasted in v. 11 with a "clean offering" (minhâ těhôrâ) brought by the nations: "'For from the rising of the sun to its setting, great is my name among the nations, and in every place incense is brought for my name, and a clean offering, for great is my name among the nations,' says Yhwh of hosts." The verb g'l , used here for the blemished sacrifices, is attested as a synonym for the more common verb tm' ("to pollute," "to be polluted") beginning in texts of the sixth century and continuing thereafter, as I have noted. The equivalence of the verbs g'l and tm' and their derivatives is suggested not only by Mal 1:7–12, but also by texts such as Neh 13:29–30; Lam 4:14–15; and Dan 1:8.[16] The association of blemished sacrificial animals with uncleanness in the polemic of Malachi 1 reflects an ideological position that contrasts with that of texts such as Deuteronomy, the Holiness Source, and the Priestly Writing; it functions as an effective means to underscore the inappropriateness and unacceptability of such sacrifices.

Lev 21:16–23, a text of the Holiness School, concerns the cultic privileges of blemished priests. Priests with defects are forbidden by this text to participate in some of the most prestigious and restricted rites of the sanctuary. They may not approach the altar of burnt offerings, bringing near Yhwh's food. The blemished high priest may not approach the curtain (pārōket) separating the holy of holies from the holy place to enter the holy of holies. The text says nothing about restricting other elite cultic rites normally performed by priests (such as offering incense). Nor does it suggest that a blemish renders the priest unfit to remain in the cultic sphere. On the contrary, the blemished priest may remain in the sanctuary. The text states that he may even continue to eat the holy and most holy foods: "The food of his god, from the most holy things and from the holy things, he may eat" (Lev 21:22). Clearly, the priest's blemish is not constructed as *generally* profaning to holy space and holy items. If it were, he would not be able to remain in the sanctuary sphere, nor would he be able to eat the holy foods brought to the sanctuary by worshipers. The priest's blemish is constructed as profaning only when he participates in the proscribed rites, as v. 23 suggests: "But to the curtain he shall not come, nor shall he approach the altar, for he has a blemish; he shall not profane (ḥll) my sanctuaries for I, Yhwh, sanctify them." Thus, the priest with a defect possesses the potential to profane holy space and holy items, but only under a restricted set of ritual circumstances.

The rites prohibited to the blemished priest are represented in various texts as some of the most privileged of the cult. A priest who is forbidden to approach the altar can neither bring near nor process meat sacrifices and other offerings, nor can he manipulate the blood or burn the fat of sacrificial victims. The blemished high priest cannot approach and enter the holy of holies on the Day of Atonement (or, Purgation).[17] Each of these interdicted priestly actions involves movement into a highly restricted locus associated most closely with the deity's presence. These are also the sites at which texts locate the most essential rites of the sanctuary. There is a degree of symmetry worth noting between the Holiness Source's proscribed loci and activity for blemished priests on the one hand, and the Priestly Writing's most restricted and prestigious sites in the tabernacle pericope on the other. According to the Priestly Writers, priests approaching the altar and entering the tent are required to wash their hands and feet and to wear their special priestly garments. To fail to do so would result in death for the offender.[18] It is interesting to notice that the rites and ritual loci forbidden to the Holiness School's blemished priest in Lev 21:16–23 are almost identical to the most restricted ritual sites of the Priestly Writers' tabernacle. The difference is that the Holiness School restricts the blemished priest's access only to the altar area and the holy of holies, while the Priestly Writers' areas requiring washing and special garments include the outer section of the tent. In any case, it is clear that the blemished priest of Lev 21:16–23 has been cut off from the majority of the sanctuary rites constructed as most privileged and most restricted in terms of access.

In 2 Sam 5:8b, the reference may be to blemished priests, though it is more likely in my view that it concerns blemished worshipers. The verse reads as follows: "Therefore they say, 'Anyone blind and lame shall not enter the house'" (ʿiwwēr ûpissēaḥ lōʾ yābôʾ ʾel habbāyit). Set off from its present context—the story of David's conquest of Jerusalem—the interpretation of this clearly marked popular saying has long challenged interpreters. Though there is a consensus among commentators that the aphorism was originally independent from its present context,[19] in the final casting of the biblical text, the narrative in which the adage is embedded serves an etiological purpose: It explains the origin of this curious saying by situating it in the circumstances of David's conquest.[20] What of the saying itself apart from its narrative context? The identification of the "house" mentioned in the adage is a good place to begin. The house that the blind and lame may not enter is most likely a sanctuary, probably the

Jerusalem temple. The word bayit, "house," is commonly used of temples. It may refer either to the temple building itself or to the larger complex of the sanctuary, including its court(s).[21] The idiom bā' 'el also suggests that the "house" of 2 Sam 5:8b is a sanctuary. This idiom and others like it[22] are frequently used to describe both priestly service at shrines and the entry of worshipers into sacred complexes.[23] Finally, the fact that entry into the "house" is restricted to persons lacking blindness and lameness points more likely to a temple setting than to any other locus. After all, the notion of restricting the use of blemished sacrificial animals or the ritual activity or locus of blemished priests is well known from a variety of other biblical texts concerned with the cult.

If the blind and the lame of 2 Sam 5:8b are priests, Lev 21:16–23 is the closest text for comparison. In that text, blemished priests cannot approach the altar or enter the holy of holies, but they may remain in the sanctuary sphere and continue to have access to holy and most holy foods and, presumably, other elite priestly rites (such as burning incense). In 2 Sam 5:8b, by contrast, the blind and the lame, if they are priests, are prohibited either from the priestly privilege of entering the temple building, or from entering the larger sanctuary sphere. It is impossible to determine which proscription might be intended by the saying of 2 Sam 5:8b, for the idiom bā' 'el is used for both privileged priestly movement (for example, entering the tabernacle or the holy of holies in Priestly narrative) *and* common entry into the larger sanctuary sphere permitted to all clean worshipers. If the idiom bā' 'el is read to suggest total exclusion from the cultic sphere, then the blind and the lame of 2 Sam 5:8b are treated far more severely than the blemished priests of Lev 21:16–23, who continue to have access to the sanctuary complex. But even if the idiom bā' 'el is read to suggest only that blind and lame priests may not enter the temple building, the text bears witness, nonetheless, to an ideology restricting the activities of blemished priests that differs from that of Lev 21:16–23. It places the whole of the building off-limits to such priests, rather than simply limiting access to the holy of holies to unblemished high priests; it also says nothing about altar rites in the courtyard, a focus of Lev 21:16–23. Thus, it is possible to understand 2 Sam 5:8b as prohibiting entry into the temple building while allowing access to the altar of burnt offerings and its associated rites.

If the blind and the lame of 2 Sam 5:8b are worshipers, Deut 23:2 (Eng., 1) is the primary text for comparison. According to that verse, "Whoever has crushed testicles and whoever has a penis cut off shall not enter the assembly of Yhwh."[24] The expression "enter the assembly of Yhwh" occurs several times in Deut 23: 2, 3, 4, 9 (Eng.,1, 2, 3, 8). Though the meaning of the expression is not entirely clear in its context, in sixth- and fifth-century texts such as Lam 1:10; Ezek 44:7, 9; and Isa

56:3–7, it is interpreted to mean "enter the sanctuary sphere." Lam 1:10 states, "She [Jerusalem] saw nations enter her sanctuary, / Those about whom you commanded: 'They shall not enter your assembly'" (lō' yābō'û baqqāhāl lāk).[25] Lam 1:10 either paraphrases Deut 23:4 (Eng., 3) or quotes a form of the text that differs from that of surviving biblical manuscripts. In either case, Lam 1:10 suggests that the idiom "enter the assembly" must mean to enter the sanctuary sphere. In Isa 56:3–7, Deut 23:2–9 (Eng., 1–8) is understood in a similar way. Like Lam 1:10, Isa 56:3–7 represents the proscription on entry into Yhwh's assembly as a ban on participation in temple worship. The text alludes to the exclusion of select aliens and men with damaged genitals in Deut 23:2–9 (Eng., 1–8), though it presumes a broadening of these restrictions, which it rejects.[26] Ezek 44:7, 9, a third example of this sort of interpretation of Deut 23:4–9 (Eng., 3–8), exclude uncircumcised aliens specifically from cultic participation.[27] If 2 Sam 5:8b prohibits the entry of blind and lame worshipers into the sanctuary sphere, it is much like Deut 23:2 (Eng., 1), which apparently proscribes worshipers with damaged genitalia. Blind, lame, and genitally mutilated male worshipers all possess a physical defect that disqualifies them from entering the temple complex.

Just as Deut 23:2 (Eng., 1) appears to prohibit men with damaged genitals from entering the sanctuary sphere, 2 Sam 5:8b, if it refers to worshipers, proscribes entry into the temple complex to those who are blind and lame. In each case, the prohibition is general and comparable to the general exclusion of sacrificial animals with blemishes witnessed in Deuteronomy (15:21; 17:1), in the Holiness Source (Lev 22:17–25), in the Priestly Writing (Lev 1:3, 10; 3:1, 6; 4:3, etc.), and elsewhere (Mal 1:8, 13). The proscription is also comparable to the exclusion of priests with similar somatic imperfections from serving at the altar or approaching the curtain to enter the holy of holies (Lev 21:16–23, a Holiness text). As M. Douglas has pointed out, Yhwh desires "whole" and "complete" sacrifices, sacrifices without a blemish, and according to the Holiness Source, he desires priests without a blemish to serve him in a set of elite ritual contexts within the sanctuary.[28] If 2 Sam 5:8b refers to worshipers, then two texts—Deut 23:2 (Eng., 1) and 2 Sam 5:8b—prohibit worshipers with certain blemishes from entering the sanctuary sphere. A third text, Isa 56:3–5, alludes to an expansive reading of the proscription of Deut 23:2 (Eng., 1), which it opposes.[29] In contrast, in other sources, a ban on blemished worshipers is not mentioned, nor is allusion made to it. It is possible that the notion of excluding blemished worshipers is alien to materials such as the Priestly Writing and the Holiness Source. Certainly the Holiness Source does not exclude blemished priests from the sanctuary, as I have argued. Alternatively, it is equally possible that a source such as the Priestly Writing, which does not speak explicitly about such a proscription, assumes it nonetheless.

Does 2 Sam 5:8b concern blind and lame priests, or blind and lame worshipers? The idiom bā' 'el, used either for worshipers entering a temple complex or for priests performing privileged rites, is of little help in determining the identity of the blind and the lame in 2 Sam 5:8b. Nonetheless, there are reasons to suspect that the text concerns worshipers. The fact that priests are not explicitly identified in the text suggests that the proscribed group is not specific but general, that "anyone blind and lame" is any Israelite afflicted with these conditions. The popular nature of the adage also suggests a general exclusion. I do not imagine that members of the populace at large were much concerned with the qualifications for priestly service. They would have a personal interest, however, in restrictions that would affect their own access or the access of household members to sanctuary rites. In a word, the evidence suggests that the blind and the lame of 2 Sam 5:8b are more likely Israelite worshipers than priests.[30] During the Second Temple period, some Jewish interpreters would read 2 Sam 5:8b as a text referring not to priests but to worshipers. The writers of the Temple Scroll, recasting the restriction of 2 Sam 5:8b and elaborating upon it, prohibit the entry of blind persons into the sanctuary city.[31] Similarly, several early rabbinic texts exclude blind and lame Jewish males from pilgrimage obligations, probably under the influence of 2 Sam 5:8b.[32]

Deut 23:2 (Eng., 1) prohibits the entry of men with damaged genitals into the sanctuary sphere, and it is likely that 2 Sam 5:8b proscribes blind and lame worshipers. Yet these two texts taken together treat only damaged male genitals, blindness, and lameness, leaving other physical defects and mutilations unaddressed. Are these particular imperfections somehow more threatening than others to the sanctity of the temple complex? Or did other blemishes also disqualify worshipers from entry into the sanctuary according to the circles responsible for 2 Sam 5:8b and Deut 23:2 (Eng., 1)? Symmetrically speaking, it would be rather odd if other physical imperfections were *not* grounds for excluding worshipers. Lev 21:18–20 contains a lengthy list of defects disqualifying a priest for service at the altar and other elite specialized activity; Lev 22:22–24 presents a similar list of blemishes disqualifying animals for sacrifice. In light of this parallel material it is rather surprising and puzzling that Deut 23:2 (Eng., 1) and 2 Sam 5:8b, together, mention only a few defects. How might this be explained?

One possible approach to the problem is to view the blind and the lame and their counterparts in Deut 23:2 (Eng., 1) as synecdoches, representative of all blemished worshipers disqualified for cultic participation according to the circles responsible for these texts. This approach has some appeal, for it produces the expected symmetry with materials excluding a host of mutilated and physically defective animals from sacrifice and with Lev 21:16–23, which restricts the activities and locus of priests with various blemishes. Furthermore, other texts such as Mal 1:8, 13 and Deut 15:21 appear to have such a synecdochic meaning. Mal 1:8, for example, names only three conditions—blindness, lameness, and sickness—which seem to stand for all disqualifying physical imperfections in sacrificial animals; Mal 1:13 mentions mutilated (?),[33] lame, and sick animals, with the same intent. Another, slightly different approach would be to view "the blind and the lame" as a dyadic pairing of two members of the same class—the blemished in this case—intended to communicate the larger totality of that class. Examples of this are found in other biblical texts, including 1 Sam 15:3. Yhwh, speaking through Samuel to Saul, orders the annihilation of the Amalekites: "Now go and strike down Amalek, and destroy utterly all that belongs to him. Do not spare him, but kill man and woman, child and infant, ox and sheep, camel and ass."[34] In this text, each pairing stands for a class of living thing: adult persons, children, clean quadrupeds, and unclean quadrupeds. The last two pairings, and possibly the second, communicate a larger totality by listing only two members of the class in question. Ox and sheep are not the only members of the class of clean quadrupeds, yet their pairing communicates the totality of this class: All are to die by the edge of the sword. Likewise, camel and ass do not exhaust the members of the class of unclean quadrupeds. (In contrast, the opposition of man and woman is inclusive of all adults.) The blind and the lame of 2 Sam 5:8b may well be a pairing of this type, emblematic and inclusive of all defective conditions of the body from head to toe. In Lev 21:18, blind and lame priests stand at the head of the long list of physically imperfect functionaries. Perhaps this suggests the importance of blindness and lameness as emblematic blemishes. Given that the locus of one condition is the eyes, at the top of the body, and the site of the other is the feet, at the bottom, the pairing "blind and lame" communicates totality quite effectively.[35]

It remains for me to explore why the blind and the lame (and probably others with blemishes) are excluded from the sanctuary sphere according to the adage of 2 Sam 5:8b. There are two possible explanations for this: The blemishes of 2 Sam 5:8b are either constructed as profaning to holiness or understood as polluting. Lev 21:23, as I have mentioned, views the blemished priest as having the potential to profane the holiness of the sanctuary, but only in a limited set of circumstances. Certainly, the text does not suggest that he is generally a threat to the sanctuary's holiness or that of various sanctified items in it. Only if the priest with physical defects approaches sites forbidden to him does he profane the sanctuary. Nothing in Lev 21:16–23 suggests that the blemished priest is understood to be a polluter. In fact, he is permitted to remain in the sanctuary and eat the holy and most holy foods; therefore, he cannot be defiled.[36] Blemished sacrificial animals are treated similarly in most of the texts that mention them. They are not fitting for sacrifice to Yhwh, but they, like clean non-sacrificial animals, may be consumed outside of a sacrificial setting (Deut 15:22). The exception to this pattern is Malachi 1, which treats blemished sacrificial animals as polluting and therefore analogous to unclean animals. What of the blind and lame of 2 Sam 5:8b? It is not possible to determine whether they are excluded because they are understood to be profaning or because they are constructed as polluting. There are no idioms of profanation or pollution present in 2 Sam 5:8b that might suggest one explanation rather than the other. I will therefore consider the implications of both possibilities.

If the blind and the lame are profaning, they are marginalized to a much greater extent than are the blemished priests of Lev 21:16–23, whose defective bodies are threatening to the holiness of the sanctuary only in certain circumstances. Their treatment is, however, comparable to that of the genitally damaged men of Deut 23:2 (Eng., 1), who may not "enter the assembly of Yhwh."[37] Two Qumran texts, 1QSᵃ II 3–10 and 1QM VII 4–5, exclude blemished men, along with those who are polluted, from the "congregation of the men of name" and the eschatological war camp.[38] Though both are treated similarly, the blemished and the polluted form two distinct groups in these two texts. In excluding completely those with physical defects, 1QSᵃ and 1QM are not unlike their predecessors Deut 23:2 (Eng., 1) and 2 Sam 5:8b and were probably influenced by them.

If the blind and the lame of 2 Sam 5:8b are polluting, they are comparable to the defiling blemished sacrificial animals of Malachi 1, and their total exclusion occasions no surprise at all. In a later era, the circles responsible for the Temple Scroll, recasting the ban witnessed in 2 Sam 5:8b, would prohibit the blind from entering Jerusalem on account of their power to pollute: "Any blind persons shall not enter it [the city] all their days; they shall not pollute the city in the midst of which I dwell."[39] The notion in the Temple Scroll that the blind are polluting may have been derived exegetically from 2 Sam 5:8b. If 2 Sam 5:8b understands blemished persons to be polluting, it is likely the earliest witness to an association of physical defects and the power to defile, witnessed later in Malachi 1 and the Temple Scroll.

Blemishes and Inequality

I begin my exploration of the hierarchical dimensions of the opposition whole/blemished with sacrificial animals. Several texts suggest the inferior standing of sacrificial animals with physical defects. Whether constructed as polluting or not, texts agree that blemished sacrificial animals are unfit for sacrificial slaughter. Mal 1:6–7 states that it is dishonoring to Yhwh to receive them as sacrifices; other texts describe them in such a way as to suggest their inferiority to their unblemished congeners (for example, Lev 22:25; Deut 17:1). Blemished sacrificial animals are fit for consumption only outside of sacrificial contexts according to Deut 15:21–22; their status in that text is analogous to that of clean nonsacrificial animals such as the gazelle and hart. Thus, though inferior to unblemished sacrificial animals, Deut 15:22 implies that they remain superior to unclean animals, which cannot be eaten at all. Are similar patterns of superiority and inferiority discernible in texts describing persons with blemishes? Several texts portray both priest and worshiper experiencing status change as a result of possessing a physical defect. The blemished priest of Lev 21:16–23 is forbidden to approach highly restricted and prestigious space within the sanctuary (such as the altar) and cannot participate in most of the elite rites that realize and communicate the superior status of priests vis-à-vis others. Cut off from such activities and their specialized sites in the sanctuary, the blemished priest loses status vis-à-vis his unblemished priestly brethren. But even though he cannot perform most of the prestigious, priest-specific rites, he remains, nonetheless, in a status position superior to that of priestly dependents and to that of nonpriests. He may still eat the most holy offerings, in contrast to all in his household who are not males of the priestly lineage; he may still eat the holy offerings, unlike persons outside of priestly households; presumably, he may still offer incense, a privileged rite, though the text says nothing directly about this.[40] In short, the blemished priest of Lev 21:16–23 continues to occupy a position of superior rank, though he has ceased to be the equal of his unblemished brethren. It seems fair, therefore, to speak of two priestly classes in Lev 21:16–23: the whole and the blemished. Each class enjoys a status superior to that of any nonpriest, and their privileges create and advertise these status differences. There is, however, a distinct difference in status between them, and this contrast in rank is also realized and communicated through the rites of the cult. By stripping the physically defective priest of many of his privileges, Lev 21:16–23 acknowledges implicitly his inferiority to priests with whole bodies. By allowing him to retain certain other privileges, the text asserts indirectly that the blemished priest remains the superior of the whole nonpriest.

If 2 Sam 5:8b concerns blind and lame (and probably other blemished) priests, it is a text that may treat such priests with far greater severity than does Lev 21:16–23. This depends on how one chooses to understand the ambiguous statement that the blind and the lame "shall not enter the house." If entering the house means entering the temple building, then the restriction of 2 Sam 5:8b is not unlike those of Lev 21:16–23: Blemished priests may remain in the sanctuary sphere, but they lose status vis-à-vis their unblemished colleagues because they are cut off from performing certain elite rites and entering certain restricted space. But if entering the house means entering the sanctuary sphere, then the restriction of 2 Sam 5:8b is far more severe than any of Lev 21:16–23. Where the blemished priests of Lev 21:16–23 lose access to some prestigious rights and privileges, in this reading, the blind and lame of 2 Sam 5:8b are completely marginalized, entirely excluded from the sanctuary. Unlike the blemished priests of Lev 21:16–23, those of 2 Sam 5:8b do not retain any of their priestly privileges. Whether because of their pollution or their potential to profane the sanctuary, they are cut off from the privileges that confer status, including the diet of holy foods mandated for them. In effect, they are no different from nonpriests who are separated from the sanctuary for whatever reason (such as pollution).

   If 2 Sam 5:8b refers to blind and lame (and probably other blemished) worshipers, as I believe it does, it marginalizes such persons by prohibiting their entry into the sanctuary sphere. As I have noted, Deut 23:2 (Eng., 1) is similar in its treatment of genitally damaged men. Whether because of their power to pollute the sanctuary or profane it, blind and lame worshipers of 2 Sam 5:8b lose access to what texts represent as the prime context for the slaughter and distribution of meat, the prime locus for the realization and communication of hierarchical social relations, and the prime site for the worship of Yhwh. The genitally damaged men of Deut 23:2 (Eng., 1) are similarly cut off. As is true of all who are excluded from the sanctuary sphere because of long-term pollution, removal because of physical defects, whether they are conceived as polluting or not, stigmatizes those removed. They are marked off as distinct from the unblemished of the community, as persons whose appearance is presumably displeasing to Yhwh in the same way that the appearance of blemished animals is said to be displeasing to him in various texts. Like the excluded alien of Deut 23:4–9 (Eng., 3–8) and Isa 56:3–7, they do not participate in the rites of the cult and therefore experience social marginalization.

Conclusion

The blemished body, whether of sacrificial animals, priests, or worshipers, is associated either explicitly or implicitly with ugliness and undesirability in various biblical passages. Texts confer inferior status on physically defective animals and persons, both of which are often contrasted directly with their physically whole counterparts. Among sacrificial animals, the physically defective may be accorded an intermediate status between whole sacrificial animals and unclean, forbidden creatures, as in

Deut 15:21–22. Or they may be assigned what amounts to the same status as unclean, nonsacrificial animals, as in Malachi 1. Not unlike the blemished sacrificial animal of Deut 15:21–22, the physically defective priest of Lev 21:16–23 occupies an intermediate position between that of the priest without a blemish and all nonpriests. Just as the physically defective sacrificial animal of Deut 15:21–22 has not become the equal of the unclean creature, so the defective priest has not become the counterpart of nonpriests. Status as a clean sacrificial animal or a priest apparently outweighs status as blemished in these texts. If I am correct that 2 Sam 5:8b concerns worshipers, the blemished worshiper, whether his defect is constructed as profaning or polluting, has effectively become the equal of the polluted person and not unlike the genitally mutilated man of Deut 23:2 (Eng., 1). Like the individual removed from the sanctuary sphere because of pollution unrelated to blemishes, the defective worshipers of 2 Sam 5:8b and Deut 23:2 (Eng., 1) are so excluded. In these texts, the effect of having a blemish is the same as that of being polluted, whether the blemished individual is constructed as polluting or not.

The opposition whole/blemished, like the other polarities examined in this study, categorizes and creates hierarchical distinctions. Physically defective sacrificial animals, priests, and worshipers are ranked in a manner inferior to their counterparts who are whole, and their inferiority is both realized and communicated in cultic settings. In light of this, it is important to note that not all alterations to the body are constructed by biblical texts as adulterations producing blemishes. Various permanent and temporary physical alterations such as piercing and shaving are not generally understood to be blemishing actions by biblical texts, and the biblical anthology frequently bears witness to these practices.[41] Circumcision is perhaps the most interesting example of a permanent alteration not constructed as blemishing. On the contrary, the very act of circumcision is described explicitly by a number of texts as a prerequisite to participation in cultic and quasi-cultic rites,[42] and circumcision eventually becomes the identity marker par excellence for male Israelites (Gen 17:9–14). Blemish and wholeness, as the example of circumcision illustrates particularly well, are constructed categories rather than transhistorical and transcultural givens. There is nothing about cutting off the male foreskin that suggests that the act should not be constructed as blemishing. Biblical texts speak of blemishes resulting from the loss of a part of the body (for example, an eye or a tooth, as in Lev 24:19–20). Certainly circumcision was viewed as blemishing by Greek and Roman writers. Yet if anything, it is the uncircumcised male, whose foreskin is fetishized in 1 Samuel 18, and whose uncircumcision is emblematic of his otherness in so many biblical texts, who is treated as if he himself were blemished.[43]

Conclusion _____

DISTINCTIONS of status, whether significant or minor, are the building blocks of hierarchy. Among the several tools employed by biblical texts to establish status distinctions among groups and individuals, the binary opposition has proved to be especially effective. In textual representations of the cult and analogous ritual settings, a number of privileged oppositions establish and mark external boundaries. The holy/common dyad, for example, distinguishes the territory of the sanctuary, constructed as holy, from other, common space. The opposition unclean/clean divides the populace into those who may enter sanctified space or participate in nonsanctuary rites requiring purity and those who must avoid all such ritual contexts without exception, either temporarily, as in the case of persons with minor pollution, or for a longer period of time. The gendered and mutable contrast circumcised/uncircumcised determines cultic and quasi-cultic access in a number of texts (such as Exod 12:43–49), as do the various forms of the more general opposition of Israelite and alien (for example, "exile" community/peoples of the land[s] in Ezra-Nehemiah). In a text such as 2 Sam 5:8b, the opposition whole/blemished is also relevant to cultic access.

Denial of access to cultic and quasi-cultic settings not only establishes boundaries around the sanctuary and its analogues but contributes to the shaping of status differences between individuals and groups. Some persons are excluded for a short period of time and have little trouble regaining access (for example, persons polluted by a seminal emission). Others may be separated for long periods of time or permanently; the sources of their exclusion may have negative cultural associations (menstrual blood, blemishes). Among those who may return, the expense, time, and effort required for purification can be daunting. Exclusion by definition marginalizes, and some groups (women of childbearing age, aliens in certain texts) are affected to a much greater degree than others (such as adult native males). Exclusion from cultic and quasi-cultic ritual settings means, in effect, separation from what texts represent as the primary locus for slaughter and meat consumption, for praising and petitioning Yhwh, the national god, and for the regular rehearsal of the national story of origins. These are ritual contexts in which the social order is made and remade. In a word, loss of access to the sanctuary and its analogues is nothing less than a serious hardship for those excluded.

The boundaries around cultic loci and their analogues may shift over time. A number of examples illustrate the way in which boundaries may change as a result of the introduction of newly privileged binary contrasts or reconceptualizations of older, boundary-generating oppositions. Perhaps the most interesting biblical example of this is the reconstitution of the categories "alien" and "native" in the fifth-century work Ezra-Nehemiah. Alienage, portrayed in most texts antedating the fifth century as a largely gendered attribute that could be overcome for the most part by means of circumcision, is transformed in striking ways in Ezra-Nehemiah. The aliens of concern in Ezra-Nehemiah are equally female and male, and, in an innovative move, are constructed as polluters who cannot be assimilated into the community under any circumstances. In addition, children born of intermarriages between Israelite men and alien women are no longer classified as Israelites. Instead, they are reconstituted as polluting foreigners subject to exclusion from community and cult because of the background of their mothers, who for the first time play a significant role in determining the ancestry of their children. Ezra-Nehemiah reflects both a redefinition of the category "alien" and its transformation through the introduction of the novel notion of alien pollution. Thus, both "alien" and "polluter" are shifting cultural constructs, the products of social processes occurring in particular historical settings.

Apart from the binary contrasts that establish and mark the external boundaries of cult and analogous contexts, there are also privileged oppositions that create status difference within the sanctuary sphere and in quasi-cultic ritual settings. In the context of the sanctuary, these include such contrasts as holy/common, Yhwh/priest, priest/nonpriest, priest/Levite, Levite/Israelite, whole priest/blemished priest (Lev 21:16–23), household head/non–household head. These oppositions generate status distinctions by limiting access to particular ritual space, ritual actions, cultic items, and food offerings that are associated with high status, prestige, and honor. They do so also by establishing an order of precedence in ritual action (see 1 Sam 2:12–17). Thus, the status of a particular person (such as the high priest) or group (such as women of childbearing age, heads of household) emerges out of a web of textually articulated multiple contrasts. Some of these contrasts determine access to the spheres of cultic and quasi-cultic rites; others determine the individual's physical locus, role in ritual action, sacrificial portion to be consumed, and place in the order of food distribution and consumption.

The head of household or elder is an example of an individual belonging to a category the status of which is determined by multiple contrasts. He performs elite, prestigious rites that establish his preeminence of status and honor vis-à-vis his dependents. He slaughters sacrificial animals and distributes their processed meat to his household at pilgrimage (1 Sam 1:4–5). Yet, he must pass along the partially processed slaughtered animal to the priests, who finish the processing (fat burning, blood manipulation, cooking the meat) and pass back the meat portions for distribution and consumption. In this scenario, the elder is contrasted with both his dependents and the priests. Though he performs rites that establish his superior status and honor with respect to his dependents, the priests, through their ritual action and his, establish and communicate their superior rank vis-à-vis the head of household. Thus, the status of the household head is determined by means of contrast with that of his dependents on the one hand and that of the priests on the other.

Thus far, I have spoken at length of the construction of status differences and of the relationship of status to honor, holiness, purity, and alienage. However, I have yet to explore in any depth the relationship of status to power in biblical materials. The representation of status differentiation in biblical texts has a close, though inexact, relationship to the exercise of power, as it often does elsewhere.[1] High-status persons draw upon economic, political, legal, and theological resources that allow them to wield significant power. This is expressed through exactions of wealth, fines, expulsions, and exclusions from sanctuary or community, executions, the imposition of curses, intimidating threats of punishment for those who challenge the status hierarchy, and cautionary tales of rebellion and retribution.

Priestly control of the sanctuary sphere results in an exalted status position for priests vis-à-vis nonpriestly cultic servants (for example, Levites in the Priestly Writing and Chronicles) and worshipers. This superior status is realized and communicated by means of elite ritual action, exclusive right of access to restricted ritual sites, the attribution of holiness to priests only, access to holy foods, and so on, as I have discussed at length. But priestly control of the sanctuary has very concrete economic dimensions as well. Priests and other cultic servants receive sacrificial animals, agricultural offerings, and horticultural offerings from worshipers. Some of this material they return fully processed to worshipers for consumption (for example, cooked meat from the well-being offering); some they burn as an offering to Yhwh (for example, the fat); but much remains in the sanctuary for their own use. Priests collect and process the holy and most holy foods for themselves and their dependents; according to certain texts, Levites receive the tithe from the people for their support. Thus, biblical law and narrative attribute to the cultic establishment, and especially its priestly elite, the power to exact significant wealth from the populace by means of obligatory offerings and the restriction of most meat processing and consumption to cultic contexts.[2] Texts suggest that power is exercised by the cultic establishment in a number of other ways as well. Gatekeepers exclude from the sanctuary individuals and animals they judge to be unclean or otherwise unqualified to enter (see Ezek 44:5, 11; 2 Chr 23:19). Fines are imposed on violators of cultic law (for example, for illegitimate profanation of a holy item), further enriching the cultic establishment (Lev 5:14–16). Priests are invested with the power to exclude persons with skin disease from the community and to readmit those judged to be healed (Leviticus 13–14). Similarly, priests put the woman accused of adultery through her ordeal, imposing a self-curse and drinking ritual on her (Num 5:11–31).

Surviving legal texts and narratives defend the privileges of the cultic elite from potential claims made by "outsiders" by means of intimidating threats and cautionary tales. Legal texts threaten violators with execution or extirpation of lineage. For example, any "outsider" who attempts to approach the altar will be put to death according to Num 18:7. Lev 7:25–27 threatens any man who eats either fat or blood with extirpation of lineage. Narrative texts such as Num 16:1–17:5 (Eng., 16:1–40), the Priestly School's story of the Levite Qorah's rebellion, send a clear warning to "outsiders" who would claim priestly status: If you do, Yhwh will kill you. The cautionary narrative of 2 Chr 26:16–20 has king Uzziah attempt to usurp control of the incense offering, only to be stricken with skin disease by Yhwh as a punishment for his offense against the established cultic order. The very act of defending privilege by means of intimidating threats or cautionary tales that claim Yhwh as the primary enforcer of the established order represents an exercise of power.

Yet the exercise of power by those of high status is only one dimension of the relationship of status to power. The privilege and power of elites may be challenged by other persons or groups who marshal their own varied resources (that is, power), sometimes successfully, in an attempt to improve their own position vis-à-vis others. Thus, power is to some extent diffuse, though it is mainly concentrated.[3] In a number of texts, cultic rites are the context par excellence for contesting the hegemonic claims of high-status groups such as the priesthood. Rites may be manipulated, offerings withheld, and exclusive privileges claimed by "outsiders." Successful challenges to the exclusive claims of elites result in a changed hierarchy of status with implications for existing power arrangements. The vast majority of surviving texts that describe challenges to the status (and power) of elite groups portray such challenges invariably as unsuccessful, even disastrous for those who dare to make novel claims. The quintessential example of this is the Priestly Writers' narrative of Qorah's destruction by Yhwh in Num 16:1–17:5 (Eng., 16:1–40), with its concrete memorial to Qorah's brazen foolishness and its words of warning to others who might imitate him and challenge exclusive Aaronid control of the priesthood. The elite writers of most surviving biblical texts have a vested interest in portraying these challenges as illegitimate failures, and so they do. Nonetheless, the odd text survives that hints at successful resistance, or even presents a counterclaim directly.

A text such as Neh 13:10–14 suggests that worshipers could, under certain circumstances, withhold offerings from the sanctuary and get away with it. Mal 3:8–12 is similar. In the latter text, the voice of Yhwh is the medium through which the cultic establishment demands its due, even promising prosperity in exchange for receipt of withheld tithes. The difficult economic times to which this text alludes are explained as the result of a curse imposed by Yhwh because he has not received what is his by right. Here is a text of elite provenance marshaling resources of power: the divine voice, promises of prosperity, and the imposition of a curse. But in this particular context, the threats and promises are not intended to prevent insurgence; they are a response to it after the fact. The system is not working: The cultic establishment lacks the power to enforce conformity, and so material exactions are being withheld by a defiant populace.

Isa 56:3–7 directly contests claims of opponents who would exclude the pious alien and the eunuch from the sanctuary on the basis of their particular expansive interpretation of Deut 23:2–9 (Eng., 1–8).[4] It resists the claims of its author's exclusivist opponents in a number of ways. First, it casts its counter message as a prophetically mediated oracle of Yhwh. Yhwh speaks authoritatively and eloquently for the inclusion of pious aliens and eunuchs, promising to act decisively to bring this about. In effect, deploying the voice of Yhwh is intended to neutralize the opponents' authoritative claims based on their reading of Deuteronomy 23. The language of challenge is interesting and revealing. Where opponents of inclusion, using charged rhetoric reminiscent of Ezra-Nehemiah, claim that Yhwh will surely "separate" (bdl) the alien from Israel, Isa 56:3–7 uses what appears to be a charged counter rhetoric of "attachment" (lwh) to subvert it. In addition, Yhwh's determination to associate pious aliens and eunuchs with his holy mountain and temple can be seen as an indirect attack on opponents who would cast the alien as a polluter, as in Ezra-Nehemiah. In all of these ways, subtle and direct, Isa 56:3–7 marshals resources of power in order to resist the claims of opponents who would act to exclude the alien and the eunuch from the cultic community and its ritual life. Thus, other voices challenge the status and hegemonic practices of certain elites.

No work of scholarship emerges out of a vacuum. As I write these words, two million immigrants—a record number—await naturalization decisions from the U.S. Immigration and Naturalization Service (INS). The INS is literally swamped with alien resident petitioners for citizenship, many of whom applied because they feared—often correctly—that they would lose benefits restricted to citizens alone by a neo-nativist Congress. Other immigrants, less well informed, applied because they feared deportation. Public, anti-gay rhetoric seems once again to be on the rise among religious conservatives and their allies. During the spring of 1998, the Senate majority leader spoke publicly of homosexuals as sinners, not unlike kleptomaniacs and alcoholics. His words emboldened various conservative Christian organizations to begin an anti-gay advertising campaign in prominent newspapers. Racial and gender issues such as affirmative action and the status of pornography continue to inform and at times monopolize public debate. While conservatives advocate restricting immigration or rolling back affirmative action, self-identified "progressives" on the left celebrate identity politics. In a word, binary modes of thought and discourse are part and parcel of contemporary American life. It is through such practices that groups and individuals within our society are ranked, privileged, marginalized, empowered, and disempowered. Binary practices also allow groups and individuals to contest the status and power of dominant elites. I did not consciously decide to write on the topic of this book because of the shape of contemporary public debate, but now that I reflect on the larger cultural setting of my project, my decision makes a lot of sense to me. The subject of hierarchy is timely, and biblical texts concerned with social differentiation, particularly those employing binary modes of thought and discourse, resonate in our contemporary context.

The Idea of Holiness in the Holiness Source

THE distribution of holiness according to materials of the Holiness Source is not easily explained. Unlike Priestly texts, in which holiness is restricted to the sanctuary sphere (including holy items and holy foods) and among persons, to the priesthood alone, holiness in the Holiness Source is more widely distributed. A number of Holness texts call upon Israel to be holy, or speak of Israel as being sanctified by Yhwh. Lev 19:2 is often presented as the paradigmatic example of the Holiness School's call to Israel to be holy: "Holy shall you be, for holy am I, Yhwh your god." Texts such as Exod 31:13; Lev 20:8; and 21:8 describe Israel as sanctified by Yhwh: "You shall keep my statutes and do them; I am Yhwh, who sanctifies you" (Lev 20:8).[1] This mix of sanctification idioms, in the indicative and the imperative,[2] is not unlike what is found in Holiness texts concerning the priesthood. In Lev 21:6 the priests are urged to be holy, as Israel is in a text such as Lev 19:2: "Holy shall they be to their god. . . . They shall be holy." In Lev 21:7, the priest is described as holy, as Israel is in a text such as Lev 20:8: "For holy is he to his god." Thus, in terms of rhetoric alone, there seems to be little if any difference between the way in which the sanctification of priests and people are described: Both people and priests are urged to be holy, and both are also described as holy.[3]

Why, then, do these texts urge people and priests to be holy if they are holy already? It would seem that to be holy means at least in part to obey Yhwh's commandments, an obligation of both priests and people (see Lev 21:7; Exod 31:13). Is there a difference between priestly sanctification and that of the people? A number of Holiness texts suggest that there is indeed. Lev 21:6, 7, 8 recognize the special status of priests and connect it to their sanctification. A priest shall not marry a prostitute or divorced woman "for holy is he to his god," says Lev 21:7. "You shall sanctify him," says Lev 21:8, "for the food of your god he brings near; holy shall he be for you, for holy am I, Yhwh, who sanctifies you." Other texts explicitly restrict access to the holy foods to priests and their dependents (Lev 22:10–13). If all Israel is holy, as Lev 22:32 and other texts seem to suggest, why must access to the holy foods be restricted, as Lev 22:10–13 makes plain? And why is the special status of the priesthood, with its attendant rights and obligations, connected to their holiness by Lev 21:6,

7, 8? If all the people are holy, what makes the holiness of the priesthood significant? The holiness of the priest in the Holiness Source must be of a different order than that of the people. The people's separation and holiness in Holiness texts does not privilege them in any concrete way vis-à-vis the priesthood; it seems mainly to be rhetorical. In contrast, some Holiness materials emphasize the privileges of priests vis-à-vis the people: they bring near Yhwh's offerings (Lev 21:6, 8); they eat holy foods (Lev 22:10–13). Thus, priestly holiness has concrete ramifications in texts of the Holiness School. It is very likely conferred through rites such as anointing, setting it apart from the holiness of the people, as some scholars have argued.[4] But however it is conferred, concrete differences in privilege distinguish priestly sanctification from that of the people. And when all is said and done, the people, though sanctified, have no greater privileges in the cultic sphere than do the people according to the Priestly Writing. They have access to neither holy foods nor priestly rites, nor can they approach restricted holy space such as that of the altar for burnt offerings. In short, there is little if any difference between the Holiness School and the Priestly Writers with respect to the place of the people in cultic hierarchy. The difference between the sources seems to be more one of approach to the rhetoric of sanctification. Where the Priestly Writers guard holiness jealously, restricting it to the priesthood alone, the Holiness School speaks of the people's holiness or their potential to be holy.[5] In doing so, the Holiness Source is not unlike other sources that attribute holiness to Israel. The holiness of Israel is mentioned as early as the Book of the Covenant and is a common theme in Deuteronomy and other materials betraying a Deuteronomistic background.[6] In addition, biblical materials of varying provenance speak of worshipers sanctifying themselves or being sanctified as a prerequisite to participation in cultic or quasi-cultic rites.[7] Whatever the meaning of this sanctification, these texts indicate that Israel's holiness in the Holiness Source had biblical antecedents. Exod 22:30 (Eng., 31) is in fact constructed much like any Holiness text calling on Israel to be holy: "Holy persons shall you be to me: torn flesh in the field you shall not eat; to the dog(s) you shall throw it." The call to holiness in this text is followed by a concrete example of obedience, not unlike Lev 11:44–45: "You shall sanctify yourselves and be holy, for holy am I; you shall not pollute yourselves with any swarming thing that moves on the ground . . . you shall be holy, for holy am I."

Notes

Introduction

1. Among philosophers, see for example E. Levinas, *Autrement qu'être ou au-delà de l'essence* (The Hague: M. Nijhoff, 1974), whose theory of alterity has been influential, and more recently, M. C. Taylor, *Altarity* (Chicago: University of Chicago Press, 1987). Among linguists, see F. de Saussure, *Cours de linguistique générale* (Paris: Payot, 1916) and R. Jakobson and M. Halle, *The Fundamentals of Language* (The Hague: Mouton, 1956). Among classicists, see especially G. E. R. Lloyd, *Polarity and Analogy: Two Types of Argumentation in Early Greek Thought* (Cambridge: Cambridge University Press, 1966) and P. Cartledge, *The Greeks: A Portrait of Self and Others* (New York: Oxford University Press, 1993). A number of anthropologists—and some sociologists—have been particularly engaged in the exploration of dyadic thought and discourse from a variety of standpoints. They range from C. Lévi-Strauss, who has argued that binary modes of thought are universal and an attribute of the human mind itself, to others who identify such modes in the cultures that they study but view these strictly as culturally specific and historically situated phenomena. See, among many possibilities, Lévi-Strauss, *Anthropologie structurale* (Paris: Plon, 1958) and *La pensée sauvage* (Paris: Plon, 1962); E. Leach, *Culture and Communication: The Logic by Which Symbols Are Connected* (New York: Cambridge University Press, 1976); R. Needham, *Symbolic Classification* (Santa Monica: Goodyear, 1979); L. Dumont, *Homo Hierarchicus: Essai sur le système des castes* (Paris: Gallimard, 1966); T. Turner, "Dual Opposition, Hierarchy and Value," in J.-C. Galey, ed., *Différences, valeurs, hiérarchie: textes offerts à Louis Dumont* (Paris: Ecole des Hautes Etudes en Sciences Sociales, 1984) 335–70; P. Bourdieu, *Esquisse d'une théorie de la pratique* (Geneva and Paris: Droz, 1972); and Needham's edited volume *Right and Left: Essays in Dual Symbolic Classification* (Chicago: University of Chicago Press, 1973). Interest in binary oppositions among anthropologists may be traced back to the work of Durkheim, Mauss, Hertz, and van Gennep. See, for example, the classic treatments of E. Durkheim and M. Mauss, "De quelques formes primitives de classification: Contribution à l'étude des représentations collectives," *Année sociologique* 6 (1901/1902) 1–72; and R. Hertz, "La prééminence de la main droite: Etude sur la polarité religieuse," *Revue philosophique* 68 (1909) 553–80.

2. E.g., C. Bell, *Ritual Theory, Ritual Practice* (New York: Oxford University Press, 1992) 36–37, 101–4, 140–41; S. K. Stowers, "Greeks Who Sacrifice and Those Who Do Not: Toward an Anthropology of Greek Religion," in L. M. White and O. L. Yarbrough, eds., *The Social World of the First Christians: Essays in Honor of Wayne A. Meeks* (Minneapolis: Fortress, 1995) 293–333, esp. 307, 310–11.

3. P. P. Jenson points this out (*Graded Holiness: A Key to the Priestly Conception of the World* [JSOTSup 106; Sheffield: Sheffield Academic Press, 1992]

63 n. 5), and lists a few exceptions, among them A. Bertholet, "Religionsge-
schichtliche Ambivalenzerscheinungen," *Theologische Zeitschrift* 4 (1948) 1–
16; J. Goldingay, "Diversity and Unity in Old Testament Theology," *VT* 34
(1984) 156–68; idem, *Theological Diversity and the Authority of the Old Testament* (Grand Rapids, MI: Eerdmans, 1987) 191–99. One might also add to
this list J. Milgrom's mapping of the relationship between holy/common and
unclean/clean (*Leviticus 1–16* [AB 3; New York: Doubleday, 1991] 731–32),
and G. A. Anderson's analysis of oppositions associated with mourning and rejoicing in biblical and rabbinic literature, with frequent reference to materials
from Ugarit and Mesopotamia (*A Time to Mourn, A Time to Dance: The Expression of Grief and Joy in Israelite Religion* [University Park, PA: Pennsylvania State University Press, 1991]). Jenson's own work focuses on the contrasts
holy/common and unclean/clean. F. H. Gorman Jr., in his *The Ideology of Ritual: Space, Time and Status in the Priestly Theology* (JSOTSup 91; Sheffield:
Sheffield Academic Press, 1991), identifies four dyadic contrasts that he believes
are operative in P ritual: clean/unclean, holy/common, life/death, and order/
chaos (207–10, 232).

   4. Cp. similarly Deut 32:39; Job 1:21.
   5. See similarly Isa 3:24–26; Amos 8:10. Anderson (*A Time to Mourn, A Time
to Dance*), presents a detailed study of the antithetical states of mourning and
rejoicing and their distinct binary vocabulary.
   6. Some readers will have noticed by now that I use the terms "opposition"
and "polarity" to describe several types of dyadic relation. Some biblical oppositions are comprehensive: They divide a group in two, classify all members of the
group in question as *either* A *or* B, and therefore allow for no intermediate possibilities. Examples of this type of polarity include male/female, unclean/clean,
holy/common, circumcised/uncircumcised, Israelite/alien, whole/blemished, and
living/dead. It is this type of opposition that will be of central interest in this study.
A second type of polarity that occurs frequently in biblical discourse brings together two antithetical terms that are not comprehensive and therefore allows for
intermediate possibilities. Examples of this second type include the oppositions
good/evil and wise/fool. In contrast to the comprehensive dyad unclean/clean,
persons in biblical thought can be other than wise or foolish, good or evil. Thus,
the antithetical terms brought together in this type of opposition, rather than
being comprehensive, represent two extremes or poles and allow for possibilities
between them. A third type of opposition describes antithetical actions or potential actions of an agent, often Yhwh, or antithetical experiences or potential experiences. An example of this type is 1 Sam 2:6–7, quoted above ("Yhwh kills and
allows to live, he causes one to descend to Sheol and he brings up"); other examples include Eccl 3:1–8 ("a time to be born, a time to die"); Job 1:21; Deut 32:39;
Amos 8:10; Isa 61:1–4, and Genesis 1. I call all three of these types of opposition
"antithetical dyadic constructions," for in each type, term B is presented as the
antithesis of term A (e.g., circumcised is the antithesis of uncircumcised, to debase
is the antithesis of to exalt, good is the antithesis of evil, to give a headdress is the
antithesis of to give ashes [Isa 61:3]). A fourth, less common type of dyadic construction brings together two members of the same category or group and is de-
ployed in texts to communicate totality or inclusivity. Sometimes, the two terms

in question are brought together in a "from . . . to" construction (min . . . wĕʿad), as in 1 Sam 15:3: "Now go and strike down Amalek, and destroy utterly all that belongs to him. Do not spare him, but kill man and woman, child and infant, ox and sheep, camel and ass" (mēʾîš ʿad ʾiššâ mēʿōlēl wĕʿad yônēq miššôr wĕʿad śeh miggāmāl wĕʿad ḥămôr). The four dyads in this example represent four classes of living things: adult persons, children, clean quadrupeds, and unclean quadrupeds. Each dyad is intended to refer to the totality of all belonging to that class (e.g., "camel and ass" [literally, "from camel to ass"] means all unclean quadrupeds, not simply camels and asses; the adult human class is, however, exhausted by man and woman). In contrast to the other types of opposition discussed, there is no sense of antithesis in this type of dyadic construction. On the variety of polar expressions in Greek materials and their classification, see Lloyd's treatment in *Polarity and Analogy*, 86–169, which was immensely helpful to me as I sought to formulate this discussion. Aristotle was the first to attempt a systematic analysis of the different modes of opposition used in Greek thought, as Lloyd points out.

7. There is no way to know just how widespread such strategies of classification were in ancient Israel, since the evidence that survives is literary and bears witness mainly to the concerns of elite literate groups such as the priesthood. This observation is noteworthy, as some anthropologists have argued that binary modes of thought and discourse are particularly characteristic of literate elites (e.g., J. Goody, *The Domestication of the Savage Mind* [Cambridge: Cambridge University Press, 1977] 52–111), though many others take no such position. On this, see further the discussion of B. Morris, *Anthropological Studies of Religion* (Cambridge: Cambridge University Press, 1987) 295–96.

8. Others who take a similar position on the power of ritual to make reality include D. I. Kertzer, *Ritual, Politics & Power* (New Haven: Yale University Press, 1988) 1–2, 12, 14, passim; S. B. Ortner, *High Religion: A Cultural and Political History of Sherpa Buddhism* (Princeton: Princeton University Press, 1989) 11–12; J. and J. Comaroff, eds., *Modernity and Its Malcontents: Ritual and Power in Postcolonial Africa* (Chicago: University of Chicago Press, 1993) xvi–xxi; and C. Bell, *Ritual: Perspectives and Dimensions* (New York: Oxford University Press, 1997), 82–83. On the problem of defining ritual, see n. 28 below.

9. E.g., L. Dumont, "The Anthropological Community and Ideology," *Social Science Information* 18 (1979) 785–817; and Turner, "Dual Opposition," 336. See also the excellent discussion of Bell, *Ritual Theory, Ritual Practice*, 101–4, which brought Turner's work to my attention.

10. The language of "privileging" oppositions is Bell's.

11. E.g., Judg 20:1; 2 Sam 3:10. Cp. similarly Esther 1:1, which describes the extent of Ahasuerus's empire with the expression "from India to Ethiopia" (mēhōddû wĕʿad kûš).

12. Reading with the versions (G, Syr, Vg); MT has experienced a haplography.

13. The missing wife has long been recognized as a crux of interpretation, and I can offer no plausible solution to explain her absence.

14. Cp. Lev 25:6–7, a list that includes the hired laborer (śākîr) and ends with animals.

15. For a brief but informative review of cross-cultural evidence for triadic constructions and other, more complex, forms of classification, see Needham, *Symbolic Classification*, 9–14.

16. The nonresident status of the nokrî is implied by contrasting him with the gēr, who is a resident.

17. L. A. Fallers, *Inequality: Social Stratification Reconsidered* (Chicago: University of Chicago Press, 1973) 27.

18. G. D. Berreman, "Race, Caste and Other Invidious Distinctions in Social Stratification," in J. B. Cole, ed., *Anthropology for the Nineties* (New York: Free Press, 1988) 485, 488. I note that "stratification" is a vexed term in the social sciences, and I shall mainly avoid using it in my own analysis, speaking instead of hierarchy or inequality. For debate about the use and definition of the term "stratification" with respect to non-Western contemporary societies, see Fallers, *Inequality*, 3–29; and Dumont, *Homo Hierarchicus*, 15, 48–49, 314–18, passim. For contemporary Western societies, see similarly J. Scott, *Stratification and Power: Structures of Class, Status and Command* (Cambridge: Polity, 1996) 15–19. P. Wason, (*The Archaeology of Rank* [Cambridge: Cambridge University Press, 1994] 57–66) provides an interesting and informative discussion of the uses of the term "stratification" in contemporary sociology and anthropology. My thanks to Theodore Lewis for bringing Wason's study to my attention.

19. For the language of "ascribed" versus "achieved" status, see, e.g., B. S. Turner, *Status* (Minneapolis: University of Minnesota Press, 1988) 4. For the language of "birth-ascribed" versus "non-birth-ascribed" status, see Berreman ("Race, Caste," 485–86), who equates these with the more conventional contrast of "ascribed" versus "achieved." Though the language of "ascribed" versus "achieved" status is commonplace among sociologists, I prefer anthropologist Berreman's distinction "birth-ascribed" versus "non-birth-ascribed" status. This contrast seems a far more apposite tool for analyzing representations of social differentiation in ancient societies, where birth and other types of ascription play so central a part, and "achievement," as sociologists understand it, even among the very talented, is rarely separable from birth-ascribed characteristics such as lineage, birth order, or gender.

20. See the discussion of Turner, *Status*, 4.

21. Turner, *Status*, 14. See, similarly, Scott, *Stratification and Power*, 4, 34.

22. Turner, *Status*, 14, 26–27, 32–33. M. I. Finley (*The Ancient Economy* [Berkeley: University of California Press, 1973] 50) notes Lukács's insight for classical antiquity. (Turner cites both Finley and Lukács.) For Finley's treatment of status, see especially 44–51; and idem, "The Servile Statuses of Ancient Greece," *Revue internationale des droits de l'antiquité* 7 (1960) 165–89.

23. C. Geertz, *Negara: The Theatre State in Nineteenth-Century Bali* (Princeton: Princeton University Press, 1980), 34. Fallers discusses relationships of the patron-client type in the context of East African Bantu kingdoms (*Inequality*, 4, 47–49). For patronage in classical antiquity, particularly Rome, see R. P. Saller, *Personal Patronage under the Early Empire* (New York: Cambridge University Press, 1982); and A. Wallace-Hadrill, ed., *Patronage in Ancient Society* (New York: Routledge, 1989). Among the essays in this volume is a more recent treat-

ment by Saller ("Patronage and Friendship in Early Imperial Rome: Drawing the Distinction," 49–62).

24. An example is David's attachment as client to Saul, which leads to his marriage into the royal family according to 1 Sam 18:17–29. See also 2 Sam 16:1–4; 19:25–40 (Eng., 24–39; cp. 9:1–13), where David rewards loyal servants with assets such as benefices and pensions after the defeat of Absalom's revolt.

25. E.g., Lev 1:3, 10, 14; 5:7, 11; cp. Deut 16:17, which is intended to clarify Exod 23:15, 17; 34:20, 23.

26. Finley, *The Ancient Economy*, 68, brought to my attention by Turner, *Status*, 32.

27. Turner, *Status*, 8, 14–16. Berreman was especially concerned to highlight resistance to stratification from those who least benefit from it ("Race, Caste," 490).

28. Bell states in her recent survey that there is "no clear and widely shared explanation of what constitutes ritual or how to understand it" (*Ritual*, x). A broadly applicable definition of ritual such as that developed by J. and J. Comaroff is for me most appealing. Contributing to the development of practice-type approaches to ritual and emphasizing ritual's historical context and innovative potential, they suggest that ritual might be defined as "formally stylized, communicative action," often "a vital element in the processes that make and remake social facts and collective identities." See further their introduction to *Modernity and Its Malcontents*, xv–xxii, esp. pp. xvi, xviii.

29. The war camp shares features in common with cultic contexts. The rules of purity apply there, as many texts suggest, due to the presence of the deity. According to Deut 23:15 (Eng., 14), the war camp is sanctified, and 1 Sam 21:6 (Eng., 5) implies that it can be so at times, but is not necessarily so (see the contrast derek ḥōl with the implied derek qōdeš). The war camp can also be a context for sacrifice, like the sanctuary.

30. On this last point, see chapter 2, n. 73.

31. On festivals and the rehearsal of the national story, see, for example, the arguments of F. M. Cross, "The Epic Traditions of Early Israel: Epic Narrative and the Reconstruction of Early Israelite Institutions," in R. E. Friedman, ed., *The Poet and the Historian: Essays in Literary and Historical Biblical Criticism* (Chico, CA: Scholars, 1983) 13–39.

32. The order of the appearance of Jesse's sons before Samuel at the sacrifice in Bethlehem is based on age and, therefore, status (1 Sam 16:6–10), as is the seating of Joseph's brothers at the meal in Joseph's house (Gen 43:33). The several references to individuals possessing greater honor than others in the households to which they belong (e.g., Gen 34:19; 1 Chr 4:9; cp. 1 Sam 22:14) are yet another indication of status differentiation among the elder's dependents. Distribution of portions at festivals is mentioned in several other texts, among them 2 Sam 6:19 and Neh 8:10.

33. Called haqqĕrû'îm, "those summoned," in the text.

34. Samuel's potential absence from cultic rites is an issue for Saul in 1 Sam 15:30. After Samuel informs Saul that Yhwh has rejected him, Saul asks Samuel nonetheless to honor him (kabbĕdēnî nā') before the elders of the people

and before Israel by accompanying him to the cultic rites that follow victory in battle.

35. E.g., Gen 28:10–22; Exod 24:3–8; Num 16:1–17:5 (Eng., 16:1–40).

36. On the Deuteronomistic History, see M. Noth, *Überlieferungsgeschichtliche Studien I: die sammelnden und bearbeitenden Geschichtswerke im Alten Testament* (Tübingen: Niemeyer, 1943). On the work of the "Chronicler," see D. N. Freedman, "The Chronicler's Purpose," *CBQ* 23 (1961) 436–42; and F. M. Cross, "A Reconstruction of the Judean Restoration," *JBL* 94 (1975) 4–18.

Chapter 1
Foundational Discourse

1. These texts include texts of the Hebrew epigraphic corpus. See, e.g., the inscription on the ivory pomegranate, the head of a small scepter whose provenance is very likely the Jerusalem temple: "Belonging to the house of [Yhw]h; a holy thing (qdš) of the priests." Cp. the inscriptions on pithoi from Tel Miqne-Ekron, which include "holy" (qdš) and "holy to Asherah/the asherah" (qdš l'šrt). On the ivory pomegranate, see further P. K. McCarter, Jr., *Ancient Inscriptions: Voices from the Biblical World* (Washington: Biblical Archaeology Society, 1996) 112–13. On the Miqne-Ekron inscriptions, see S. Gittin, "Seventh Century B.C.E. Cultic Elements at Ekron," in A. Biran et al., eds., *Biblical Archaeology Today, 1990: Proceedings of the Second International Congress on Biblical Archaeology, Jerusalem, June–July 1990* (Jerusalem: Israel Exploration Society/The Israel Academy of Sciences and Humanities, 1993) 250–51. For the evidence concerning sanctification and defilement from Mesopotamia, see E. Jan Wilson, *"Holiness" and "Purity" in Mesopotamia* (AOAT 237; Neukirchen-Vluyn: Neukirchener; Kevelaer: Butzon and Bercker, 1994).

2. By implicit, I mean that a text may mention only one member of the binary pair, or neither, though its discourse is clearly shaped by the opposition in question. The statement in Lev 21:12 concerning the high priest and the sanctuary is an example of what I mean by the implicit presence of a binary pairing in a biblical text. The verse states: "From the sanctuary (miqdāš) he shall not go forth; he shall not profane (yĕḥallēl) the sanctuary of his god." Neither holy (qōdeš) nor common (ḥōl) occurs in this text, but the term sanctuary (miqdāš, literally "holy place") and the verbal form "to profane" (ḥll) indicate that the holy/common binary underlies the prohibition.

3. The text seems to imply that to drink alcohol would impair the judgment of the priests when they are called upon to draw the distinctions described and teach Yhwh's statutes. Cp. Ezek 44:21, which is similar. Ezekiel's apparent close relationship to the Holiness School is frequently noted. See, among others, A. Hurvitz, *A Linguistic Study of the Relationship between the Priestly Source and the Book of Ezekiel* (CahRB 20; Paris: Gabalda, 1982) 77.

4. See, e.g., Lev 7:19–21; 19:8; 22:3, 9; Num 18:32; 19:13, 20; Josh 7. For the interpretation of kārēt ("cutting off") as an idiom for extirpation of lineage, see D. J. Wold, "The *Kareth* Penalty: Rationale and Cases," *SBLSP* 1 (1979) 1–45; T. Frymer-Kensky, "Pollution, Purification, and Purgation in Biblical Israel," in C. L. Meyers and M. O'Connor, eds., *The Word of the Lord Shall Go Forth:*

Essays in Honor of David Noel Freedman in Celebration of His Sixtieth Birthday (Winona Lake, IN: ASOR/Eisenbrauns, 1983) 404–5; J. Milgrom, *Leviticus 1–16* (AB3; New York: Doubleday, 1991), 457–60.

5. The text is part of a hypothetical source narrative, the "History of David's Rise," used by the Deuteronomists to construct their history. On the "History of David's Rise," see further P. K. McCarter, *I Samuel* (AB 8; Garden City: Doubleday, 1980) 27–30.

6. The mention of avoiding women suggests the issue is the purity of David's men, since seminal emissions are defiling (see Exod 19:15; Lev 15:16–18; Deut 23:11–12 [Eng., 10–11]). It is not clear in this text whether the holy bread (elsewhere known as the "bread of the presence," leḥem pānîm) was normally off limits to nonpriests, though this seems likely. On the bread of the presence in the Priestly Writing, see Exod 25:30; 35:13; 39:36; 40:23. Besides the opposition of holy bread and common bread, 1 Sam 21:6 also speaks of a "common journey" (derek ḥōl) versus, by implication, a sanctified one, in the context of the travels of a military band.

7. See, e.g., Deut 26:12–14 on the tithe, especially v. 14, in which the offerer confesses that he has not had contact with the holy offering while unclean. Deut 23:11–12, 13–15 (Eng., 10–11, 12–14) concern preserving the holiness of the camp from pollution. Two examples from epic narrative are worth noting. In Gen 35:2–3 (E), Jacob's dependents are ordered to purify themselves and change their garments before ascending to Bethel to erect an altar there to Yhwh. Exod 19:10–15 (J) is a text in which Moses is ordered by Yhwh to sanctify the people of Israel, who must wash their garments and be clean in preparation for Yhwh's theophany at Sinai/Horeb. The mountain itself is off-limits to the people in this latter text, upon pain of death. Epigraphic evidence such as that mentioned in n. 1 above confirm the impression given by biblical texts from various eras that these distinctions are fundamental to cultic life from early on.

8. E.g., Exod 19:10, 14; Num 11:18 (J); Josh 3:5; 7:13; 1 Sam 16:5; Joel 2:16; 2 Chr 30:17–18; cp. Isa 66:17. See ahead for discussion of the idiom hitqaddēš.

9. Other pairings include what I call secondary binary pairings such as most holy/holy or the gradations of impurity implicit in many biblical texts. On gradations of holiness and impurity, see ahead for discussion. Degrees of holiness are the central topic of P. P. Jenson, *Graded Holiness: A Key to the Priestly Conception of the World* (JSOTSup 106; Sheffield: Sheffield Academic Press, 1992).

10. Others have taken positions similar to mine on the connection of purity and pollution to holiness and the cult. E.g., J. Neusner (*The Idea of Purity in Ancient Judaism* [SJLA 1; Leiden: Brill, 1973] 8–11, 16, 20–21, 28–29) concludes on the basis of a survey of relevant texts that "all matters of purity attain importance because of the cult. No other occasion for attaining or preserving purity is considered" (20). See similarly D. Wright, "Unclean and Clean (OT)," *ABD* 6:729: Impurity is "that which is a threat to or opposes holiness, and hence must be kept separate from that sphere." Wright, like Neusner and others, rejects the notion that impurity in biblical representation has a demonic character (cp. B. A. Levine, *In the Presence of the Lord: A Study of Cult and Some Cultic Terms in Ancient Israel* [SJLA 5; Leiden: Brill, 1974]). In other cultures with purity con-

cerns, pollution is not necessarily bound to any conception of holiness, though this does generally seem to be the case in ancient west Asian examples.

11. Thus, one might attempt to define holiness in its biblical representation as the divine quality par excellence, which is distributed spatially and among persons, offerings, and other items in a selective manner. Jenson's attempt at a definition of holiness emphasizes association of the sanctified item with the deity: "that which belongs to the sphere of God's being or activity" (*Graded Holiness*, 48).

12. Milgrom has argued that holy/unclean is the primary contrast in biblical texts with cultic interests, though he acknowledges that formally speaking, the antithesis of holy is common and that of unclean is clean. Holy and unclean, according to Milgrom, are both dynamic; common and clean are static (*Leviticus 1–16*, 731–32). Here Milgrom develops the insights of W. Paschen, who argued that "clean" is negatively defined as simply "freedom from pollution," in contrast to "unclean" and "holy," which are transferable (*Rein und Unrein: Untersuchung zur biblischen Wortgeschichte* [Studien zum Alten und Neuen Testament 24; Munich: Kösel, 1970] 64, cited by Milgrom in *Leviticus 1–16*, 732). Certainly Milgrom has a point when he speaks of holiness and impurity sharing a dynamic character and when he speaks of the absolute antagonism between the holy and uncleanness. But in the binary rhetoric of biblical materials, unclean is not properly the opposite of holy, though it is threatening to it (on this last point, see similarly F. H. Gorman, Jr., *Ideology of Ritual: Space, Time and Status in the Priestly Theology* [JSOTSup 91; Sheffield: Sheffield Academic Press, 1991] 209–10). The category holy cannot exist without the category common, against which its distinct character is constructed; similarly, clean cannot exist without unclean, good without evil, light without darkness, native without alien. But holy *can* exist as a distinct category without unclean, demonstrating that the two terms are not inextricably bound one to the other. Holy does not need unclean to emerge as a distinct category as it needs common. Others have attempted to make sense of the relationship among the holy, the common, the unclean and the clean. See, for example, J. Barr's brief discussion in "Semantics and Biblical Theology—A Contribution to the Discussion," in *Congress Volume: Uppsala 1971* (VTSup 22; Leiden: Brill, 1972), 15–16; and, recently, Jenson, *Graded Holiness*, 43–55. Jenson argues that "holiness (and its opposite, the profane) represents the divine relation to the ordered world, and the clean (with its opposite, the unclean) embraces the normal state of human existence in the earthly realm. The holy-profane pair represents (positively and negatively) the divine sphere, and this may be distinguished from the human sphere (which is marked by the opposition between clean and unclean). The presence of a holy God and a holy sanctuary in the midst of Israel ensures that these two points of view overlap in a complex way" (47–48). It is not clear to me why Jenson believes that the common has any relation whatsoever to the divine sphere, or why he describes it as a negative representation of that sphere. Only holiness has such an association, and the contrast between the holy and the common in fact delimits the extent of sanctification, as I have argued. There is nothing negative about the common in itself. In certain purity constructions (e.g., that of the Priestly Writing), common individuals may enter the sanctuary sphere as long as they are clean, though they are not properly of that sphere.

With respect to the contrast clean/unclean, I am uncertain why Jenson believes it is properly "at home in the life of Israel outside the cult" (53). The whole point of the contrast is the determination of access to the sphere of the cult and quasi-cultic rites, or, as Jenson himself puts it, purity "is of significance primarily in that it is a presupposition for approaching the holy" (53). Jenson speaks frequently of what he calls a "holiness spectrum": very holy, holy, clean, unclean, very unclean (e.g., 40, 44, 63–65, 88). He derives the idea of a spectrum from the work of J. Lyons (*Semantics* [2 vols.; Cambridge: Cambridge University Press, 1977] 283, 290). I find this approach to the binary contrasts present in biblical materials rather unhelpful and unrepresentative of the evidence. In my view, the textual rhetoric tends to be binary in structure, primary pairings giving rise to secondary pairings (e.g., most holy/holy) and, occasionally, triadic constructions. These are intended to produce distinctions *within* particular categories (e.g., most holy/holy produces distinction within the category holy). Jenson acknowledges that his "spectrum" cannot accommodate the category common, a crucial defect he cannot explain or justify convincingly (44–45). It is better either to discard the spectrum schema entirely or to speak of several spectra rather than a single spectrum: most holy/holy/common, most unclean/unclean/clean, native/resident outsider/ nonresident alien. These spectra are essentially the same as the triadic constructions about which I have spoken in the introduction.

13. Some useful treatments of holiness include D. P. Wright, "Holiness (OT)," *ABD* 3:237–49; Jenson, *Graded Holiness*; Y. S. Licht, qōdeš, qādôš, qĕdûšâ, *EM* 7:44–62 (Hebrew); C. B. Costecalde, "Sacré et Sainteté dans l'Ancien Testament," *DBSup* 10 (1985) 1393–1432; M. Haran, *Temples and Temple Service in Ancient Israel* (Oxford: Clarendon, 1978) 175–88; I. Knohl, *The Sanctuary of Silence: The Priestly Torah and the Holiness School*, trans. J. Feldman and P. Rodman (Minneapolis: Fortress Press, 1995) 180–86; and J. G. Gammie, *Holiness in Israel* (OBT; Minneapolis: Fortress, 1989), though Gammie's book has some weaknesses. M. Douglas, "The Abominations of Leviticus," in idem, *Purity and Danger* (1966; reprint, Boston: Ark, 1984) 41–57, though flawed in some details, is a landmark study by a noted anthropologist that has had a notable influence on the way specialists in the biblical field view holiness and purity.

14. On Yhwh's holy name, see, among many examples, Lev 20:3; 22:2, 32; Amos 2:7; Ezek 20:39; 36:20, 21, 22; Ps 33:21; 103:1; 105:3; 145:21; on his holy arm, see Isa 52:10; Ps 98:1; on his holy word(s), see Jer 23:9; Ps 105:42; on his holy spirit, see Isa 63:10, 11.

15. E.g., Isa 1:4; 5:19, 24; 10:20; 41:14, 16, 20; 43:3, 14; 55:5.

16. Zech 14:5; Ps 89:6, 8 (Eng., 5, 7); Job 5:1; 15:15; Dan 8:13; cp. Deut 33:2.

17. Exod 20:8, 11//Deut 5:12; Exod 31:14, 15; 35:2; Isa 56:2, 6; 58:13; Neh 9:14; 10:32 (Eng., 31). Note that Exod 23:12 and 34:21, probably the two oldest Sabbath law formulations, do not mention the holiness of the Sabbath, nor does Exod 31:16–17, a Priestly text following the Sabbath formulation of the Holiness Source in Exod 31:12–15.

18. On these texts and their development, see further Knohl, *Sanctuary of Silence*, 19–40. The earliest formulations of the festival calendar do not mention the holiness of the festivals (see Exod 23:14–17; 34:18, 20c, 22–23).

19. The camp's holiness is explicit in Num 5:2–4 and implicit in Num 12:14. Lev 13:46; 14:8 require the exclusion of persons with skin disease from the camp, though the camp as a whole is not constructed as holy. On the basis of these texts, Knohl has argued that the camp lacks holiness for the Priestly Writers, except for the tabernacle; the Holiness School, in contrast, attributes holiness to the whole camp (*Sanctuary of Silence*, 184–85). Knohl views Num 5:1–4 as an H response to P's toleration of the presence of certain polluters in the camp. (P requires only the person with skin disease to leave the camp [Lev 13:46; 14:8]; the man or woman with a discharge and the person who has had contact with a corpse are not removed from the camp by P.)

20. A number of texts describe the Ark of the Covenant, Yhwh's throne, present with the Israelites in camp and in battle (e.g., 1 Sam 4:3–8; cp. Num 10:35–36). The ark's wanderings ceased, however, with the building of Solomon's temple in Jerusalem, in which it was permanently installed.

21. Other terms for sanctuary: hêkāl, māqôm, bāmâ.

22. The oldest cultic calendars speak of three pilgrimage festivals, at which every male Israelite was required to be present with offerings. See Exod 23:14–17; 34:18, 20c, 22–23. Cp. Deut 16:16–17, which adapts Exod 23:15b, 17, and includes the requirement that all males appear before Yhwh with offerings. The offerings of the cult are described in detail by P (with H supplementation) in the first seven chapters of Leviticus. Earlier sources also bear witness to a variety of offering types, though without the complexity and detail of the description in Leviticus 1–7. See, e.g., Gen 8:20–21; Exod 20:24; 24:5; Deut 33:10; 1 Sam 11:15. On offering types, see Levine, *In the Presence of the Lord*; and the extended discussion in Milgrom, *Leviticus 1–16*, 133–489.

23. The sanctified offerings, or holy foods, reserved for the priests and their dependents, are discussed in the P text Lev 10:12–20 and the H texts Lev 22:2–16 and Num 18:8–19; they are enumerated in detail in the latter text. According to H, the tithe is given to support the Levites; it is not holy since it is not intended for the priests. Only the best tenth of it, given by the Levites to the priests, is considered holy in H's schema (Num 18:29, 32). In contrast, the tithe in D is holy, and to be given to the Levite, the resident alien, the fatherless, and the widow (Deut 26:12–15).

24. I read the tabernacle texts not as a source for reconstructing cult before Israel's emergence in Canaan, but as a valuable source for the Priestly circle's own cultic ideology, which they present as normative, projecting it back to the Sinai revelation. The P description of the tabernacle may well be intended to evoke the cult of the Jerusalem temple, though this remains uncertain. On this, see the argument of Haran, *Temples and Temple Service*, 189–94.

25. For a recent survey, see A. Mazar, *Archaeology of the Land of the Bible (10,000–586 B.C.E.)* (New York: Doubleday, 1990) 492–502.

26. See also Jer 33:18, 21, 22. Cp. Judg 17:7–13.

27. See Ezek 40:46; 43:19; 44:10–14, 15–31; 48:11.

28. See further Mazar, *Archaeology*, 496–98.

29. Exod 37:16 claims the table served to display vessels; 40:22–23 say the table displayed bread.

30. On kippēr as "to purge" or "wipe away" and kippûr as "purgation," see Levine, *In the Presence of the Lord*, 56–67, 123–27; and Milgrom, *Leviticus 1–16*, 1079–84. Thus Yom Kippur is more properly the "Day of Purgation."

31. This is the so-called long house, an architectural pattern well known from various west Asian sites of the second and first millennia BCE. See further Mazar, *Archaeology*, 377.

32. See 1 Kgs 6:16; 7:50; 8:6. These texts refer to the inner chamber of the temple as qōdeš qodāšîm, "most holy" or "holy of holies."

33. Though never stated explicitly, 2 Chr 4:6 implies that both the lavers and the sea stood in the court, since the lavers are used to rinse the elements of the burnt offering, a process that would certainly have occurred in the courtyard rather than in the house itself.

34. Haran (*Temples and Temple Service*, 192–93) has argued that originally, only one courtyard surrounded the temple. The first mention of two courts, he claims, comes in texts such as Isa 1:12 and 2 Kgs 21:5; 23:12. Given the difficulties of the description in 1 Kings 6–7, this argument is certainly worthy of consideration, though problems remain. Even if we choose to discount the expression ḥāṣar bêt yhwh happěnîmît in 1 Kgs 7:12 as Haran does, the inner court (ḥāṣēr happěnîmît) mentioned in 1 Kgs 6:36 nonetheless suggests the existence of an outer court associated with it. Is that outer court necessarily the same court that surrounded both the temple and palace complexes and therefore not truly a court of the temple, as Haran maintains? This remains unclear.

35. Ezek 8:16; 10:3 (cp. v. 4) speak of an "inner court" (ḥāṣēr happěnîmît) beside the entry into the temple. A number of texts speak generally of a plurality of courts (e.g., Ezek 9:7; 1 Chr 28:12; 2 Chr 23:5). Several texts remain unclear. Jer 36:10 speaks of an "upper court" (ḥāṣēr hāʿelyôn) where the populace gathered, which was at the entry of the new gate of the house of Yhwh, and 2 Chr 20:5 speaks of a "new court" (ḥāṣēr haḥădāšâ). What was the relationship of the "upper court" of Jer 36:10 and the "new court" of 2 Chr 20:5 to the two courts of the temple mentioned in other texts?

36. E.g., 2 Kgs 15:35; 2 Chr 23:20 on the Upper Gate; Jer 20:2 on the Upper Gate of Benjamin; Jer 26:10; 36:10 on the New Gate.

37. Jer 36:10 mentions a room (liškâ) assigned to Gemaryahu son of Shaphan in the upper court at the opening of the New Gate of Yhwh's house.

38. See n. 32 above.

39. Following the lead of H. Gese (*Der Verfassungsentwurf des Ezechiel (Kap. 40–48) traditionsgeschichtlich untersucht* [BHT 25; Tübingen: Mohr/Siebeck, 1957]), many scholars believe that the text of Ezekiel 40–48 in its extant form is composite, having been expanded and supplemented over the course of the sixth century. A more recent assessment sympathetic to Gese's perspective is that of W. Zimmerli, *Ezekiel 2*, trans. R.E. Clements (1969; Philadelphia: Fortress, 1983) 547–53. J. Z. Smith (*To Take Place: Toward Theory in Ritual* [Chicago: University of Chicago Press, 1987] 47–73), offers an interesting analysis of what he calls "the ideology of place" in Ezekiel 40–48. He calls the pericope "an endeavor in mapping the social configurations of an ideal cultic place" (48), and identifies "four ideological maps" in it.

40. There were two forms of the cubit in use during the period when biblical texts were written. The long cubit equaled approximately 52.5 cm; the short cubit 44.5 cm, as Mazar notes. The measurements present in descriptions of Ezekiel's temple and Solomon's temple may assume the long cubit. See further Mazar, *Archaeology*, 376.

41. 42:20 (MT) seems to contradict 45:1, in that it states that the wall around the temple complex is intended to separate holy from common, yet the territory of the holy district immediately outside the complex is hardly common according to 45:1! LXX of 42:20 does not speak of the wall separating holy from common, but speaks of division between the sanctuary and the "outer wall" (proteichismatos, reading *ḥēl for *ḥōl, as others have observed [e.g., G. A. Cook, *The Book of Ezekiel* (ICC; Edinburgh: T. and T. Clark, 1936) 462]). The LXX may reflect an attempt to harmonize disparate views about holy and common now present in the composite text of Ezekiel 40–48 (Ibid.).

42. See the earlier discussion in this chapter on the Levites in P, H, Ezekiel, and Chronicles/Ezra-Nehemiah.

43. Also called the "holy place" (qōdeš) in 41:23.

44. The most thorough exploration of the evidence for gradations of holiness is Jenson's *Graded Holiness*. Though the author's focus is P, he does make reference to gradations of holiness as represented in other biblical sources. Haran's *Temples and Temple Service* also includes a careful study of gradations in P's tabernacle pericope.

45. Exod 28:43; 30:17–21; 40:32.

46. E.g., Exod 35:12 and 40:21 on the pārōket hammāsāk; 26:36–37 and 40:5 on the screen (māsāk) at the entrance to the tent; 27:16 and 40:8 on the screen at the entrance to the sanctuary complex.

47. See further the detailed argument presented by Haran, *Temples and Temple Service*, 158–63.

48. 1 Kgs 6:16; 7:50; 8:6 on the designation "holy of holies" for the děbîr (cp. 2 Chr 3:8, 10); 1 Kgs 6:31–32 on the doors of the holy of holies.

49. As mentioned, 2 Chr 4:9 speaks of a priests' court and a great court, the latter "great" presumably because it was larger than the priests' court and contained the worshiping populace. The great court is also mentioned, albeit in a slightly different form, in 1 Kgs 7:12, where it is paired with the inner court of the house of Yhwh.

50. I am not depending on the use of the expression "most holy" (qōdeš qodāšîm) to determine relative degrees of holiness in Ezekiel's temple and its surroundings, since the expression is used in a confusing and contradictory way in Ezekiel 40–48, in contrast to its precise use in the Priestly descriptions of the tabernacle. The expression "most holy" is used for a number of areas of the sanctuary complex in the final form of Ezekiel 40–48: the innermost room of the temple (41:4); the larger sanctuary complex, including the two courts (43:12; 45:3); and the priestly share of the holy territory within which the temple was located (48:12). This usage makes little or no sense. How can the whole temple complex (let alone the large territory outside its walls) be "most holy"? If this were so, it would suggest that all parts of the temple complex have an equal, high degree of holiness, and therefore the various walls, gates, and doors marking the

boundaries between each area of the temple complex would serve no purpose. Also, the prohibition preventing the people and the Levites from entering the inner court would make no sense if the inner court were not more holy than the outer. Perhaps "most holy" in Ezekiel 40–48 is used as a rhetorical device to highlight the holiness of a particular part of the sanctuary complex or the complex as a whole rather than a technical term intended to mark off one or more areas as more holy than other areas. See similarly, Milgrom, *Leviticus 1–16*, 321. (I reached this conclusion before encountering Milgrom's treatment.)

51. As pointed out by Milgrom, *Leviticus 1–16*, 732.

52. E.g., Lev 19:12; 20:3; 22:31–32.

53. I have benefited from Milgrom's treatment of this text, which clarifies a number of points with respect to ma'al, qodšê Yhwh and Piel šlm. I follow him in translating 'āšām as "reparation offering" and yĕkappēr as "effects expiation." See further *Leviticus 1–16*, 319–20, 327, 328.

54. Numbers 18 is probably to be attributed to the Holiness School. See further n. 67 below on 18:1–7; and Knohl, *Sanctuary of Silence*, 53–54.

55. On the difficult 'et miqdĕšô mimmennû of v. 29, see the discussion of B. A. Levine, *Numbers 1–20* (AB 4; New York: Doubleday, 1993) 452–53. LXX to hēgiasmenon ap' autoû suggests, as Levine notes, a Hebrew Vorlage with mĕquddāšô, "its sanctified portion."

56. On the ḥērem, see further Num 18:14; Deut 7:2, 26; Josh 7:1–26 (cp. 6:17); 1 Sam 15:3, 21; 1 Kgs 20:42, among others.

57. This is not true of all texts. See Exod 13:2 and 22:28–29 (Eng., 29–30), the latter of which is very likely the oldest formulation of the law of the firstborn: "The firstborn of your children [or, perhaps, "sons"] you shall give to me. Thus shall you do with your cattle and your sheep. Seven days it shall remain with its mother, but on the eighth day, you shall give it to me."

58. E.g., Exod 13:12–15; 34:19–20; Num 18:15–18. Exod 13:12–15 (D) expands upon the older Exod 34:19–20, adding an historical explanation for the practice of selected obligatory redemption. Aside from redeeming human firstborn, these two texts speak of redeeming the firstborn of the ass. Num 18:15, in contrast, requires the redemption of the firstborn of unclean beasts generally, in addition to the firstborn of humans.

59. Animal substitution is stated explicitly in the case of the ass in Exod 34:20 and 13:13; it is implied for the firstborn of humans. Num 18:16 requires payment of a valuation to redeem the firstborn after they have lived one month. Presumably, this verse, with its delay of redemption for one month, concerns only the human firstborn, though this is not stated explicitly. See, however, Num 3:40, which supports this interpretation.

60. Num 3:11–13 is very similar to this text. See also Num 3:40–51.

61. On the law of the firstborn and its development, see further G. Brin, *Studies in Biblical Law: From the Hebrew Bible to the Dead Sea Scrolls* (JSOTSup 176; Sheffield: Sheffield Academic Press, 1994) 166–237.

62. The position that all male Levites are priests is assumed in this text as well as Deut 18:1–8; 33:8–11 and Jer 33:18, 21–22. Eventually, it would come to be challenged successfully by Aaronid claimants to exclusive priesthood, though it is difficult to determine when. The Aaronid challenge to a pan-Levitic priesthood is

reflected in such texts as P, H, Ezekiel, and Chronicles/Ezra-Nehemiah. On these conflicting visions of the legitimate priesthood and the way in which they are manifest in biblical narratives, see F. M. Cross, "The Priestly Houses of Early Israel," in his *Canaanite Myth and Hebrew Epic* (Cambridge, MA: Harvard University Press, 1973) 195–215.

63. Though Knohl has recently argued that the non-J material in Num 16:1–17:5 (Eng., 16:1–40) is to be assigned to the Holiness Source rather than to the Priestly Writing, I cannot accept his position (*Sanctuary of Silence*, 73–82). The whole point of the non-J material in this pericope is the restriction of holiness to the priesthood alone; neither the Levites nor the congregation have any claim whatsoever to holiness or to the priestly prerogatives that are tied to it according to this text. This is a position compatible with what we know of P from other passages, though not with H, which does not restrict the rhetoric of holiness to the priesthood. In H materials, the whole congregation are holy, though H does reserve priestly obligations and privileges for the priesthood alone (see further Lev 22:10–13 and probably Num 18:1–7, as well as the appendix). Since the non-J material in Num 16:1–17:5 (Eng., 16:1–40) concerns both rhetorical claims to holiness (e.g., 16:3: "All of the congregation, all of them, are holy and in their midst is Yhwh") and ritual action (incense presentation), it seems to me that this pericope fits better with the Priestly Writing than with the Holiness Source. Though both P and H would presumably oppose the usurpation of priestly prerogatives (i.e., incense presentation), it is difficult to imagine H opposing a claim by the congregation or the Levites to holiness, since all are sanctified according to H. There are other reasons to favor assignment of the material in question to P. First, there is no distinct H rhetoric in the non-J sections of the chapter. The use of qṣp in v. 22, which Knohl believes suggests H, does not; it occurs also in Lev 10:16, a text he himself assigns to P. Though miškan yhwh (v. 9) may be an expression distinct to H as Knohl argues, maḥtôt (v. 6) with the meaning "censers" is very likely an expression distinct to P (see Lev 10:1; 16:12, the only other examples of this usage, both P). In fact, Num 16:6–7 is worded much like Lev 10:1, a P text even in Knohl's view (cp. also Num 16:35 and Lev 10:2). Linguistic analysis of the non-J material in Num 16:1–17:5 (Eng., 16:1–40) points more readily to P than to H, as does analysis of the content.

64. On the holiness of the priests in P, see Exod 28:3, 40–41; 40:12–15; Lev 8:30; in Ezekiel 40–48, see Ezek 42:13–14; 44:19; and 46:20, where it is implied, and 48:11, where it is stated explicitly. On their separation from other cultic servants, see especially Num 16:10; 17:5 (Eng., 16:40); Ezek 44:13, 15–16, and my discussion of these two texts ahead. H also speaks of the sanctification of the priests, though it does not restrict its rhetoric of holiness to the priesthood. On the priests' sanctification in H, see Lev 21:6, 7, 8; on H's rhetoric of holiness and the interpretive challenges it poses, see the appendix.

65. On qrb, "to approach" (legitimately) or "be brought near," as well as "to encroach," or invade, see Milgrom, "The Encroacher and the Levite," in his *Studies in Levitical Terminology I* (University of California Publications: Near Eastern Studies 14; Berkeley: University of California Press, 1970) 16–37.

66. Though Knohl believes Num 8:5–22 is an H text, I am not certain about its assignment, as it contains idioms that appear to be characteristic of P on the

one hand and H on the other (*Sanctuary of Silence*, 71–73). The use of the verb nzh (Hiphil), "to sprinkle," (v. 7) is characteristic of P (see, e.g., Exod 29:21; Lev 4:6, 17; 8:11, 30; 14:7, 16, 27, 51; 16:14, 15, 19; Num 19:4, 18, 19, 21b) and never used by H. In contrast, the expression wayyithattĕ'û has parallels in H material (Num 19:12, 13, 20; 31:19, 20, 23) though not in P.

67. Knohl assigns Num 3:5–10 to H, though there are no distinct H idioms in the passage (*Sanctuary of Silence*, 72). I am inclined to believe the pericope is P, even given the parallels Knohl adduces with Num 18:1–7, a text that may well be the work of H. Differences in idiom between the two texts are as worthy of note as their parallels. See, e.g., 18:2 wĕyillāwû ʿālêkā (cp. v. 4 wĕnilwû ʿālêkā) where 3:6 has wĕhaʿămadtā 'ōtô; lipnê 'ōhel hāʿēdūt in 18:2 where 3:7 has lipnê 'ōhel môʿēd. The expression 'ōhel hāʿēdūt appears to be characteristic of H, as Knohl has argued (108). Perhaps Num 18:1–7 is indeed an H text, a recasting of P material in Num 3:5–10, in which H confirms Aaronid hegemony over the Levites. Nothing is said in Num 18:1–7 about the distribution of holiness among cultic servants, though the Levites are forbidden to usurp priestly prerogatives, as they are in Lev 22:10–13. On the privileges of the priesthood in H, see the appendix.

68. Cp., however, 2 Chr 23:6, where both the Levites and priests are described as holy.

69. On this alternative schema of Chronicles, see further the comments of Wright, "Holiness (OT)," 238.

70. E.g., Exod 19:10, 14; Num 11:18 [J]; Josh 3:5; 7:13; 1 Sam 16:5; Joel 2:16; 2 Chr 30:17–18; cp. Isa 66:17.

71. The sanctification mentioned in 2 Chr 30:17 is associated closely with purification: "For there were many among the assembly who had not sanctified themselves and as for the Levites, they were in charge of the slaughter of the Passover for all who were not clean, in order to sanctify it to Yhwh." Many of the other texts that mention the requirement of sanctification for worshipers associate it with purification as well. For example, in Exod 19:10, 14, the command to sanctify is paired with the command to wash garments, an act tied to purification elsewhere (e.g., Lev 15:13). In 2 Sam 11:4, the vocabulary of sanctification is used of Bathsheba in a noncultic context where we would expect an idiom of purification: "As for her, she was sanctifying herself from her [menstrual] uncleanness." It is as if sanctification in this text were not much more than purification. Nonetheless, Isa 66:17 speaks clearly of sanctification and purification together, as if they were separate actions, suggesting that it is unlikely that sanctification of worshipers in these non-P, non-H, and non-Ezekiel contexts means simply purification. Compare Milgrom, *Leviticus 1–16*, 965–68, who argues that hitqaddēš is simply the non-Priestly term for purification by bathing.

72. On H and sanctification, see the appendix.

73. On the assignment of Num 16:1–17:5 (Eng., 16:1–40) in its final form to P, see n. 63 above.

74. Much of this text in its final form is P material focusing on the rebellion of Qorah and his allies. This narrative is, however, fused with J elements (vv. 12–15, 25, 26 [?], 27b, 28–34) concerning a rebellion of Dathan and Abiram against the authority of Moses (see further M. Noth, *A History of Pentateuchal Traditions*, trans. B. W. Anderson [1948; Chico, CA: Scholars, 1981] 32). Within the P mate-

rial concerning Qorah and the Levites, there are fragments that suggest the presence of a third narrative about a revolt of Israelite leaders (vv. 2–4, parts of vv. 17,
35). In this latter narrative, as in the Qorah story, the issue is holiness: The rebel
leaders claim that the whole congregation is holy (v. 3). This claim stands in
tension with the Levite challenge to Aaronid holiness, which, by implication, was
a claim to holiness not for the whole congregation, but for the Levites. Yet, because of the nature of the text in its final form, this claim is never made directly by
Qorah; instead, the claim of holiness for the whole congregation in v. 3 serves,
oddly, as the Qorahite claim, though it stands in tension with it. The link between
v. 3 and the Qorahite claim to holiness and thus, priesthood, is made through the
repetition of rab lākem ("enough") in v. 7, as others have pointed out (e.g.,
Knohl, *Sanctuary of Silence*, 77).

All three stories have the rebels making similar claims concerning status, and
this may explain why they were fused in the redactional process. In the P narrative, Qorah and his allies challenge the Aaronid claim to exclusive priesthood by
challenging their exclusive claim to holiness, which brings them elevated status
(e.g., vv. 5–7, 10); in the fragments concerning the revolt of the Israelite leaders,
the leaders accuse Moses (and Aaron? The accusation is plural in its present
form.) of magnifying himself (themselves?) over the assembly (v. 3); in the J narrative, Dathan and Abiram accuse Moses of making himself a prince over them (v.
13; kî tiśtārēr ʿālênû gam hiśtārēr). On the difficulties of this chapter, and for a
different view of the extent of the narrative of the revolt of the leaders, see Knohl,
Sanctuary of Silence, 75–83.

75. Cp. Num 8:14 on the dedication of the Levites to Yhwh. Here, Yhwh
orders the Levites "separated" from the congregation to serve in the sanctuary.

76. The priests are "set apart" for sanctification (1 Chr 23:13) and are
"brought near" to Yhwh when sanctified (Exod 29:4, 8; 40:12, 14); they are
described as "near Yhwh" (Lev 10:3b; Ezek 42:13; 43:19), and they alone "approach" to "bring near" Yhwh's offerings (Lev 21:6, 17, 21; Ezek 44:15; cp.
Num 17:5 [Eng. 16:40]). Derivatives of the root qrb and the causative of the root
bdl occur often in narrative concerning the privileges and duties of the priests.

77. See Num 16:10; 17:5 (Eng., 16:40); cp. 16:5, 7.

78. The priesthood is therefore more narrowly defined here than it is in P, H,
and Chronicles/Ezra-Nehemiah, where all Aaronid males are priests. Zadok was
Solomon's high priest, the progenitor of the high priests of the temple. By claiming that only Zadokites are priests, texts such as Ezek 44:15 in effect restrict the
priesthood to the high priestly line alone (see also Ezek 40:46; 43:19; 48:11). On
Zadok himself, see further Cross, *Canaanite Myth*, 207–15; and S. M. Olyan,
"Zadok's Origins and the Tribal Politics of David," *JBL* 101 (1982) 177–93.

79. See Ezek 46:2–3 on restricted access of the prince and of the people.
Though no text explicitly states that the Levites may not enter the inner court, this
is implied in various passages that speak of that court's holiness and the required
practices of the priests when entering it (e.g., they must wear their holy garments,
surely off-limits to the Levites).

80. See similarly Ezek 42:14, which states explicitly that the priestly garments
are holy.

81. Slaughter is here transferred from the worshiper to the Levites. Thus, according to this text, heads of household on pilgrimage would lose control of an

important ritual function that they had previously enjoyed. On slaughter performed by the household head, see, e.g., 1 Sam 1:3–5 and my discussion in the
introduction to this book. Lev 1:5, 6, 9, 11, 13, among other texts, speak of the
worshiper laying his hand on the head of the victim, slaughtering it, skinning it,
and cutting it up; in addition, the worshiper is said to wash its entrails and shins
(following Milgrom [*Leviticus 1–16*, 159–60] on kĕrāʿayim, often translated
"legs" [e.g., RSV]). Verse 11 specifies that the slaughter occurs by the side of the
altar. In certain circumstances, texts suggest that a person (male or female) other
than a head of household could offer sacrifice (e.g., Lev 12:6; 14:10; 15:14, 29;
Num 6:10, 14). On the series of sacrificial rites described in Leviticus 1, see further the detailed treatment in Milgrom, *Leviticus 1–16*, 150–51, 154–60.

82. The verb used in Ezek 44:13 is ngš, a synonym of qrb.

83. A rather vague charge, but frequently made in the Book of Ezekiel. See,
e.g., 14:1–5, 6–11.

84. They control access through their gatekeeping responsibilities.

85. On the fat and the blood and their handling by the priest, see Lev 1:5, 8,
11–12, 15; 3:16b; 7:22–27; 17:6, 10–14, among other texts. Manipulation of
blood is a central priestly function.

86. Num 16:9–10 speaks of Yhwh bringing the Levites near to him, but not in
the manner of the priests.

87. Other passages also treat the holy foods. See, e.g., Lev 6:7–11 (Eng., 14–
18) on the cereal offering; 6:18–23 (Eng., 24–30) on the purification offering;
7:1–6 on the reparation offering.

88. Num 18:9–10; Lev 10:12–13, 16–20. Cp. Lev 22:3–9, which states outright the requirement of purity when approaching any of the holy foods. This is
assumed in Leviticus 10 and Numbers 18 concerning the eating of the most holy
offerings. With respect to the cereal offering, Lev 10:12 requires that it be eaten
in the form of unleavened bread beside the altar. Verse 13, somewhat awkwardly,
is not as specific: It says it must be eaten in a holy place. Cp. Lev 6:7–11 (Eng.,
14–18), 18–23 (Eng., 24–30); 7:1–6.

89. In a detailed treatment, Milgrom (*Leviticus 1–16*, 461–73) argues for the
translation "elevation offering." Cp. the comments of Levine (*Numbers 1–20*,
276), who translates "presentation offering." Both agree that the verb lĕhānîp
means "to raise" rather than "to wave." Thus, the tĕnûpâ is a "raised offering."

90. Num 18:11–15, 17–18. Cp. the brief enumeration in Lev 10:14–15, which
mentions only the breast of the tĕnûpâ and the thigh of the tĕrûmâ (from the
well-being offering) of the items to be eaten both by males and females in a clean
place.

91. E.g., Exod 30:33; Num 3:10, 38; 17:5 (Eng., 16:40); 18:4, 7. In Num
1:51, zār refers to one who does not have the Levitic privilege of setting up and
taking down the tabernacle.

92. I cannot imagine that "progeny" means here anything other than an adult
son, who would be in a position to provide for his mother and therefore eliminate
the need for her to return to her own father's house.

93. Perhaps also to an adult son, though the text is not clear about this possibility. See n. 92 above.

94. This is true if male, foreign slaves were to be circumcised, as were all
Israelite males according to Gen 17:12–13. No doubt there were other rites of

transition that functioned to erase the slave's previous identity (including lineage bonds), leaving the slave little more than an extension of the master's person, but extant texts make no reference to such rites. On the status of the slave, the slave's rites of transition, and the slave's eating holy foods, see further my discussion in chapter 3.

95. This expression obviously refers to others besides sons and daughters (e.g., wives or slaves).

96. E.g., as in Lev 22:3–9.

97. This would even be true for H, which attributes holiness of a different order to the whole congregation. Priestly sanctification, acquired through anointing and other rites, is presumably what establishes the priestly claim on the holy foods, and this is what is symbolically extended to priestly dependents in these texts. See further the appendix.

98. The tithe is, however, holy in D, and distributed among Levites, resident outsiders, widows, and the fatherless (Deut 26:13). Though Neh 13:10–14 associates the tithe with the Levites, the Priestly Writing makes no mention of this privilege.

99. See n. 30 above on kippēr and kippûr.

100. Lev 16:2–19 (P), 29–34 (H).

101. See Exod 29:7, 29; Lev 8:12–13; 16:32; 21:10; Num 35:25 on the anointing of the high priest. These texts seem to suggest that anointing was a unique characteristic of the high priest. An alternative tradition, evidenced in texts such as Exod 28:41; 30:30; 40:13, 15; Lev 7:36; Num 3:3, claims explicitly that both the high priest and the priests were anointed.

102. Exod 28:2–39; 29:29; 39:1–31.

103. On the Urim and Tumim, see Exod 28:30; Lev 8:8; Num 27:21; Deut 33:8; 1 Sam 14:41; 28:6. The Ephod of P is a garment to be worn by the high priest (e.g., Exod 28:6–14), but earlier sources describe a garment of linen routinely worn by other priests (1 Sam 22:18) or even by David in a ritual setting (2 Sam 6:14). Judg 8:27 speaks of a very different kind of Ephod: an object of gold made by Gideon, which he sets up in his city, Ophrah. On the Ephod, see further, C. Meyers, "Ephod," *ABD* 2:550; and M. Haran, "The Ephod According to Biblical Sources," *Tarbiz* 24 (1955) 380–91 (Hebrew).

104. Lev 21:13–14; cp. 21:7. Ezek 44:22 allows the regular priest to marry only a priest's widow among widows.

105. There are several other contexts in which an explicit connection is made between holiness and honor. See, e.g., Isa 58:13, where the Sabbath, described as Yhwh's "holy day," is honored by Israelites when they cease to do labor on it. According to P, Aaron's holy garments are made "for honor and for beauty" (Exod 28:2). After killing Aaron's sons Nadab and Abihu, Yhwh states that "among those near to me I will be sanctified ('eqqādēš), and in the presence of all the people I will be honored ('ekkābēd)" (Lev 10:3).

106. The root kbd (Piel), "to honor," is contrasted with a number of roots, among them qll (Hiphil), "to diminish"; bzh (Qal), "to despise," klm (Hiphil), "to shame." On the rhetoric of honor and dishonor, see S. M. Olyan, "Honor, Shame and Covenant Relations in Ancient Israel and its Environment," *JBL* 115 (1996) 201–18.

107. bēn yĕkabbēd 'āb wĕ'ebed 'ădōnāyw wĕ'im 'āb 'ānî 'ayyēh kĕbôdî.

108. hakkōhănîm bôzê šĕmî.

109. leḥem mĕgō'āl. The verb g'l and its derivatives are used beginning in sixth-century texts to indicate pollution. See, e.g., Isa 59:3; Lam 4:14; Ezra 2:62 (=Neh 7:64); Neh 13:29; Dan 1:8. On g'l, see further I. Zatelli, *Il campo lessicale degli aggetivi di purità in ebraico biblico* (Florence: Istituto di linguistica e di lingue orientali, Università di Firenze, 1978) 93. In the context of Malachi 1, Yhwh objects to receiving blemished sacrifices (see 1:8, 13). Blemished sacrificial animals are not polluting in other sources, though they appear to be here. See Mal 1:11, where the blemished offerings are contrasted with minḥâ ṭĕhôrâ, "a clean offering," suggesting the issue is one of defilement, and my discussion of Malachi 1 in chapter 4.

110. The narrative in vv. 12–17 accuses the sons of Eli of corrupt cultic practices; the material in v. 29 implicates Eli as well.

111. Determining exactly what the priests have taken is rather difficult, given the state of preservation of v. 29. The text seems to assume that all or a portion of the first fruits (rē'šît) belong to Yhwh rather than to the priests and that the priests have plundered them. In other materials, the first fruits are generally assigned to the priesthood (Num 18:12–13; Deut 18:4; Ezek 44:30), though P bears witness to a practice whereby a portion of the cereal offering (the 'azkārâ of the minḥâ) is burned to Yhwh before the priests receive the remainder for their own use (Lev 2:2–3, 9–10, 16; 6:8–9 [Eng., 15–16]). On the text-critical dimensions of v. 29, see the helpful treatment of McCarter, *I Samuel*, 87–88.

112. kî mĕkabbĕday 'ăkabbēd ûbōzay yēqāllû. The verb yēqāllû is sometimes translated "they will be cursed," as if it were a Pual (e.g., McCarter, *I Samuel*, 86), though it is a Qal.

113. On the covenant background of this notion of reciprocal honor and its hierarchical dimensions, see Olyan, "Honor, Shame and Covenant Relations," 204–8. Though reciprocal honor between unequal covenant partners is a common enough theme, many texts foreground only the honor owed to a superior by an inferior, as in Mal 1:6–7.

114. wattĕhî ḥaṭṭa't hannĕ'ārîm gĕdôlâ mĕ'ōd 'et pĕnê yhwh kî ni'ăṣû hā'ănāšîm 'et minḥat yhwh. On this sense for n'ṣ (Piel), see the entry n'ṣ in *THAT* 2:3–6.

115. Mal 2:1–9 is similar, in that Yhwh promises to curse, shame, and make despised (nibzîm) and abased (šĕpālîm) before all the people the very priests who have despised him by not following his teachings.

116. By encroaching, I mean illegitimate approach to holy items or space. On this, see further n. 65 above.

117. E.g., Num 18:3, 7, 32, which threaten death to the violator.

Chapter 2
Admission or Exclusion

1. The bibliography for the biblical representation of purity and pollution is extensive. Among useful studies are W. Paschen, *Rein und Unrein: Untersuchung zur biblischen Wortgeschichte* (Studien zum Alten and Neuen Testament 24; Mu-

nich: Kösel, 1970), 19–81, 195–97; Zatelli, *Il campo lessicale degli aggetivi di purità in ebraico biblico* (Florence: Istituto di linguistica e di lingue orientali, Università di Firenze, 1978); H. Cazelles, "Pureté et impureté: Ancien Testament," *DBSup* 9 (1979) 491–508; T. Frymer-Kensky, "Pollution, Purification, and Purgation in Biblical Israel," in C. L. Meyers and M. O'Connor, eds., *The Word of the Lord Shall Go Forth: Essays in Honor of David Noel Freedman in Celebration of His Sixtieth Birthday* (Winona Lake, IN: ASOR/Eisenbrauns, 1983); D. P. Wright, *The Disposal of Impurity: Elimination Rites in the Bible and in Hittite and Mesopotamian Literatures* (SBLDS 101; Atlanta: Scholars, 1987); idem, "Unclean and Clean (OT)," *ABD* 6:729–41; M. Douglas, *In the Wilderness: The Doctrine of Defilement in the Book of Numbers* (JSOTSup 158; Sheffield: Sheffield Academic Press, 1993) and her earlier, influential essay "The Abominations of Leviticus," in *Purity and Danger* (1966; reprint, Boston: Ark, 1984), 41–57. In addition, volume 1 of Milgrom's commentary on Leviticus is chock full of insightful discussion and useful references, and his influence on my work will be readily evident to readers. Two other works of interest that deal in part with biblical notions of purity and impurity are J. Neusner, *The Idea of Purity in Ancient Judaism* (SJLA 1; Leiden: Brill, 1973), 7–31; and E. Feldman, *Biblical and Post-biblical Defilement and Mourning: Law as Theology* (New York: KTAV/Yeshiva University, 1977) passim. Concern with pollution is known from other ancient west Asian and Mediterranean cultures. See, for example, M.-J. Seux, "Pur et impur en Mésopotamie," *DBSup* 9 (1979) 451–59; D. Meeks, "Pureté et purification en Égypte," *DBSup* 9 (1979) 430–51; K. van der Toorn, *Sin and Sanction in Israel and Mesopotamia* (Assen: van Gorcum, 1985) 17–18, 27–36; Wilson, *"Holiness" and "Purity" in Mesopotamia* (AOAT 237; Neukirchen-Vluyn: Neukirchener; Kevelaer: Butzon and Bercker, 1994); Wright, *Disposal of Impurity*; Robert Parker, *Miasma: Pollution and Purification in Early Greek Religion* (Oxford: Clarendon, 1983). For a survey of views on purity and pollution in the history of religions, see J. Henninger, "Pureté et impureté: l'histoire des religions," *DBSup* 9 (1979) 399–430.

2. Examples of the explicit contrast of clean (ṭāhôr) and unclean (ṭāmē') include Lev 10:10 (H); 11:47 (P); 14:57; 20:25; Num 19:19; Deut 12:15, 22; 15:22; Ezek 22:26; 44:23; Job 14:4; Eccl 9:2. Cp. Gen 7:2, 8, which contrasts "clean quadrupeds" with those that are "not clean" (habbĕhēmâ 'ăšer lō' ṭĕhōrâ or habbĕhēmâ 'ăšer 'ênennâ ṭĕhōrâ). In a few texts, ṭāhôr is contrasted not with ṭāmē' but with another word such as mĕgō'āl (e.g., Mal 1:7; cp. v. 11). On ṭāhôr in contrast to expressions such as lō' ṭāhôr or mĕgō'āl, see further Zatelli, *Il campo lessicale degli aggetivi di purità*, 93–94, including nn. 85–86. Zatelli (95) notes the rhetorical precedence of ṭāmē' before ṭāhôr in most of the texts contrasting the two terms explicitly, though there are exceptions to this pattern (e.g., Lev 20:25). She identifies a comparable order in the pairing of qōdeš and ḥōl. The reason for this ordering of binary pairs may have something to do with what Paschen identified as the positive content of impurity (it is transferable, like holiness) in contrast to purity's negative definition as "what is not polluted" (*Rein und Unrein*, 64).

3. E.g., Num 9:6 (cp. Exod 12:1–11, 46); 1 Sam 20:26.

4. These "alien gods" are presumably iconic representations.

5. This is implied by their sanctification and their washing of garments.

6. Among the variety of literary materials apart from P, H, and Ezekiel evidencing purity concerns, see, e.g., Deut 23:10–12 (Eng., 9–11); Judg 13:7, 14; 2 Sam 3:29; Isa 6:4–7; 64:5 (Eng., 6); 66:20; Jer 2:7; Hos 9:3; Hag 2:11–14; Ps 106:38–39; Job 14:4; Eccl 9:2; Lam 4:14–15.

7. See, e.g., Lev 15:17; Num 31:20, 22–23.

8. See, e.g., m. Kelim 1:1–4; b. Baba Qama 2b. H. K. Harrington deals with classical rabbinic materials in *The Impurity Systems of Qumran and the Rabbis: Biblical Foundations* (SBLDS 143; Atlanta: Scholars, 1993) 113–260.

9. E.g., Ezek 44:11; 2 Chr 23:19.

10. E.g., Lev 10:10–11; Ezek 22:26; 44:23. See also Lev 14:57, which does not mention the priests explicitly, though it concerns them nonetheless, as it is their responsibility to make judgments concerning skin disease. Cp. Deut 33:10, regarding the Levitic priests: "They shall teach your ordinances to Jacob, and your torah to Israel."

11. In an interesting twist, Ezek 9:7 has Yhwh abandon his sanctuary and then order its defilement with corpses after he has determined that he will destroy Jerusalem and scatter Judah's populace. Other biblical texts bear witness to the ruin of sanctuaries polluted purposely by their enemies. See, e.g., Josiah's destruction of the high places, the sacred precinct for child sacrifice (the tōpet) outside of Jerusalem, and the Bethel temple by means of the introduction of polluting agents such as bones or corpses (2 Kgs 23:8, 10, 13, 15–20; only vv. 13–20 are specific about which polluting agent was used).

12. Propaganda in the Book of Haggai supporting the temple's rebuilding (ca. 520 BCE) explains Judah's continuing impoverishment by the lack of a temple cult in Jerusalem and promises prosperity and blessing if the temple were to be rebuilt (Hag 1:2–11).

13. See, e.g., the texts cited in n. 6 above.

14. E.g., no biblical text suggests that urine, perspiration, saliva, or vaginal fluids are themselves polluting, though saliva is a conductor of pollution in Lev 15:8. In contrast, semen, the fluids of parturition, menses, and, in some purity constructions, excrement are defiling.

15. The most popular explanation relates all sources of defilement either directly or symbolically to death (e.g., W. Kornfeld, "Reine und Unreine Tiere im Alten Testament," *Kairos. Zeitschrift für Religionswissenschaft und Theologie* 7 [1965] 146–47; Paschen, *Rein und Unrein*, 63–64, 195; Feldman, *Defilement and Mourning*, passim; G. Wenham, ["Why Does Sexual Intercourse Defile] (Lev 15 18)?" *ZAW* 95 [1983] 433–34; H. Eilberg-Schwartz, *The Savage in Judaism* [Bloomington: Indiana University Press, 1990] 183–86; Milgrom, *Leviticus 1–16* (AB 3; New York: Doubleday, 1991) 46, and "The Rationale for Biblical Impurity," *JANES* 22 [1993] 107–11; and Douglas, *In the Wilderness*, 23). Corpses, carcasses, bones, and graves share an obvious connection to death. A case can be made for establishing a symbolic association of skin disease and death in Israelite culture on the basis of Num 12:12. A similar case can be made for a symbolic association of wasted semen and death on the basis of Gen 38:9. (When Onan spilled his seed, says the text, he "destroyed toward the ground, so as not to give progeny to his brother.") The vocabulary of cleansing rites may provide some

indirect evidence in support of the death hypothesis. Cleansing waters are occasionally called "living waters" (mayim ḥayyim), perhaps implying that they bring "life" to polluted persons who may be understood to be symbolically "dead." See, similarly, Milgrom, *Leviticus 1–16*, 924. The death hypothesis has some points in its favor, but it has clear limitations as an explanatory tool. It is not at all evident that Israelites associated all sources of defilement, even symbolically, with death. Furthermore, it is unclear to me what it is about all unclean animals that would associate them with death on a symbolic level in this culture (not all are scavengers or carnivores; cp. Paschen, *Rein and Unrein*, 195). And what of cases of ejaculation leading to conception? All semen effusions are polluting, yet some lead to pregnancy (similarly, Eilberg-Schwartz, *The Savage in Judaism*, 186; cp. Wenham ["Why Does Sexual Intercourse Defile"], who argues that semen should be seen as a "life liquid" [like blood] and associates its loss with loss of life and therefore impurity).

16. For example, P never mentions excrement as a source of defilement, but other materials such as Ezek 4:9–15; Zech 3:3–5; 2 Kgs 10:27 suggest that it is in certain non-Priestly purity constructions. Though P speaks of adultery as defiling (Num 5:11–31 passim), H and related texts bear witness to the idea that a variety of cultic and noncultic behavioral offenses are polluting (e.g., various sexual acts [Lev 18:24; Ezek 22:11]; murder [Ps 106:38–39]; turning to ghosts and spirits [Lev 19:31]; child sacrifice [Lev 18:21, cp. 18:24]; or making "idols" [Ezek 22:3]). Such defiling behaviors threaten Israel's presence in its land according to the Holiness School (Lev 18:24–25, 27–28; 20:22–23). As others have noted, texts do not generally speak of purification procedures that might remove impurity caused by behavioral offenses (e.g., Frymer-Kensky, "Pollution, Purification, and Purgation," 404, 407–8).

17. On biblical dietary restrictions, see especially Douglas, "The Abominations of Leviticus," 41–57; Kornfeld, "Reine und Unreine Tiere," 134–47; W. Houston, *Purity and Monotheism: Clean and Unclean Animals in Biblical Law* (JSOTSup 140; Sheffield: Sheffield Academic Press, 1993); and the extended discussion of Milgrom, *Leviticus 1–16*, 643–742. For dietary prohibitions in Mesopotamia, see van der Toorn, *Sin and Sanction*, 33–36.

18. The much longer version in Leviticus 11 is made up of a Priestly core (vv. 1–23, 41–42, 46) that has been supplemented by both additional P material (vv. 24–40, 47) and H framing material (vv. 43–45), as is widely recognized. The version in Deuteronomy 14 may well be dependent on the core of Leviticus 11. See further the detailed treatment of Milgrom, *Leviticus 1–16*, 691–704. Houston assigns a considerable portion of Leviticus 11 to H (*Purity and Monotheism*, 55).

19. Milgrom has argued that pollution caused by contact with the carcass of a clean animal is a late development, reflected only in vv. 39–40 in this chapter, and not otherwise in (earlier) P material or in H. See further Milgrom's argument in *Leviticus 1–16*, 681–82, 694.

20. According to H and Ezekiel, priests are forbidden to eat any carcass. See Lev 22:8; Ezek 4:14; 44:31, and contrast Lev 17:15, which, like Leviticus 11, does not actually prohibit nonpriests from eating carcass meat, as pointed out by Houston, *Purity and Monotheism*, 222.

21. Relevant P and H materials include Num 5:2–4 (H); 9:6 (H); 19:1–10a (P), 10b–13, 20–21a (mainly H), 14–19, 21b–22 (P); 31:19–24 (H). For D, see Deut 26:14; 2 Kgs 23:14, 16; perhaps also Deut 21:23. See also Hag 2:13, which knows of such defilement. On the division of Numbers 19 into sources, see the treatment of I. Knohl (*The Sanctuary of Silence: The Priestly Torah and the Holiness School*, trans. J. Feldman and P. Rodman [Minneapolis: Fortress Press, 1995] 93), with which I concur for the most part. Lam 4:14–15 bears witness to the notion that the blood of a wound defiles any person who has contact with it. Cp. Isa 59:3; 63:3. Blood is not mentioned in H and P materials detailing the sources of death-related defilement. Pollution from corpse contact and the shedding of blood is known from Mesopotamian sources (van der Toorn, *Sin and Sanction*, 15–16, 36–37).

22. On the use of the verb ḥṭ' (Hitpael) here, see the discussion of B. A. Levine, *Numbers 1–20* (AB 4; New York: Doubleday, 1993) 465–66.

23. "Living water" is usually explained as water that is flowing rather than standing (e.g., in a cistern). See, e.g., Levine, *Numbers 1–20*, 468; and Milgrom, *Leviticus 1–16*, 836–37, 923–24.

24. See Paschen, *Rein und Unrein*, 51; Levine, *Numbers 1–20*, 221 n. 6; and J. Milgrom, *Numbers* (Philadelphia: Jewish Publication Society, 1990) 44. They point out the similarities between Nazirite restrictions and those of the high priest.

25. The identity of "man who grasps the spindle" (maḥăzîq bappelek) is obscure, though he may be a gender nonconformist, given the gendered representation of spinning in biblical and related sources. See Prov 31:19, where spindle and distaff are associated with the labor of the ideal wife. Various parallels in west Asian literatures attest not only to the gendering of items such as the spindle or the sword, but also to their magical power as gendered items. On this, see further H. Hoffner, "Symbols of Masculinity and Femininity: Their Use in Ancient Near Eastern Sympathetic Magic Rituals," *JBL* 85 (1966) 326–34. Hoffner believes that the man grasping the spindle in David's curse is one who has lost "masculine attributes and power," rather than a man who actually does "women's work."

26. Though not mentioned explicitly for the woman, the text suggests subtly and indirectly that her rites are the same as those of the man. In all other ways the texts are symmetrical, except that the long section detailing the different ways that the affected man's pollution can be communicated is not reproduced for the woman in any detail (cp. Lev 15:4–12 vs. 15:26–27). Therefore, if the section on the woman's potential to communicate impurity is abbreviated, why not the section on her purification rites as well?

27. For Mesopotamian parallels, see van der Toorn, *Sin and Sanction*, 31–32.

28. Many examples could be cited. For such pollution in Mesopotamia, see van der Toorn, *Sin and Sanction*, 31. For Greece, see Parker, *Miasma*, 48–53, 100–103. For the "Sambia" of the New Guinea highlands (a pseudonym), see G. Herdt, *Guardians of the Flutes* (1981; reprint, Chicago: University of Chicago Press, 1994) 159–202, esp. pp. 189–99; for the Hua, another people of highland New Guinea, see A. Meigs, "A Papuan Perspective on Pollution," *Man* 13 (1978) 305, 309. Milgrom cites many examples from various cultures in *Leviticus 1–16*, 750, 949–52.

29. The text uses the verb hitqaddēš, "to sanctify oneself," apparently with the meaning "to purify oneself" here. On this, see further my discussion in chapter 1, n. 71.

30. It is not clear from the passage when the seven-day period begins. Is the text speaking of seven days of impurity from the first signs of the woman's period? Or seven days of uncleanness after the period has ended? These questions vexed traditional Jewish interpreters, who are divided in their views. See further the comments and citations of Milgrom, *Leviticus 1–16*, 935.

31. Milgrom (ibid., 923–24, 934–36) argues that rites of bathing and washing clothes are to be assumed for the woman with a discharge, the menstruant, and the parturient. He provides various arguments to support his case. For example, he argues that if seminal emissions, which only cause impurity until evening, require bathing, how much more so should pollution lasting a week or more. Since washing clothes is required for other cases of defilement lasting seven days (or more), then it must be mandated also for the menstruant, parturient, and woman with an abnormal discharge. These are certainly valid points, though more can be said. It is interesting to note the way Leviticus 15 as a whole deals with rites of purification. The sections in the first half of the chapter concerning pollution caused by men detail the rites of purification required for the polluter himself as well as those defiled secondarily (vv. 2–15, 16–18). Yet the sections dealing with pollution caused by women (vv. 19–24, 25–30) speak only of the rites required of those who are secondarily defiled by polluted women. And in the case of the man who takes on the menstruant's primary pollution through sexual congress with her, nothing is stated explicitly about his rites of purification (he is treated, in other words, just like the women who are primary polluters in this chapter). Perhaps Milgrom is correct to argue that the text simply assumes that the reader understands that the menstruant and the woman with a discharge must wash their clothes and bathe in order to be clean. (I would add the man to whom menstrual pollution is transferred through intercourse.)

32. See the expression děmê ṭohŏrâ, "the blood of purification," in vv. 4, 5.

33. There are, however, rabbinic traditions that posit a connection, e.g., b. Niddah 31b. See further Milgrom, *Leviticus 1–16*, 744.

34. Paschen believes that the parturient must avoid physical contact with others while in process of purification (*Rein und Unrein*, 60).

35. Though later Jewish tradition understands the child to be clean, this may not be so, given the text's understanding of parturition as polluting. Cp. Ezek 16:4, 6, which seem to understand bathing in order to wash off blood as the normal procedure mandated for a newborn. This may indicate that the newborn is unclean until purified by bathing.

36. The term ṣāraʿat appears to be used for a group of skin conditions rather than a single affliction, but these have yet to be identified with any confidence. See further the detailed discussion of Milgrom (*Leviticus 1–16*, 774–76, 816–26), who attempts to identify the afflictions in question, and cites E. V. Hulse, "The Nature of Biblical 'Leprosy' and the Use of Alternative Medical Terms in Modern Translations of the Bible," *PEQ* 107 (1975) 87–105; J. Wilkinson, "Leprosy and Leviticus: The Problem of Description and Identification," *Scottish Journal of Theology* 30 (1977) 153–69; and idem, "Leprosy and Leviticus: A

Problem of Semantics and Translation," *Scottish Journal of Theology* 31 (1978) 153–66. Van der Toorn discusses Mesopotamian parallels in *Sin and Sanction*, 30–31.

37. Num 12:1–16 presents a number of difficulties for the interpreter. In v. 1, Aaron and Miriam speak against Moses on account of his Kushite wife; in v. 2, they challenge what the text at this juncture presents as Moses' exclusive claim to prophecy. The issue of prophecy remains a focus of the narrative after v. 2. The Kushite woman, at issue in v. 1, is never mentioned again in the narrative.

38. See similarly Feldman (*Biblical and Post-Biblical Defilement and Mourning*, 37–41), who also points out that the association of the person with skin disease and the dead goes back to the rabbis (b. Nedarim 64b; Midr. Rab. Bereshit 1:9); Frymer-Kensky, "Pollution, Purification, and Purgation," 400; and F. H. Gorman, Jr., *The Ideology of Ritual: Space, Time and Status in the Priestly Theology* (JSOTSup 91; Sheffield: Sheffield Academic Press, 1991) 131–32, 153.

39. Many others have pointed this out. The verbs prm and prʿ are used for priests and mourning in Lev 10:6 and 21:10; cp. Ezek 44:20. Ezek 24:16–17, 22–23 allude to covering the upper lip and allowing the hair to hang loose among other mourning rites.

40. See Milgrom (*Leviticus 1–16*, 782), who attributes this insight to D. Wright.

41. The fact that the verb sgr in Num 12:14–15 is a Niphal rather than a Hiphil is, in my view, insignificant. The narrative simply uses a passive construction at that point ("Let her be shut up seven days outside of the camp").

42. This is Milgrom's view, in *Leviticus 1–16*, 779–80, 782. It goes back to the rabbis.

43. On the release of the living bird and its role in the ritual, see the interpretations of Frymer-Kensky, "Pollution, Purification and Purgation," 400; and Wright, *The Disposal of Impurity*, 75–86. The discussion of Gorman (*Ideology of Ritual*, 169–71) is also helpful.

44. Gorman offers an assessment of the stages in the aggregation process similar to what follows (*Ideology of Ritual*, 157–61).

45. For Mesopotamian parallels, see van der Toorn, *Sin and Sanction*, 17–18.

46. The Hebrew reads ʾaḥărê ʾăšer huṭṭammāʾâ.

47. This position is taken also by Paschen, *Rein und Unrein*, 36. Houston is probably correct to claim that this type of contingent impurity is witnessed elsewhere as well (e.g., Lev 21:7, 14; see *Purity and Monotheism*, 42).

48. Gen 49:4 and 1 Chr 5:1 are also relevant to this discussion (cp. Gen 35:22). They speak of Reuben polluting his father's bed. Presumably, these texts allude to an event narrated in Gen 35:22, when Reuben slept with his father's concubine Bilhah. On the verb ḥll with the meaning "to pollute," see ahead and n. 54.

49. See immediately ahead for a discussion of excrement as a source of defilement.

50. The idea that Yhwh's worship is restricted to the land of Israel is found intermittently in pre-exilic materials. See, e.g., 1 Sam 26:19; Ruth 1:15. Cp. 2 Kgs 5:17, where Naaman the Aramean exports a cartload of earth from Israel to Syria in order to be able to worship Yhwh there.

51. For other examples of the pollution caused by "idols," see Jer 7:30 (=32:34); Ezek 5:11; 20:30; 22:3, 4; 23:7, 30. The following may also have such defilement in mind: Hos 5:3; 6:10; Jer 2:23; Ps 106:39.

52. See further my more detailed treatment of this passage in chapter 3. There are other ways that Dinah's pollution might be explained, e.g., the defilement that results from forbidden sexual contact, as in Num 5:11–31 (cp. Lev 18:20, 23; for this interpretation, see Frymer-Kensky, "Pollution, Purification, and Purgation," 407).

53. Reading the expression ʿārēl wĕṭāmēʾ as a hendiadys construction ("[the] uncircumcised [person who is] unclean") rather than as two separate substantives ("[the] uncircumcised [person] and [the] unclean [person]"), as the singular verb suggests. Cp. Joel 4:17 (Eng., 3:17): "Jerusalem will be holy, and aliens (zārîm) will not again pass through it," suggesting that the alien invaders are in some way a threat to the city's holiness, presumably because of their uncleanness. Ps 79:1 may be read to suggest that aliens polluted the temple by their presence: "God, nations invaded your inalienable tract, they polluted your holy temple, they turned Jerusalem into ruins." See also Jer 51:51, though it does not mention pollution directly: "We are ashamed, and have heard reproach; humiliation covers our face, for aliens (zārîm) have entered the holy places of the house of Yhwh." On Isa 52:1, see further my discussion in chapter 3.

54. On this, see Milgrom (Leviticus 1–16, 37), who cites Lev 21:12 and 22:9 as examples of the use of ḥll where ṭmʾ is expected. Lev 21:4 is another clear example not mentioned by Milgrom, as is Ezek 23:39. A number of other passages in Ezekiel probably use ḥll in this way (e.g., 7:22, 24; 24:21), and Lev 21:7, 14 may as well. Several other texts of varying provenance also appear to know this meaning of ḥll (e.g., Gen 49:4; 1 Chr 5:1; Dan 11:31).

55. See Neh 13:4–9, 28–30; Ezra 9:2 lends itself to a similar interpretation. Ezra 6:21; 9:11 may also suggest that aliens themselves defile. See further my detailed discussion of these texts in chapter 3.

56. On the prophetic symbolic act, see the discussions of G. Fohrer, Die symbolischen Handlungen der Propheten (Zurich: Zwingli, 1953), and the more recent discussion of M. Greenberg, who cites Fohrer (Ezekiel 1–20 [AB 22; Garden City: Doubleday, 1983] 122–28).

57. Just as animal carcasses are less polluting than human corpses, so animal dung appears to be less polluting than human excrement.

58. On the symbolism of excremental pollution, see B. Halpern, " 'The Excremental Vision': The Doomed Priests of Doom in Isaiah 28," HAR 10 (1986) 109–21. Though many scholars have failed to notice the texts evidencing excremental defilement, Houston (Purity and Monotheism, 18–19, 220) includes a cogent though brief discussion. In this, he criticizes M. Weinfeld for his claim that "there is no Biblical reference to the effect that human excrement defiles" (Deuteronomy and the Deuteronomic School [Oxford: Oxford University Press, 1972] 238).

59. The rabbis recognized this (see further n. 8 above).

60. E.g., shaving, sprinkling with a special purifying agent, a second round of bathing, and washing garments.

61. E.g., Leviticus 14 distinguishes between the "person with skin disease" (hammĕṣōrāʿ or haṣṣārûaʿ) and the "person being purified" (hammiṭṭahēr). The

latter term replaces the former in the text once the purification process has begun with the priest's command of v. 2.

62. That "evening" in these texts refers to sunset is made clear in Deut 23:12 (Eng., 11): "At the coming of evening, he shall wash in water, and when the sun has set, he may come into the midst of the camp." See also Lev 22:7, which is similar.

63. This is pointed out by Milgrom, *Leviticus 1–16*, 773. Only the individual with skin disease is put out of the camp according to P (Lev 13:46; 14:3). Milgrom believes that this is because the person with skin disease can pollute others simply by being in the same confined space with them, as can a corpse (977, 992; see Num 19:14–16 on the corpse). H, in contrast, assumes the camp is holy and excludes other polluters as well, specifically those having contact with the dead and those with discharges (see Num 5:2–4; 31:19–24). Holiness texts do not mention how those polluted by menstruation, by parturition, or by contact with semen are to be treated.

64. lipnôt ʿereb, literally "at the turn of evening."

65. Lev 15:5–11, 19–23, 27.

66. See n. 30 above on the question of when the seven days of uncleanness begins for the menstruant.

67. E.g., Num 19:11; 31:19, 24 (H); 19:14, 17–19 (P).

68. Ashes of the red cow mixed with "living waters" according to P; "waters of purification" (mê niddâ) according to H. On the latter, see Levine, *Numbers 1–20*, 463–64.

69. See further n. 26 above on this point.

70. It is possible, however, that H assumes their removal.

71. Though not stated explicitly, this is the implication of D's exclusion of the man who has had a seminal emission (Deut 23:11 [Eng., 10]).

72. Even on the eighth day, when the offerings are presented, the formerly afflicted individual is still referred to as "the one being purified" (hammiṭṭāhēr) and the priest as "the one purifying" (ham[mĕ]ṭahēr), suggesting that the process continues until the completion of the sacrificial stage.

73. However, these contexts are not the exclusive loci. Deut 12:15, 22 imply that before centralization of the cult, clean game were slaughtered and eaten outside of cultic and quasi-cultic contexts by the clean and unclean alike. Deut 15:22 enjoins that blemished sacrificial animals not be sacrificed, but eaten like clean game. Deuteronomy's program of cult centralization results in the innovation of noncultic slaughter and the possibility of consumption of some sheep, goats, and cattle for those who live far from Jerusalem. Like the slaughter of game, this new noncultic slaughter is permitted to both clean and unclean (Deut 12:15–18, 20–27).

74. On the clan's yearly sacrificial feast (zebaḥ mišpāḥâ), see 1 Sam 20:29 and Haran's discussion in *Temples and Temple Service in Ancient Israel* (Oxford: Clarendon, 1978) 304–14.

75. This is true at least for males, though some texts are ambiguous. See, e.g., Deut 16:16; Exod 12:47; 2 Chr 30:17. Deut 16:16 requires pilgrimage of all males three times a year. Exod 12:47 speaks of the Passover as an obligation of "all the assembly of Israel."

76. The Hebrew reads hišbattā miṭṭŏhorô // wĕkis'ô lā'āreṣ miggartā. Note, however, that miṭṭŏhorô is often emended. On its emendation, see further Paschen, *Rein und Unrein*, 19, with citations.

77. On the fate of the dead, see similarly Ps 6:6 (Eng., 5); 28:1; 115:16–18, among others.

78. E.g., corpse contact while in mourning, apparently expected of the mourner.

79. Reduced frequency of menstruation would have been the result of greater frequency of pregnancy and time spent nursing, and inferior health and nutrition, as pointed out by Milgrom, *Leviticus 1–16*, 953.

80. Milgrom believes that "the biblical woman, who was generally in a state of pregnancy or nursing, was rarely excluded from participating in the cult" (ibid). "Rarely excluded" seems too strong to me, if "the biblical woman" was frequently giving birth and if texts such as Lev 12:1–8 reflect actual practice.

81. On the Hua, see Meigs, "Papuan Perspective," 309; on the "Sambia," see Herdt, *Guardians of the Flutes*, 159–202, esp. 189–99.

82. On women and prophecy, see Exod 15:20; Judg 4:4; 2 Kgs 22:14; Isa 8:3; Neh 6:14. On the Nazirite vow, by means of which a man or woman becomes sanctified for a period of time, see Num 6:1–21 (P). On the similarity of Nazirite practice and that of the high priest, see Paschen, *Rein und Unrein*, 51; Levine, *Numbers 1–20*, 221n. 6; and Milgrom, *Numbers*, 44. It is not at all clear how commonplace women prophets and Nazirites were in Israelite society. The biblical text rarely speaks of women in prophecy and only theoretically of female Nazirites.

83. See my discussion of this text earlier in the chapter.

84. For a very different assessment of the significance of priestly restrictions prescribed in H texts such as Lev 21:1–15, see R. A. Kugler, "Holiness, Purity, the Body, and Society: The Evidence for Theological Conflict in Leviticus," *JSOT* 76 (1997) 25–26. Kugler argues that such restrictions suggest ambivalence on the part of H circles toward the priesthood. I discuss Kugler's views in the appendix, n. 5.

85. The text says nothing about any limitations on the length of the Nazirite vow, or whether it can be repeated, though it seems to assume that the vow is temporary (e.g., Num 6:13). Other biblical material, however, bears witness to the possibility of lifelong Nazirite status (e.g., Samson, Judg 13:7).

86. The Nazirite must avoid all products of viticulture at all times. No text makes this demand of the high priest, though Ezek 44:21 states that priests may not drink wine when they enter the inner court of the temple.

87. The enhanced status of the Nazirite is implied in Amos 2:11: "I raised up some of your children as prophets, and some of your young men as Nazirites." See also Judg 13:5; 16:17, which suggest that Samson's heroic abilities are tied to his Nazirite status.

Chapter 3
Generating "Self" and "Other"

1. Some recent examples in Judaic studies include J. Shapiro, *Shakespeare and the Jews* (New York: Columbia University Press, 1996); and L. J. Silberstein and R. L. Cohn, eds., *The Other in Jewish Thought and History: Constructions of*

Jewish Culture and Identity (New York: New York University Press, 1994). For discussion of the role of the self and the other in anthropological ethnographic work, see R. S. Khare, "The Other's Double—The Anthropologist's Bracketed Self: Notes on Cultural Representation and Privileged Discourse," *New Literary History* 23 (1992) 1–23; J. Clifford and G. E. Marcus, eds., *Writing Culture: The Poetics and Politics of Ethnography* (Berkeley: University of California Press, 1986).

2. E.g., Shapiro, *Shakespeare and the Jews*, 1, 5; Khare, "The Other's Double," 1; L. J. Silberstein, "Others Within and Others Without: Rethinking Jewish Identity and Culture," in *The Other in Jewish Thought*, 1–34; S. L. Gilman, "The Jewish Nose: Are Jews White? Or, the History of the Nose Job," in *The Other in Jewish Thought*, 365; Clifford, "Introduction," in *Writing Culture*, 23–24; and J. Z. Smith, "What a Difference a Difference Makes," in E. S. Frerichs and J. Neusner, eds., *"To See Ourselves as Others See Us": Christians, Jews, "Others" in Late Antiquity* (Chico, CA: Scholars, 1985) 10, 46–47.

3. I derive the language of "project" from Smith, "What a Difference," 46, 48: "'Otherness' is not a descriptive category, an artifact of the perception of difference or commonality. Nor is it the result of the determination of biological descent or affinity. It is a political and linguistic project, a matter of rhetoric and judgement" (46).

4. It is important to keep in mind that the other about whom we learn through the medium of a group's self-defining discourse is little more than a component of that group's own project of self-definition. The representation of the Canaanite in biblical discourse tells us much about how the biblical writers and their constituencies constitute themselves over against a Canaanite other, but it says little about the Canaanites themselves. On this, see further R. A. Oden, Jr., "Religious Identity and the Sacred Prostitution Accusation," in his *The Bible without Theology* (San Francisco: Harper and Row, 1987) 131–53; and R. L. Cohn, "Before Israel: The Canaanites as Other in Biblical Tradition," in *The Other in Jewish Thought*, 74–90.

5. E.g., the native, white, male, Protestant, married, heterosexual with children has been an abiding normative construct of self in American society, while the other has included women, Jews and Catholics, unmarried persons, sexual nonconformists, people of color, immigrants, and childless persons.

6. According to some theorists, the most threatening other is the one who is least distinguishable from the dominant group and therefore most difficult to contain. See further the brief but widely quoted comments of Smith, "What a Difference," 47; and I. M. Young, *Justice and the Politics of Difference* (Princeton: Princeton University Press, 1990) 145–46. It remains to be seen whether this claim can be validated on the basis of cross-cultural studies.

7. The passive participle mûl occurs twice in biblical narrative (Josh 5:5; Jer 9:24).

8. There are several manifestations of the Israelite/alien contrast in Ezra-Nehemiah. In addition to the opposition "exile" community/peoples of the land(s), I note the following: Israel/persons of mixed background ('ēreb), which occurs in Neh 13:3; seed of Israel (zeraʿ yiśrāʾēl)/aliens (běnê nēkār), which occurs in Neh 9:2; and holy seed (zeraʿ haqqōdeš)/peoples of the lands, which occurs in Ezra 9:2.

9. Issues in the dating of each of these texts will be discussed as the individual text is examined.

10. The text is conventionally assigned to the Yahwist, though several verses (4, 6, 8–10, 15–17, 20–23, 27, 28) were thought by Noth to be secondary (*A History of Pentateuchal Traditions*, trans. B. W. Anderson [1948; Chico, CA: Scholars, 1981] 30 n. 99). These include vv. 9, 16, and 21, which sound strikingly like Deut 7:3 in reverse and may be much later than the original J narrative. (Where Deut 7:3 says wĕlōʾ tithattēn bām bittĕkā lōʾ tittēn libnô ûbittô lōʾ tiqqaḥ libnekā, Gen 34:9 says wĕhithattĕnû ʾōtānû bĕnōtēkem tittĕnû lānû wĕ'et bĕnōtēnû tiqḥû lākem.) The verses most of interest to me, e.g., vv. 5, 13, and 14, are assigned by Noth to the original J narrative, as is the circumcision of the Shechemites and its aftermath (e.g., vv. 24–26). I favor an early date (tenth or ninth century) for J rather than a date in the sixth century, though such an early dating has been and continues to be challenged, especially in Europe. The triumphalist tone of so many J texts suggests to me a date for J not in the exile, as some revisionists would have it, but in the period of the empire, when Israel came to dominate its immediate neighbors, or soon after, when such domination apparently continued. This domination is presented in J as fulfillment of divine promises to the ancestors, as others have pointed out before me. On J's triumphalism, see, e.g., Gen 9:18–27; 12:1–3; 15:17–21; 19:30–38; 22:15–18; 25:21–26a; 27:27–29, 39–40. The last mentioned text, Gen 27:39–40, speaks both of Edom's domination by Israel and of its eventual rebellion. There is debate about how to understand this reference to Edom's rebellion, since the Deuteronomistic History refers to rebellion both at David's death (1 Kgs 11:14–22, 25 [?]) and in the middle of the ninth century (2 Kgs 8:20–22). Obviously, the dating of the rebellion mentioned in Gen 27:39–40 will have ramifications for the dating of J as a whole. The following review articles summarize discussion on the subject of the Yahwist's date and provenance: D. A. Knight, "The Pentateuch," in D. A. Knight and G. M. Tucker, eds., *The Hebrew Bible and Its Modern Interpreters* (Philadelphia: Fortress; Chico, CA: Scholars, 1985) 277–82; A. de Pury, "Yahwist ("J") Source," *ABD* 6:1012–20; and R. Rendtorff, "Directions in Pentateuchal Studies," *Currents in Research: Biblical Studies* 5 (1997) 43–65, though Rendtorff's presentation is not as evenhanded as it ought to be.

11. It is not entirely clear to what the feminine pronoun hîʾ refers. S. J. D. Cohen will argue in a future publication that hîʾ refers ambiguously either to the foreskin itself or to the act of giving a daughter in marriage to an uncircumcised man (oral communication). My own preference is to see the foreskin, a grammatically feminine noun, as the antecedent of the feminine pronoun "it" (hîʾ). This understanding may find support in Josh 5:9, where the expression ḥerpat miṣrayim probably refers to the foreskin, as Victor Hurowitz has pointed out to me (oral communication). On this, see further the discussion in n. 12 below. Rashi seems to understand ḥerpâ hîʾ to refer to the foreskin, though he is not entirely clear in this regard.

12. The word ḥerpâ is elsewhere associated with circumcision in Josh 5:2–9. In Josh 5:2, Yhwh orders Israelite males born in the wilderness to be circumcised (MT adds "a second time," though this is missing in LXX). Once this is accomplished, Yhwh states cryptically: "Today I have removed the disgrace (ḥerpâ) of

Egypt from upon you" (v. 9). Though "the disgrace of Egypt" seems to refer to the foreskin here, it is not clear why it should be associated with Egypt in this text, given that the text states explicitly that those who came out of Egypt were indeed circumcised. (In addition, the biblical tradition associates the practice of circumcision with Egypt. See Jer 9:24–25 [Eng., 25–26].) J. Sasson's suggestion that ḥerpat miṣrayim refers to the Egyptian method of circumcising with a dorsal slit is not convincing, since the text clearly states that those born in the desert, in contrast to those born in Egypt, were uncircumcised. The issue is nowhere one method of circumcising versus another, as Sasson suggests ("Circumcision in the Ancient Near East," *JBL* 85 [1966] 474).

13. The text does not seem to understand the pollution of Dinah as a temporary thing, yet we know from other sources—early and late—that effusions of semen are temporarily polluting, including those that occur during intercourse. See Exod 19:15; 1 Sam 21:2–7, esp. 5 (Eng., 1–6, esp. 4); 2 Samuel 11 (?); and Lev 15:16–18, which specifies that the polluted state of the man and his partner lasts until evening of the day on which intercourse occurred (cp. Deut 23:11–12 [Eng., 10–11]). The observation that the pollution of Dinah mentioned in Genesis 34 is of a long-term nature has also been made by J. Klawans, "Notions of Gentile Impurity in Ancient Judaism," *AJS Review* 20 (1995) 290 n. 25.

14. Gen 34:5, 13, 27. S. J. D. Cohen will argue this in a future publication (oral communication).

15. See, e.g., Deut 24:1–4, which uses the root ṭm' to describe the pollution of the twice-married woman who would return to her first husband. In addition, various texts of the Holiness School understand illicit sexual activity to result in pollution that is apparently long-term (e.g., Lev 18:24–30 passim; Num 5:11–31 passim).

16. A cogent argument for an early dating of 2 Sam 1:19–27 may be found in P. K. McCarter, Jr., *II Samuel* (AB 9; Garden City: Doubleday, 1984) 78–79. On the pre-Deuteronomistic literary materials of 1 Samuel, see P. K. McCarter, Jr., *I Samuel* (AB 8; Garden City: Doubleday, 1980) 12–30, esp. pp. 27–30 on the "History of David's Rise."

17. As in Judg 15:18; 1 Sam 14:6; 31:4; 2 Sam 1:20. Cp. Judg 14:3; 1 Sam 17:26, 36, where "Philistine" or "Philistines" is modified by the adjective "uncircumcised."

18. Jer 9:24–25 (Eng., 25–26) lists the circumcised nations: Egypt, Judah, Edom, Ammon, Moab, and desert dwellers. Were the Canaanite- and Aramaic-speaking populations of Phoenicia and Syria circumcised? Some relevant evidence survives in mythological texts (Philo of Byblos on El and his allies, *Praeparatio evangelica* 1.10.33 in H. W. Attridge and R. A. Oden, Jr., *Philo of Byblos, The Phoenician History: Introduction, Critical Text, Translation, Notes* [CBQMS 9; Washington: Catholic Biblical Association of America, 1981] 56–57) and among material remains (see the circumcised male figurines from early third millennium Syria [Amuq Valley] discussed by Sasson, "Circumcision," 473–76, and those from Tel Judeideh [near Alalakh] and elsewhere in O. Negbi, *Canaanite Gods in Metal* [Tel Aviv: Tel Aviv University, 1976] 14, 108, and plate 17). Herodotus 2.104 claims that the Phoenicians were circumcised, learning the practice from the Egyptians. On circumcision in Egypt, see C. de Wit, "La circoncision chez les

anciens Egyptiens," *Zeitschrift für Ägyptische Sprache und Altertumskunde* 99 (1972) 41–48; F. Jonckheere, "La circoncision des anciens Egyptiens," *Centaurus* 1 (1951) 212–34; and Sasson, "Circumcision," 473–74, who cites Jonckheere. The evidence from Egypt is not extensive, and it is not known how widely circumcision was practiced there, or when. Josephus claims that Egyptian priests practiced circumcision (*Against Apion*, 2.141). On circumcision in Judah and its environs during the Second Temple period, see S. J. D. Cohen, *The Beginnings of Jewishness: Boundaries, Varieties, Uncertainties* (Berkeley: University of California Press, 1999) 44–46, 115–16.

19. On Philistine origins in the Aegean or Asia Minor, see T. Dothan, *The Philistines and Their Material Culture* (Jerusalem: Israel Exploration Society, 1982).

20. David describes himself as a "poor man" of low status in v. 23 ('îš rāš wĕniqleh) and suggests that his family is not sufficiently important to intermarry with the king (v. 18).

21. Reading *kî 'im with LXX all ē.

22. Texts portray alien servants of David (with gēr status?) entering Yhwh's sanctuaries and related settings. Some, such as Doeg the Edomite, who was "detained before Yhwh" at Nob (1 Sam 21:8 [Eng., 7]), belong to a people associated with the practice of circumcision (see Jer 9:24–25 [Eng., 25–26]). Others, such as Uriah the Hittite, who carefully observes the purity obligations of the army at war (2 Samuel 11), do not. Obededom, a Philistine (?) of Gath, cares for the Ark of the Covenant before it is brought to Jerusalem, and the text tells us that he more than meets Yhwh's expectations as a caretaker for this holy object (2 Sam 6:10–12). The text says nothing about his circumcision or lack of same. Other foreigners from peoples not associated with the practice of circumcision are said to serve in the sanctuary (e.g., the Gibeonites as hewers of wood and drawers of water in Josh 9:27). David's personal guard of alien mercenaries is drawn from the Philistines and related peoples not associated with circumcision (e.g., Keretites, Peletites, Gittites). Yet they go to war for the king, and we know from other sources that the war camp can be constructed as a quasi-cultic setting where purity regulations apply, since Yhwh is present with the army (e.g., Num 5:2–4; 12:14; Deut 23:10–12, 13–15 [Eng., 9–11, 12–14]; 1 Sam 21:5–7 [Eng., 4–6]). These texts suggest that uncircumcision might not have been an impediment preventing an alien's participation in cultic and quasi-cultic activity early on. Then again, if alien males did indeed participate in Israel's cult and its analogues, they might have been circumcised before their participation was permitted. The evidence is just not clear on this matter.

23. The locus classicus for the claim that circumcision is a "sign of the covenant" is Gen 17:9–14. Though the chapter is traditionally attributed to the Priestly Writers, I believe that the Holiness School is responsible for at least some of the material in vv. 9–14, if not most of it. Frequent change of person and number, repetitions, and the H cliché "that life will be cut off from its people" point to such a conclusion. (On this cliché as a marker of H, see I. Knohl, *The Sanctuary of Silence: The Priestly Torah and the Holiness School*, trans. J. Feldman and P. Rodman [Minneapolis: Fortress Press, 1995] 13, 52, 102 n. 145.) Sorting out the source-critical dimensions of vv. 9–14 is, however, no simple task.

I propose division of the verses as follows: 8b, 10, 11–12, 13b, 14 are from H; 9, 10b (frg.), 12b (frg.), 13a (cp. 7–8a) are from P. Some of the material in these verses uses the second masculine plural pronoun -kem with second masculine plural verbal forms; other material uses the second masculine singular pronoun -kā with second masculine singular verbal forms. The second masculine plural pronoun is found in the expression lĕdōrōtêkem; the second masculine singular is linked to the expression lĕdōrōtām (e.g., v. 7: wahăqīmōtî ʾet bĕrîtî bênî ûbênekā ûbên zarʿăkā ʾaḥărêkā lĕdōrōtām bĕrît ʿôlām). The expression "sign of the covenant" occurs in v. 11 and is linked consistently in that verse to second masculine plural pronouns and verbal forms. Is the second masculine plural usage H or P? The plural usage—including the expression lĕdōrōtêkem—is found in H material in Lev 23:14, 21, 31, and 41, as Knohl has pointed out (*Sanctuary of Silence*, 12–13). It is also present in H material concerning the Sabbath in Exod 31:12–15, which closely resembles the material I would attribute to H in Genesis 17: ʾak ʾet šabbĕtōtay tišmōrû kî ʾôt hîʾ bênî ûbênêkem lĕdōrōtêkem lādaʿat kî ʾănî yhwh mĕqaddiškem. In contrast, the doublet of the Sabbath legislation in Exod 31:16–17, which I would attribute to P, uses lĕdōrōtām bĕrît ʿôlām. Thus, it is on the basis of differing usage that I divide Gen 17: 9–14, and attribute v. 11, which mentions the "sign of the covenant," to H. Raising circumcision to a "sign of the covenant" has long been associated with the Judean elite's sixth-century exile in Bablyon, where they lived among uncircumcised peoples. Pre-exilic biblical materials mentioning circumcision make no such association (e.g., Gen 34:14; Exod 4:24–26; Josh 5:2–9). Obviously, I am led to conclude that at least some H material has an exilic provenance.

24. On the date of H, see n. 23 above and the discussion ahead in the text.

25. Cp. Deut 16:2, 5–7, where the sacrifice takes place at the central shrine, and Israelites are explicitly forbidden from making it at home, as was the older practice (Exod 12:21–22 [J]; cp. 12:3–4, 7 [H according to Knohl, *Sanctuary of Silence*, 19]).

26. The hypothetical gēr in question in Exod 12:48 is clearly an alien, since he is uncircumcised.

27. See v. 7: bahăbîʾăkem bĕnê nēkār ʿarlê lēb wĕʿarlê bāśār lihyôt bĕmiqdāšî lĕḥallĕlô ʾet bêtî. On the use of the verb ḥll in H as the equivalent of ṭmʾ, see Milgrom's discussion in *Leviticus 1–16* (AB 3; New York: Doubleday, 1991) 37. H uses ṭmʾ more broadly than does P (including for moral violations) and seems to understand ḥll to mean at times ṭmʾ. Examples given by Milgrom of H's use of ḥll with the sense of ṭmʾ include Lev 21:12 and 22:9. Lev 21:4 is another good example, as is H-related Ezek 23:39. Other probable examples in Ezekiel are 7:22, 24; 24:21. See also Gen 49:4; 1 Chr 5:1; Dan 11:31, where this usage is attested. Though Klawans acknowledges this meaning of ḥll in certain contexts, he does not believe that it is present in Ezek 44:7 ("Gentile Impurity," 292 and n. 33).

28. It is not at all clear who these uncircumcised aliens are. Some commentators have thought they are descendants of foreign temple slaves such as the Gibeonites mentioned in Josh 9:23, 27 (e.g., M. Haran in G. Brin, ed., *Yehezqel* [Olam Ha-Tanakh 14; Tel Aviv: Davidzon-Iti, 1993] 224). Traditional Jewish commentaries often mention the view that they are priests (e.g., *Sepher Yehezqel*

[Jerusalem: Harav Kook, 1985] 36). The text of v. 8 is problematic and not easily understood, but it is evident that access to "holy things" (e.g., holy space, items, foods), restricted to priests elsewhere, is in question.

29. Though the term gēr is not used, the reference to resident foreigners seems very likely. The text uses ben nēkār, a person who is distinct from the gēr in H materials such as Exod 12:43–48. If ben nēkār here refers to a resident of the land, the usage is similar to that of Ezra-Nehemiah, which also does not speak of a gēr class, but refers to foreign residents as běnê nēkār (e.g., Neh 9:1–3).

30. Though in this particular text, the uncircumcised persons in question are very likely foreign conquerors rather than alien residents who come to worship.

31. Cp. similarly tôšāb wěśākîr lō' yō'kal bô in Exod 12:45.

32. See Jer 9:24–25 (Eng., 25–26), which states that other Canaanite speakers (Ammonites, Moabites, Edomites), the Egyptians, and desert dwellers practiced circumcision. See further n. 18 above.

33. J. Z. Smith anticipates me in pointing out that circumcision is a problematic "taxic indicator" in that it is not distinctive to Israel ("Fences and Neighbors: Some Contours of Early Judaism," in W. S. Green, ed., *Approaches to Ancient Judaism, Volume II: Essays in Religion and History* [Chico, CA: Scholars, 1980] 11).

34. S. J. D. Cohen makes all three of these observations in his treatment of circumcision among Judeans in the Second Temple period (*Beginnings of Jewishness*, 30, 39, 44–46, 47, 67).

35. In a number of H texts, the term tôšāb is used apparently in place of gēr; in others, gēr wětôšāb is used. The meaning of gēr, gēr wětôšāb and tôšāb in these texts appears to be the same. The word tôšāb is most accurately rendered "resident," and gēr wětôšāb "resident outsider," interpreting the expression as a hendiadys construction.

36. See Lev 25:35, 39–40; Deut 18:6 (concerning the Levites); Judg 17:7, 8, 9; 19:16; and 2 Chr 15:9. In some of these examples, verbal forms of the root gwr occur rather than the noun gēr. C. van Houten (*The Alien in Israelite Law* [JSOTSup 107; Sheffield: JSOT Press, 1991] 160) recognizes the possibility that the resident outsider could be either a foreigner or a displaced Israelite. C. Bultmann (*Der Fremde im antiken Juda* [FRLANT 153; Göttingen: Vandenhoeck and Ruprecht, 1992]) has argued that gēr is always used in legal texts of a displaced Israelite, and never of a foreigner. He even interprets a text such as Deut 14:21a in this way (92). In contrast, P.-E. Dion understands the gēr of Deuteronomy to be a foreign immigrant ("Israël et l'étranger dans le Deutéronome," in M. Gourgues and G.-D. Mailhiot, eds., *L'altérité: Vivre ensemble différents* [Montréal: Bellarmin; Paris: Cerf, 1986] 223).

37. The long-term residency of the gēr or tôšāb is illustrated by a number of texts, including several that mention the gēr or tôšāb who fathers children in the land (Lev 25:45; Ezek 47:22–23; cp. Ps 39:13 [Eng., 12]; 1 Chr 29:15). Elsewhere, the gēr is contrasted with the temporary wage laborer (tôšāb wěśākîr) and with nonresident aliens (nokrî and ben nēkār). What distinguishes the resident outsider of foreign origin from other foreigners is his long-term residency. Y. A. Seeligmann sees the gēr as a resident of the land where the nokrî is not ("gēr," *EM* 2:546 [Hebrew]).

38. The term is used consistently of males in our text, which gives the impression that residence was patrilocal and inheritance and descent patrilineal. Normally, a man remained at the locus of his patrimonial property, importing a wife from the outside and eventually becoming head of his own household. While the movement of a male away from his clan and their landholding appears to have been unusual in the Israelite context, the movement of women was not. Perhaps this explains the apparent gender-specific use of the term gēr in our texts. A woman from elsewhere does not belong to a special class, where a man who is an outsider would. On descent and inheritance, see the literature cited in n. 39 below.

39. The gēr has no claim to any local property holding, in contrast to local males. Nor does he possess local kinship connections, which could potentially benefit him in any number of ways (e.g., if he were to become encumbered by debt and was forced to sell himself into slavery, there would be no kinsman present to redeem him). On the lineage-patrimony system, which was characterized by patrilocal residence in a multiple-family household, and patrilineal descent and inheritance, see among others L. Stager, "The Archaeology of the Family in Ancient Israel," *BASOR* 260 (1985) 1–35, esp. pp. 18–23; C. Meyers, *Discovering Eve: Ancient Israelite Women in Context* (New York: Oxford University Press, 1988) 124–38; R. Westbrook, *Property and Family in Biblical Law* (JSOTSup 113; Sheffield: Sheffield Academic Press, 1991) 11–23; and S. Bendor, *The Social Structure of Ancient Israel* (JBS 7; Jerusalem: Simor, 1996).

40. "Potentially" because he is sometimes described as better-off than some Israelites and therefore in a position to take them on as dependents (see Lev 25:47–54), though this was apparently not the norm, given the many texts that speak of the gēr as a vulnerable person subject to special protection.

41. Evidence for the dependency of resident outsiders on patrons is to be found in many passages. Often, the resident outsider is said to be "with you" (Lev 25:23) or he is described as "your resident outsider" (Deut 5:14=Exod 20:10; Deut 29:10 [Eng., 11]; 31:12), suggesting a relationship of clientage. (The "you" addressed by the legal materials is a head of household, or elder.) Elsewhere, the resident outsider is said to be "in your towns" (Deut 14:21; 16:14), or "in your/ their midst" (Lev 17:13; Deut 16:11; 26:11), expressions which can be combined with the possessive "your resident outsider," as in Deut 5:14 or 31:12. See further Seeligmann's treatment of this manner of speaking about the resident outsider ("gēr," 547–48).

42. See n. 37 above.

43. For example, Exod 12:48 speaks of the circumcision of "every male" belonging to the gēr in the same language used by Gen 17:10, 12 for the circumcision of all males in Israelite households, including slaves, though Exod 12:48 does not specifically mention slaves belonging to the gēr.

44. "Native" appears to have nothing to do with birthplace and everything to do with lineage. Foreign resident outsiders can be born in the land and still not be natives, as several texts demonstrate (e.g., Lev 25:45–46; cp. Deut 23:4–9 [Eng., 3–8], which speak of generations of Moabites, Ammonites, Edomites, and Egyptians born in the land of Israel). "Native" is a constructed category, like "alien." Thus, I do not translate 'ezrāḥ "native-born," since place of birth does not deter-

mine "native" status (contrast, for example, van Houten, *The Alien in Israelite Law*, 163).

45. Knohl presents arguments for the H provenance of Exod 12:1–20, against its traditional assignment to P (*Sanctuary of Silence*, 19, 52).

46. See Knohl's treatment, ibid., 21, 27–28.

47. See Knohl's treatment, ibid., 53.

48. P material in Num 19:1–10a describing the ritual of producing purifying waters has been supplemented by H material in vv. 10b–13, as Knohl has argued (ibid., 93). Thus, I speak of the final H casting of the text, which opens the ritual to the resident outsider of alien background.

49. tôrâ 'aḥat (ûmišpāṭ 'eḥād) yihyeh lā'ezrāḥ (or, lākem) wĕlaggēr haggār bĕtôkĕkem (or, 'ittĕkem): Exod 12:49; Num 15:16, cp. 15:29; ḥuqqâ 'aḥat (yihyeh) lākem wĕlaggēr (ûlĕ'ezrāḥ hā'āreṣ): Num 9:14; 15:15; kaggēr kā'ezrāḥ: Lev 24:16, 22; Josh 8:33 (cp. Num 15:15 kākem kaggēr); baggēr ûbĕ'ezrāḥ hā'āreṣ: Exod 12:19.

50. The MT reads haqqāhāl ḥuqqâ 'aḥat lākem wĕlaggēr haggār at this juncture. Clearly, 'ittĕkem ought to be restored after haggār with the versions and the sense of the passage. The word haqqāhāl is an awkward addition to the H cliché beginning ḥuqqâ 'aḥat or tôrâ 'aḥat. LXX reflects the presence of haqqāhāl in its Vorlage, though it associates haqqāhāl with the preceding verse, and adds kurios as indirect object: hon tropon poieite humeis, houtō poiēsei hē sunagōgē Kuriōi.

51. Ezekiel, active during the early exile, shares a distinct ideology and vocabulary with H, as do later materials in the book of Ezekiel. If Gen 17:10–14 is in the main to be attributed to H, this may be taken as evidence of H activity during the exile. On this, see n. 23 above.

52. E.g., Isa 56:3–7; Ezek 44:4–9; 47:13–23; Ezra-Nehemiah.

53. A careful examination of the contexts in which the integrationist clichés occur suggests that these are very often secondary glosses on earlier H materials. In Lev 18:26, the cliché "the native and the resident outsider who resides in your midst" disrupts the flow of the sentence. In Exod 12:19, "whether resident outsider or native of the land" dangles at the end of the verse, a common type of gloss (cp. Lev 20:10). Lev 16:29 is similar to Exod 12:19, with "the native and the resident outsider in your midst" as a dangling gloss at the end of the verse. See also Lev 24:16, in which "the resident outsider and native alike" disrupts the flow of the verse, and Lev 17:15, which is similar.

54. In contrast, Knohl argues that the integrationist material in H is early (eighth century), though he does believe that H activity spanned several centuries, from the eighth century to the Persian period (*Sanctuary of Silence*, 199–220); Milgrom sees the Holiness corpus as wholly pre-Persian period, with a final redaction during the exile (*Leviticus 1–16*, 27). Knohl believes that the Holiness Source's eighth-century context was characterized by a struggle against the influence of foreign cults and alien social practices in Israel (*Sanctuary of Silence*, 204–6). H, he believes, grants the resident outsider "equal cultic and judicial status [as a] . . . defense measure against the incursion of idolatrous practices into the land" (220).

55. See W. Zimmerli, *Ezekiel* 2:526, 532. He dates both the gloss and the larger text to the late exile, at a time of planning a new entry into the land. There is no reason to assume, however, that the gloss does not date to a later time.

56. E.g., "They shall be for you like the native among the children of Israel" (v. 22).

57. On returning to kin and patrimony, see, e.g., Lev 25:10, 13.

58. On Zerah as Judah's "second clan" after Perez, see 1 Chr 2:4; Gen 38:30, but cp. 1 Chr 1:37; Gen 36:13, 17, where Zerah is Edomite. On Judahite Qenaz, see Num 32:12; Josh 14:6, 14; Judg 1:13, where Caleb is said to be a Qenizzite, but cp. Gen 15:19; 36:11, 15; 1 Chr 1:36, which know Qenaz as an Edomite group. On Jerahmeel as the son of Hezron, the son of Perez, see 1 Chr 2:9, 25, 27, but cp. the distinct and separate "Negeb of the Jerahmeelites" and "Negeb of Judah" in 1 Sam 27:10. In 1 Sam 30:29, the cities of the Jerahmeelites are listed among Judahite cities, pointing to their absorption.

59. For evidence of the secondary nature of the integrative material, see n. 53 above.

60. E.g., Deut 1:16; 10:19; 14:21; 23:8 (Eng., 7); 24:14; 28:43–44; Josh 20:9.

61. See Deut 16:11, 14; 26:11; 29:10; 31:12.

62. Scholars have yet to explain convincingly why the head of household's wife is not present in these dependent lists.

63. On the assembly, see, among many others, Y. Liver, "qāhāl," EM 7:66–70 (Hebrew); H. P. Müller, "qāhāl—Versammlung," THAT 2:609–19. The term qāhāl is used in biblical texts to refer both to local councils of elders who execute justice, divide property, and muster young men for war, and to larger assemblies drawn from the whole nation. Sometimes the term is used for the whole community subject to covenant obligations, including dependents (e.g., Josh 8:35 and Neh 8:2 explicitly, and elsewhere by implication [e.g., Deut 31:10–13; Neh 13:1]).

64. The resident outsider is excluded from the covenant because he is obviously not subject to the curse in Deut 28:43–44 in which he prospers and Israelites decline.

65. See, e.g., Deut 15:3; 17:15; 23:20–21 (Eng., 19–20), in which the term "brother" is contrasted with "alien" (nokrî). This point was brought to my attention by Dion, "Israël et l'étranger," 221.

66. Note that Lev 19:33–34 builds on Exod 22:20 (Eng., 21) and speaks clearly of a foreign resident outsider, whose ideal treatment is compared to that of the native.

67. Various texts speak of the resident outsider as a vulnerable person deserving of special protection along with the widow and the fatherless. These include Exod 22:20 (Eng., 21); 23:9; Lev 19:33–34; Deut 10:18–19; 14:29; 24:17, 19–21; 26:12–13; 27:19.

68. The avenger is the relative of someone who has been murdered. He is responsible to avenge the death. See Num 35:9–34; Deut 19:1–13; Josh 20:1–9; 2 Sam 14:11.

69. On "rejoicing" as cultic activity, see G. A. Anderson, A Time to Mourn, A Time to Dance: The Expression of Grief and Joy in Israelite Tradition (University Park, PA: Pennsylvania State University Press, 1991) 19–26.

70. Here, I read with LXX and other versions. MT reads "your heads, your tribes."

71. The emphasis is mine. The idiom in Hebrew is kaggēr kā'ezrāḥ, and it is found elsewhere in H material that speaks of the resident outsider (Lev 24:16, 22

[cp. Exod 12:19; Num 15:15]). The idiom and others like it are not, however, found in D or other sources.

72. See E. Nielson (*Deuteronomium* (HAT I/6; Tübingen: Mohr/Siebeck, 1995) 219–20) for discussion of the views of various scholars on this passage. A classic treatment is that of K. Galling, "Das Gemeindegesetz in Deuteronomium," in W. Baumgartner et al., eds., *Festschrift Alfred Bertholet zum 80. Geburtstag* (Tübingen: Mohr/Siebeck, 1950) 176–91.

73. See, e.g., Lam 1:10 and Ezek 44:7, 9, texts of the sixth-century. The presence of sixth-century exegesis of Deut 23:4–9 (Eng., 3–8) suggests that the text is probably pre-exilic in date. Isa 52:1, a text of the late exile, also seems to allude to Deut 23:4–9 (Eng., 3–8) but understands it to support a ban on the entry of uncircumcised aliens into Jerusalem, conceived as holy.

74. On the acquisition of clients as a way to enhance status and increase honor in the Roman context, see P. Veyne, *The Roman Empire* (Cambridge, MA: Harvard University Press, 1997) 89–91. On Roman clientage generally, see also the works cited in n. 23 of my introduction.

75. On the problems dating the missions of Ezra and Nehemiah, as well as scholarly debate about the dating of the books and their component parts, see the review of R. W. Klein, "Ezra-Nehemiah, Books of," *ABD* 2:731–42, with literature cited. An older review article of Klein's is still useful: "Ezra and Nehemiah in Recent Studies," in F. M. Cross, W. E. Lemke, and P. D. Miller, Jr., eds., *Magnalia Dei: The Mighty Acts of God* (Garden City: Doubleday, 1976) 361–76. Ezra's mission is typically dated either to 458 or 398 (the seventh year of either Artaxerxes I or II), while Nehemiah's mission is generally dated to 445 (the twentieth year of Artaxerxes I). The books, in their final form, are probably to be dated to the end of the fifth century, or the beginning of the fourth century. See further F. M. Cross, "A Reconstruction of the Judean Restoration," *JBL* 94 (1975) 4–18, who opts for ca. 400.

76. E.g., Ezra 6:21 describes those eating the Passover sacrifice as "the children of Israel who had returned from the exile and all who had separated themselves from the defilement of the nations of the land to them in order to seek Yhwh, god of Israel." See also Neh 10:29–31 (Eng., 28–30), where those who had separated themselves from the peoples of the lands enter a covenant that emphasizes opposition to intermarriage, implicitly separating themselves from other Judeans who do not embrace their separatist program.

77. See Ezra 10:8, which concerns the returnee who defies the command of the "exile" community's leadership with respect to assembly: "All his property will be confiscated and as for him, he will be separated (yibbādēl) from the assembly of the exile community."

78. The term gēr does not occur once in Ezra-Nehemiah. Terms such as nēkār, běnê nēkār, nāšîm nokriyyôt, gôyê or ʿammê hāʾāreṣ/ʾărāṣôt are used in these books to refer to those classed as foreigners, including longtime residents of the land.

79. The classic treatment of the exegetical elaboration of texts such as Lev 18:24–30, Deut 23:4–9 (Eng., 3–8), and Deut 7:1–6 in Ezra-Nehemiah is that of M. Fishbane, *Biblical Interpretation in Ancient Israel* (Oxford: Clarendon, 1985)

114–29. I am indebted to Fishbane's treatment of the exegetical dimensions of Ezra-Nehemiah, though I do not agree with all of his conclusions and believe that there is more that can be said about the material in question.

80. A number of scholars have asserted that aliens themselves are not polluting in any biblical source. Recently, Klawans has made this argument ("Gentile Impurity," 290–91). He mentions Ezra-Nehemiah in passing, claiming that the text "explicitly connect[s] the prohibition of intermarriage with the defiling *behavior* of local Gentiles," but without argument (291; my emphasis). He ignores a text such as Neh 13:4–9, which is surely relevant to debate about this issue, given that it suggests that aliens themselves are polluting and has nothing to say about Neh 13:28–30, though he lists it as evidence that alien behavior defiles (291 n. 29). On these two texts, see my argument ahead.

81. Presumably, the high priest Elyashib of Neh 13:28 is not the same individual who gave Tobiah the Ammonite a chamber in the temple according to Neh 13:4–5.

82. Ezra 2:59–62 (= Neh 7:61–64), though allegedly a list of returnees from Babylon at the first return, speaks of the exclusion of priests from priestly duties and privileges who could not prove their Israelite lineage; they are considered polluted according to the text (waygō'ălû min hakkĕhunnâ). Though assigned to the era of the first return, the issues of concern in this text are those of the fifth century.

83. As Fishbane points out, it is probably derived from Isa 6:13 (*Biblical Interpretation*, 123).

84. See similarly, ibid., 121; and J. Kugel, "The Holiness of Israel and the Land in Second Temple Times," in M. V. Fox et al., eds., *Texts, Temples and Traditions: A Tribute to Menahem Haran* (Winona Lake, IN: Eisenbrauns, 1996) 23–24.

85. Exod 19:6 is D supplementary material according to Noth, *A History of Pentateuchal Traditions*, 31 n. 112. Verse 5 looks particularly like D with respect to style, mentioning sĕgullâ mikkol hā'ammîm. Other D occurrences of the idea of Israel as a holy people include Deut 7:6; 14:21; 26:19; 28:9. H occurrences include Lev 11:44–45; 19:2; 20:7–8. Fishbane notes the connection to older texts describing Israel as holy (*Biblical Interpretation*, 121–23), as does Kugel, "The Holiness of Israel," 23–24. Kugel shows how earlier conceptions of Israel's holiness were not constructed as "genetic," in contrast to what emerges in fifth-century texts such as Ezra 9:1–2. He argues convincingly that the prohibition of mixing two kinds of agricultural seed informs this novel notion of a holy seed mixing with the peoples of the land, thereby giving the mixing "the resonance of a violation of cultic law" (ibid., 24; cp. Lev 19:19; Deut 22:9).

86. The use of niddâ with the general sense of "defilement" rather than the specific sense of "menstrual discharge" is characteristic of H rather than P, as Milgrom has pointed out (*Leviticus 1–16*, 38).

87. G. Alon, "The Levitical Uncleanness of Gentiles," in his *Jews, Judaism and the Classical World: Studies in Jewish History in the Time of the Second Temple and Talmud*, trans. I. Abrahams (Jerusalem: Magnes, 1977) 146–89, originally *Tarbiz* 8 (1937) 137–61 (Hebrew).

88. E.g., Gen 35:2; Jer 7:30 (= 32:34); Ezek 5:11; 20:30; 22:3, 4; 23:7, 30; 36:18. Several other texts may also refer to the polluting power of "idols." These include Hos 5:3; 6:10; Jer 2:23; Ps 106:39, among others.

89. E.g., Hos 9:3–4; Amos 7:17; Ezek 4:13; perhaps Ps 137:4. See my earlier discussion in chapter 2.

90. See especially Fishbane, *Biblical Interpretation*, 114–29 with references.

91. The reading mnšh (with suspended nun) for mšh in some Hebrew manuscripts must be secondary and apologetic in intent. See further Cross, "The Priestly Houses of Early Israel," in his *Canaanite Myth and Hebrew Epic* (Cambridge, MA: Harvard University Press, 1973) 197–98; and E. Tov, *Textual Criticism of the Hebrew Bible* (Minneapolis: Fortress; Assen/Maastricht: Van Gorcum, 1992) 57.

92. E.g., David's genealogy is traced back through Obed to Boaz and eventually Perez in Ruth 4:18–22. Genealogies typically record male generations. Daughters and wives are occasionally mentioned, though they play no central role in the genealogies.

93. Cp. Num 26:29–33 on Asriel, Machir, and Gilead. There, Asriel is a "son" of Gilead and a Gileadite clan. Other examples of the son(s) of a concubine counted in the father's lineage include Gen 22:20–24; 36:12 (cp. 1 Chr 1:36); 2 Sam 21:8; and most famously, Gen 35:22b–26, where the sons of Jacob are listed, including the sons of the slaves Bilhah and Zilpah. Cp., however, texts in the Abraham narrative that suggest the possibility of excluding sons of a concubine from a father's inheritance (Gen 21:10; 25:5–6). Mesopotamian law treats several circumstances in which children born of a concubine might receive inheritance from their father. In LH 170–71, a father must embrace his children by a slave in order for them to inherit; they have no claim if he does not. Cp. MAL A 41, which suggests that the children of a concubine whose status has been raised to that of an ashutu-wife may inherit, though a concubine's children may not unless the father dies without sons. On concubinage, see further Z. Falk, "pîlegeš," *EM* 6:456–57 (Hebrew), with bibliography; W. Kornfeld, "Mariage," *DBSup* 5:916–17.

94. See the citations in n. 39 above.

95. On the family tomb, see Stager, "Archaeology of the Family," 23; and E. Bloch-Smith, *Judahite Burial Practices and Beliefs about the Dead* (JSOT/ASOR Monograph Series 7; Sheffield: Sheffield Academic Press, 1992) 111–12. Among the texts often cited in this regard are Josh 24:30 and Judg 2:9.

96. Such rites include setting up a stela and invoking the father's name. See 2 Sam 18:18.

97. See Gen 38:11; Lev 22:13.

98. See similarly the comments of D. Daube, *Ancient Jewish Law* (Leiden: Brill, 1981) 3–5, brought to my attention by Fishbane, *Biblical Interpretation*, 118.

99. See Seeligmann ("gēr," 546) on the main reasons for the movement of people in ancient west Asia.

100. Fishbane (*Biblical Interpretation*, 125–26) dates 1 Kgs 11:1–4 to the early post-exilic period. He argues that the text expands on the earlier 1 Kgs 11:6–7, drawing on Deut 23:4–9 (Eng., 3–8) to fashion the "pseudo-Pentateuchal citation" of 1 Kgs 11:2 and to add the Ammonites, Moabites, Edomites, and

Egyptians to the "old Canaanite population roster" of Deut 7:1. Fishbane, however, does not mention that the MT of 1 Kgs 11:1 also lists Hittites and Sidonians among the alien wives of Solomon (LXX has, in addition, Arameans). Though the Hittites occur in the list of Canaanite groups in Deut 7:1, the Sidonians (and Arameans) do not. Thus, the exegete responsible for 1 Kgs 11:1–4 goes beyond what is found in Deuteronomy 7 and 23 and condemns Solomon's other intermarriages as well. Nonetheless, Fishbane is probably correct to see the influence of Deut 23:4–9 on 1 Kgs 11:1–4. After formulating my response to Fishbane's understanding of the development of 1 Kgs 11:1–2, I came across the critique of G. N. Knoppers, "Sex, Religion, and Politics: The Deuteronomist on Intermarriage," *Hebrew Annual Review* 14 (1994) 121–39, who makes some similar points.

101. According to Ezek 44:22, a priest is to marry only an Israelite virgin or another priest's widow. Lev 21:7 does not forbid priests to marry foreign women, though Lev 21:13–14 allows the high priest to marry only an Israelite virgin.

102. I am indebted to Fishbane (*Biblical Interpretation*, 114–29) for much of what follows concerning the expansive exegesis of Ezra-Nehemiah.

103. Others (e.g., NJPS) see the peoples as the subject of the relative clause and prefer to translate approximately as follows: ". . . and because of their abominations with which they have filled it end to end with their uncleanness." LXX also understands the peoples as the subject.

104. See Fishbane, *Biblical Interpretation*, 114–23.

105. See ibid., 119–20, on the use made of the framing materials of Leviticus 18 in Ezra 9:11–12; see pp. 116–17 on the use made of Deut 23:7 (Eng., 6).

106. Fishbane points out that the influence of Deut 23:7 (Eng., 6) is unmistakable here (ibid., 117, 117n. 32).

107. ʿēreb is probably to be understood as a person of mixed heritage, given the use of the verbal form hitʿārēb in Ezra 9:2: kî nāśĕʾû mibbĕnōtêhem lāhem wĕlibnêhem wĕhitʿārĕbû zeraʿ haqqōdeš bĕʿammê hāʾărāṣôt. See similarly J. Blenkinsopp, *Ezra-Nehemiah* (OTL; Philadelphia: Westminster, 1988) 351–52. Fishbane translates ʿēreb "foreigner," but does not explain why he does so. He identifies the passage as a longstanding crux (*Biblical Interpretation*, 126).

108. As Fishbane points out, the grounds for this exclusion are not entirely clear (*Biblical Interpretation*, 117–18).

109. Sources other than H do not make use of this combination of ideas and rhetoric. The rhetoric of separation to Yhwh from the other peoples is found outside of H in 1 Kgs 8:53, but without the idea of the people's holiness and without the purity rhetoric. There, Israel is separated by Yhwh to be his patrimony (naḥălâ). In Deut 14:1–3, Israel is described as a holy people and a special possession (ʿam sĕgullâ) of Yhwh, but the rhetoric of separation is absent, as is the purity rhetoric.

110. Compare other H texts such as Lev 11:44–47; 19:2, which are similar in their call to Israel to be holy, and D texts such as Deut 14:2. See further the discussion in the appendix.

111. Cp. Kugel ("The Holiness of Israel," 22), who also points out that Israel's holiness in H materials, as in other texts antedating the fifth century, is maintained by proper behavior.

112. On the separation of cultic servants, see Num 8:14; 16:9; Deut 10:8. The rhetoric of separation and distinction, as well as the rhetoric of holiness, is derived from the cultic-priestly realm of life, as is commonly noted.

113. See Ezra 6:21 with reference to the uncleanness of the nations; 9:1 with reference to their abominations; and 10:11; Neh 9:2; 10:29 (Eng., 28); 13:3.

114. The debate in fact goes back to the early part of the century and is inseparable from one's view of the unity or disunity of the text of Isaiah 56–66 and the pericope 56:1–8 itself. Some scholars have argued that vv. 3–8, which concern the alien, are a secondary addition to vv. 1–2 (e.g., K. Elliger, *Die Einheit des Tritojesaia [Jesaia 56–66]* [Stuttgart: Kohlhammer, 1928] 125). Some have assigned 56:1–8 or 3–8 to the fifth century. (E.g., B. Duhm, *Die Theologie der Propheten als Grundlage für die innere Entwicklungsgeschichte der israelitischen Religion* [Bonn: Adolph Marcus, 1875]. J. Blenkinsopp ["Second Isaiah—Prophet of Universalism," *JSOT* 41 (1988) 97] considers seriously the possibility of a fifth-century date for 56:1–8.) C. Westermann (*Isaiah 40–66* [OTL; Philadelphia: Westminster, 1969] 306) argued that 56:1–8 belongs to Third Isaiah's final stage of redaction in the post-exilic period, but did not go so far as to date Isa 56:3–7 to the fifth century. See further the review of C. Seitz, "Isaiah, Book of (Third Isaiah)," *ABD* 3:501–7, with bibliography.

115. The referent of this term is unclear. Many scholars believe that a mamzēr is the issue of a forbidden sexual union. See further the discussion of S. E. Loewenstamm, "mamzēr," *EM* 5:1–3 (Hebrew), with bibliography.

116. The proscription on the eunuch represents an expansive reading of Deut 23:2 (Eng., 1), which refers not to eunuchs per se, but to men with crushed testicles and/or men with a cut-off penis. It is a small exegetical step to expand this prohibition to include the eunuch as well, since he shares with the prohibited persons mentioned both genital damage and an inability to procreate.

117. Ezra 6:21; 9:1; 10:11; Neh 9:2; 10:29 (Eng., 28); and 13:3 all use the idiom of separation with respect to aliens. If Isa 56:3–7 is not responding to fifth-century opponents, it is certainly responding to their predecessors, as Westermann suggests (*Isaiah 40–66*, 313).

118. The Hebrew reads wayyibbādĕlû zeraʿ yiśrāʾēl mikkol bĕnê nēkār. Cp. Neh 13:30, where Nehemiah claims to have purified the priestly and Levitic lineages "from all things alien" (mikkol nēkār). Notice also that in both Isa 56:3–7 and in Ezra-Nehemiah, the aliens in question, though presumably resident in the land, are not referred to as gērîm.

119. See, e.g., Fishbane, *Biblical Interpretation*, 118, 128; Blenkinsopp, "Second Isaiah," 96; and J. D. W. Watts, *Isaiah 34–66* (Word Biblical Commentary 25; Waco, TX: Word Books, 1987) 249.

120. Furthermore, though šārēt is used for priestly and Levitical service at the sanctuary in a number of other texts (e.g., Num 3:6; 8:26; Deut 10:8; 17:12), it is also used commonly for noncultic service (e.g., Gen 39:4; 2 Kgs 6:15; 2 Sam 13:17, 18). One passage survives in which the verb šrt is apparently used for the activities of worshipers, albeit worshipers of gods other than Yhwh. Ezek 20:32 describes Israelites who want to be like the other nations, serving (šrt) wood and stone. Though one can show that the verb šrt is used often for priestly and Levitical service in the sanctuary, it seems that it is used at least once for the cultic

service of worshipers and frequently for noncultic service. Therefore, there may not even be an allusion in Isa 56:6 to the potential cultic servanthood of the admitted aliens in question. Later exegetes, however, seem to have understood the text to refer to the service of aliens as cultic functionaries.

121. Cp. Esther 9:27, which speaks of the attachment of others to the Judeans.

122. This text, however, concerns Israelites and their god, not aliens. See also Ps 83:9 (Eng., 8), which is similar, but concerns a covenant alliance made by foreign nations with one another. The related verb sph is used of the Israelite's relationship to Yhwh as worshiper and to Yhwh's land as resident. See 1 Sam 26:17–19, especially v. 19, where David the fugitive says "they have driven me today from being attached (mēhistappēaḥ) to the patrimony of Yhwh, saying 'Go, worship other gods.'"

123. Isa 14:1 speaks of Yhwh having compassion and choosing Israel again as a future event, suggesting an exilic date for this pericope. Zechariah 2 is generally dated to the period 520–515.

124. E.g., Neh 13:1–3, 4–9, 28–30; Ezra 9:2, 11–12.

125. F. Barth, "Introduction," in his *Ethnic Groups and Boundaries: The Social Organization of Culture Difference* (Bergen and Oslo: Universitets Forlaget; London: George Allen and Unwin, 1969), 22 speaks of "cultural mechanisms to implement . . . incorporation." I have modified his language here when I speak of mechanisms of alien incorporation. By incorporation, I mean the assignment of a social niche within the corporate entity rather than outside of it.

126. There is a vast literature on rites of transition. The classic monograph is A. van Gennep's *Les rites de passage* (Paris: Emile Nourry, 1909). Van Gennep introduced the basic terminology of the rites de passage still in use (rites de séparation, rites de marge, rites d'agrégation). See also V. Turner, "Betwixt and Between: The Liminal Period in Rites de Passage," in his *The Forest of Symbols: Aspects of Ndembu Ritual* (Ithaca: Cornell University Press, 1967) 93–111; idem, *The Ritual Process: Structure and Anti-Structure* (Chicago: Aldine, 1969); E. Leach, *Culture and Communication* (New York: Cambridge University Press, 1976) 77–79; and J. S. La Fontaine, *Initiation* (Manchester: Manchester University Press, 1985) 24–29, who includes a survey of post–van Gennep elaboration and modification of van Gennep's rites de passage model.

127. See Exod 21:2–6, 7–11; Lev 25:39–43; Deut 15:12–18. On debt slavery, see G. Chirichigno, *Debt-Slavery and the Ancient Near East* (JSOTSup 141; Sheffield: Sheffield Academic Press, 1993).

128. Slaves could also be manumitted. Manumission of foreign slaves by adoption was common in ancient west Asia. See F. W. Knobloch, "Adoption," *ABD* 1:77–78 and the examples discussed there, including an Elephantine text (Kraeling 8) that refers to the manumission and adoption of a young male bearing a Yhwistic name. On the formulae of adoption, see S. M. Paul, "Adoption Formulae: A Study of Cuneiform and Biblical Legal Clauses," *MAARAV* 2 (1979/80) 173–85.

129. See Lev 25:44–46, which speaks of slaves acquired both from the surrounding nations and from foreign long-term residents in the land and their descendants.

130. O. Patterson, *Slavery and Social Death: A Comparative Study* (Cambridge, MA: Harvard University Press, 1982) 4–5, my emphasis. Patterson also claims that the slave was utterly powerless vis-à-vis the master, "the ultimate human tool, as imprintable and as disposable as the master wished" (7). This generalization is not supported in biblical materials, which impose limits on the master's arbitrary power. Deut 21:10–14 limits the master/husband when he wishes to be rid of the woman he captured in war if he no longer desires her: he must allow her to go where she wishes; he may not sell her nor may he abuse her because he raped her. Another example is Exod 21:26–27, which rewards with freedom a male or female slave whose eye or tooth has been destroyed by the master. It is, however, not clear whether the slave in question is a Hebrew slave or a foreigner.

131. Patterson, *Slavery and Social Death*, 8–9.

132. For an insightful treatment of the various problems of the text: the meaning of hā'ĕlōhîm, the locus of the ritual, the significance of the door/door-post, and the signification of the ear boring, see V. Hurowitz, " 'His Master Shall Pierce His Ear with an Awl' (Exodus 21.6)—Marking Slaves in the Bible in Light of Akkadian Sources," in N. Sarna, ed., *Proceedings of the American Academy of Jewish Research LVIII* (Jerusalem and New York: American Academy of Jewish Research, 1992) 47–77.

133. The thesis that ear boring functions here as a sign of enslavement goes back to Rashbam; see also I. Mendelsohn, *Slavery in the Ancient Near East* (New York: Oxford University Press, 1949); I. Cardellini, *Die biblischen "Sklaven"-Gesetze im Lichte des keilschriftlichen Sklavenrechts* (BBB 55; Bonn: Hanstein, 1981) 243–51; and others cited by Hurowitz, " 'His Master Shall Pierce His Ear,' " 52 n. 12. The alternative view, that the ear boring is a punishment, is highly unlikely in my view. Hurowitz adduces a parallel to Exod 21:6 from a Mesopotamian ritual text and suggests that "piercing the ear signifies purchasing the slave, establishing and publicly proclaiming ownership, now permanent because of the slave's own volition and protestations of loyalty" (76).

134. Patterson, *Slavery and Social Death*, 4–5.

135. I understand tôšab kōhēn wĕśākîr to be a hendiadys construction comparable to tôšāb wĕśākîr with the addition of a modifier indicating possession.

136. Here, I read with the versions and in agreement with the following pronoun and verb.

137. According to Num 18:8–19, the holy foods of the priesthood include grain, wine, oil, the first fruits, the qorbān, minḥâ, ḥaṭṭā't and, 'āšām.

138. My thanks to Barry Eichler for emphasizing to me the importance of the practical needs of the slave and the master's obligation to meet them (oral communication).

139. There is no reason to assume that the slave of this law has been adopted by his master. No evidence suggests this. On adoption of slaves in ancient west Asia, which was paired with manumission, see M. David, "Adoption," *RA* 1:37–39; and Knobloch, "Adoption," 78.

140. The text says "do" her nails (wĕ'āśĕtâ 'et ṣippornêhā).

141. It is not clear to what the expression "garment of captivity" (śimlat šibyāh) refers. Many commentators have understood it to be the garment the

woman was wearing when she was captured rather than a special garment given
to prisoners of war to mark them off from others. See, e.g., P. Craigie, *The Book
of Deuteronomy* (Grand Rapids, MI: Eerdmans, 1976) 281; A. D. H. Mayes,
Deuteronomy (NCB; London: Oliphants, 1979) 303; and R. Clifford, *Deuteronomy* (Old Testament Message 4; Wilmington, DE: Michael Glazier, 1982) 113.
Heather McKay has suggested to me that the garment of capture itself would very
likely mark the prisoner as an alien, since the garment and other forms of adorn-
ment would probably differ from those utilized by women of the victors' culture
(oral communication). Most of the literature on the treatment of prisoners of war
in west Asia focuses on the Mesopotamian evidence, which is considerably more
extensive than that of small Levantine states such as Israel. On this, see S. I. Feigin,
"The Captives in Cuneiform Inscriptions," *AJSL* 50 (1934) 217–45; I. J. Gelb,
"Prisoners of War in Early Mesopotamia," *JNES* 32 (1973) 70–98; and B. Oded,
Mass Deportation and Deportees in the Neo-Assyrian Empire (Wiesbaden:
Reichert, 1978).

142. The thirty-day mourning period is significantly longer than the more
widely attested seven-day period, though as commonly noted, it is found in other
biblical texts (e.g., Num 20:29; Deut 34:8).

143. In the MT, the verbs glḥ, ʿśh and swr (Hiphil) are third feminine singular,
indicating that the woman performs the ritual actions herself; in LXX, they are
second singular, indicating that these rites are performed on the woman.

144. The woman's social status after her marriage has been a matter of debate.
C. Carmichael (*The Laws of Deuteronomy* [Ithaca: Cornell University Press,
1974] 59, 61) argues that the woman is "prima facie a slave," though she receives
special treatment; her status is "more like that of a full wife than a concubine." He
cites G. R. Driver and J. C. Miles, eds. and trans., *The Assyrian Laws* (Oxford:
Clarendon, 1935) 127–28, on the legal status of captive women in a late second
millennium Assyrian context (these could be slaves, concubines, or full wives). In
contrast, see J. Tigay (*Deuteronomy* [JPS Torah Commentary; Philadelphia: Jewish Publication Society, 1996] 194), who does not regard the captured woman as
a slave; and W. L. Moran ("Deuteronomy," in R. C. Fuller et al., eds., *A New
Catholic Commentary on Holy Scripture* [London: Thomas Nelson and Sons,
1969] 271), who believes the captive has the legal status of a concubine. (Moran's
commentary was brought to my attention by Tigay's work.) See also Feigin, "The
Captives in Cuneiform Inscriptions," 244, who saw the captive as a concubine.
The word "concubine" (pîlegeš) is not used in this text, though ʾiššâ is used elsewhere of a woman also called pîlegeš. On concubinage, see Falk, "pîlegeš," 456–
57, with bibliography; and Kornfeld, "Mariage," 916–17.

145. C. R. Hallpike, "Social Hair," *Man* 4 (1969) 258; cp. similarly T. H.
Gaster, *Myth, Legend and Custom in the Old Testament* (New York: Harper and
Row, 1969) 438; and Moran, "Deuteronomy," 271. Assyriological evidence
lends support to this understanding of the symbolic value of hair and nails. Texts
from a number of periods mention the use of nail marks on clay tablets in place
of a seal, pointing to a symbolic location of personhood in the nail. See further the
entry "ṣupru" in *CAD* 16:251 for specific citations.

146. See P. Buis and J. Leclercq, *Le Deutéronome* (Paris: Gabalda, 1963) 147;
Moran, "Deuteronomy," 271; Craigie, *The Book of Deuteronomy*, 281; Mayes,

Deuteronomy, 303. Each takes the position that the captive's acts erase her old identity. For two texts from Mari that are not dissimilar to Deut 21:12–13, see *ARM* 1.8, 75 and the discussion of M. Du Buit, "Quelques contacts bibliques dans les archives royales de Mari," *RB* 66 (1959) 576–77. I wonder if there is not a magical dimension to these acts of nail cutting and shaving, given the incantations and other rituals that survive from Mesopotamia in which nails or hair are cut off in order to effect the removal of an individual's sin or to avert various kinds of portended evil. For an example of a namburbû (apotropaic) ritual involving the shaving of body hair, intended like other such rituals to prevent a portended evil, see F. Thureau-Dangin, *Rituels accadiens* (Paris, 1921; reprint, Osbarück: Otto Zeller, 1975) 36. Other examples of namburbû rituals are found conveniently in R. I. Caplice, *The Akkadian Namburbu Texts: An Introduction* (Malibu: Undena, 1974). My thanks to Gary Beckman for providing clarification concerning namburbû rituals and for suggesting Caplice's monograph.

147. A. Berlin, "Hair," *The HarperCollins Bible Dictionary*, ed. P. J. Achtemeier (San Francisco: HarperCollins, 1996) 398; and L. G. Herr, "Shave," *International Standard Bible Encyclopedia* (4 vols.; Grand Rapids, MI: Eerdmans, 1979–88) 4:454. Craigie considers the possibility that shaving and the other rites performed by the captive are mourning rites (*The Book of Deuteronomy*, 281). As Tigay points out, this explanation goes back to antiquity; he cites Josephus, *Ant.* 4.257 and Nahmanides (*Deuteronomy*, 194).

148. B. B. Schmidt, *Israel's Beneficent Dead: Ancestor Cult and Necromancy in Ancient Israelite Religion and Tradition* (Winona Lake, IN: Eisenbrauns, 1996) 166 n. 132; and J. J. M. Roberts, "Shaving," *HarperCollins Bible Dictionary*, 1005.

149. Nail cutting is never mentioned as a component of mourning rites or rites of purification in biblical sources, let alone in combination with shaving rites. Shaving the head and other forms of hair and beard manipulation are, however, well-attested mourning rites in biblical texts (e.g., Isa 15:2; 22:12; Jer 16:6; 41:5; 48:37; Amos 8:10; Job 1:20), and shaving also functions as a component of purification rites in certain contexts (e.g., Lev 14:8; Num 8:7).

150. See D. Daube (*Ancient Jewish Law*, 5), who anticipates me in reaching a similar conclusion regarding the significance of these rites. Daube points out that the woman's incorporation is accomplished through her marriage.

151. It seems very likely that rites producing and signaling status change of this type could have played an important part in Israelite life. Analogous rites of subordination (e.g., vassalage in covenant contexts) are described in other biblical contexts.

152. In contrast, much evidence survives from Rome. See Veyne, *The Roman Empire*, 71–93, esp. 89–91. Clients paid homage each morning to their patron and protector; to fail to appear at the patron's home was to "disavow one's bond of clientage." Clients appeared in special attire, and each received a symbolic gift of food. The order of admission to the patron's antechamber was regulated by hierarchical considerations. Thus, the household functioned as a locus for competition between groups of retainers and between individual clients.

153. E.g., Gen 43:34; 2 Sam 11:8; 19:43. On reciprocal honoring and the competition for honor among the vassals of a suzerain, see S. M. Olyan, "Honor,

NOTES TO CHAPTER 4

Shame and Covenant Relations in Ancient Israel and Its Environment," *JBL* 115 (1996) 201–18.

154. Exclusion from the Passover sacrifice probably should be understood to mean exclusion from sacrifice period, though we cannot be certain of this.

155. On the history of American self-definition, see recently R. M. Smith, *Civic Ideals: Conflicting Views of Citizenship in U.S. History* (New Haven: Yale University Press, 1997); and J. Rosen's review article "America in Thick and Thin: Exclusion, Discrimination, and the Making of Americans," *The New Republic* 4.329/330 (Jan. 5 and 12, 1998) 29–36. Also highly informative is P. H. Schuck and R. M. Smith, *Citizenship without Consent* (New Haven: Yale University Press, 1985).

156. Changes in German law (in 1991, 1993) have made naturalization easier for immigrants and their children who meet a specific set of residency and other requirements. My information on recent changes to German citizenship and naturalization was obtained in June 1998, from the web site of the German Information Center, a unit of the German government (http://www.germany-info.org). On the history of German citizenship and nationality up to the early nineties, see R. Brubaker, *Citizenship and Nationhood in France and Germany* (Cambridge, MA: Harvard University Press, 1992), esp. pp. 75–84, 114–37, 165–78. My thanks to Maud Mandel for suggesting Brubaker's interesting study.

157. Earlier citizenship law made descent from an American father determinative of a child's status. Present law, in contrast, recognizes a mother's status as equally relevant to that of a father in cases where lineage is determinative (e.g., when a child is born abroad).

158. On the routine exclusion of free blacks and American Indians living in their tribal settings from citizenship before the Civil Rights Act (1866) and the Fourteenth Amendment (1868), see Schuck and Smith, *Citizenship without Consent*, 42–74. The Chinese Exclusion Act (1882) explicitly denied Chinese immigrants and their American-born children citizenship until *U.S. v. Wong Kim Ark* (169 U.S. 649 [1898]), in which the Supreme Court confirmed the citizenship of an American-born child of Chinese immigrant parents in California. See further Smith, *Civic Ideals*, 359–63, 439–40.

159. See Schuck and Smith, *Citizenship without Consent*, 51.

160. E.g., Exod 12:43–49; Lev 22:10–13; Deut 21:10–14.

161. Even in an H text such as Exod 12:43–49, the resident outsider who chooses to be circumcised and thus to become more fully integrated into the cultic life of the community remains a resident outsider. He has a place in the community and its ritual life, though he remains an entity different from the native.

Chapter 4
The Qualified Body

1. Lev 24:19–20 seems to speak of intentional disfigurement, describing it as mûm.

2. For lists of blemishes, see Lev 21:18–20; 22:22–24. A number of the blemishes mentioned in these two lists are obscure. For discussion of the blemishes listed, see J. Milgrom, *Leviticus 1–16* (AB 3; New York: Doubleday, 1991) 722–

23; and B. A. Levine, *Leviticus* (Philadelphia: Jewish Publication Society, 1989) 145–46. Lev 24:19–20 presents a modified talion series as a list of blemishes. Sick animals (ḥōleh) are mentioned with other blemished sacrificial animals in Mal 1:8, 13, but the text says nothing about the nature of their sickness. "Mutilated" is probably the meaning of gāzûl in Mal 1:13 (cp. Mic 3:2).

3. See similarly Y. Leibowitz and Y. S. Licht, "mûm, m(ʾ)ûm," *EM* 4:726 (Hebrew), who believe that all are externally marked.

4. This distinction is not made explicitly in biblical texts describing blemishes, though it is present in Qumran materials (e.g., 1QM VII 4–5 mentions the permanent blemish [mûm ʿôlām] and by implication, the temporary blemish. For this text, see E. Lohse, *Die Texte aus Qumran* [3rd ed.; Munich: Kösel, 1981] 196).

5. The discussion of blemished bodies in this chapter owes much to the conceptualization of M. Douglas. She has emphasized the paradigmatic idea of "wholeness" or "completeness" as characteristic of holiness and the symmetry of the cultic exclusion of animals and restriction of priests with physical defects (*Purity and Danger* [1966; reprint, Boston: Ark, 1984] 50–52; idem, "Deciphering a Meal," *Daedalus* 101 [1972] 76–77). I develop this line of thinking further here.

6. On this, see further S. M. Olyan, "Why an Altar of Unfinished Stones? Some Thoughts on Ex 20,25 and Dtn 27,5–6," *ZAW* 108 (1996) 161–71.

7. Lev 22:25: kî mošḥātām bāhem mûm bām lōʾ yērāṣû lākem; Mal 1:14: wĕʾārûr nôkēl wĕyēš bĕʿedrô zākār wĕnōdēr wĕzōbēaḥ mošḥāt laʾdōnāy.

8. Its antonym "good" (ṭôb) also has a physical sense and is best translated "beautiful" in contexts in which the physical sense is intended. See, e.g., Dan 1:4.

9. Here I read šĕnûʾê nepeš dāwīd with the qere.

10. E.g., Lev 1:3, 10; 3:1, 6; 4:3, 23; 5:15, 18, 25 (Eng., 6:6); 22:19, 21; 23:12; Num 6:14; 19:2. Cp. Ezek 43:22, 23; 45:18; 46:4, 13.

11. Verse 23, probably a modifying gloss on the text, allows the ox or sheep with a limb too long or short to be used for a free-will offering, but not a vow, thereby contradicting v. 21.

12. Both texts have experienced glossing intended to define more precisely the meaning of "blemish." The gloss in Deut 17:1 defines "blemish" as "any disfiguring thing" (kol dābār rāʿ); the double gloss of Deut 15:21 provides specific examples of blemishes, probably intended to function synecdochically, with an added notation intended to make that function unambiguous ("lame or blind, [that is] any disfiguring blemish").

13. The holiness of sacrificial animals is not stated directly in this text, though it is clear in those texts that speak of the holy and most holy foods assigned to the priesthood and their dependents (see, e.g., Num 18:8–19).

14. On the date of Malachi, see the recently published discussion of A. E. Hill, *Malachi* (AB 25D; New York: Doubleday, 1998) 51, 80–84. Hill himself prefers a date of ca. 500.

15. Cp. Mal 1:13, which is similar.

16. Derivatives of the verbs gʾl and ṭhr are contrasted in Neh 13:29–30 (goʾŏlê hakkĕhunnâ/wĕṭihartîm mikkol nēkār), and Lam 4:14–15 essentially equates nĕgōʾălû baddām and ṭāmēʾ. Dan 1:8 uses a form of the verb gʾl in a manner

equivalent to a common use of ṭmʾ, that is, to speak of the polluting power of food and drink served by aliens.

17. On the meaning of the verb kippēr, see the citations in chapter 1, n. 30.

18. See Exod 28:43; 30:17–21; 40:32.

19. See, e.g., A. Caquot and P. de Robert, *Les livres de Samuel* (CAT 6; Geneva: Labor et Fides, 1994) 403; P. K. McCarter, *II Samuel* (AB 9; Garden City: Doubleday, 1984) 137; H. W. Hertzberg, *I and II Samuel* (OTL; Philadelphia: Westminster, 1964) 269; and C. Schäfer-Lichtenberger, *Stadt und Eidgenossenschaft im Alten Testament* (BZAW 156; Berlin: de Gruyter, 1983) 385.

20. One might compare 1 Sam 5:5, an etiology explaining the origin of a Philistine cultic custom, which is embedded within the "Ark Narrative." Both etiologies, not atypically, begin with the formula ʿal kēn. On biblical etiologies, see B. O. Long, *The Problem of Etiological Narrative in the Old Testament* (BZAW 108; Berlin: Töpelmann, 1968).

21. For bayit used to refer specifically to the temple building, see, e.g., 1 Kgs 6:2; 1 Chr 28:10. For bayit used to refer to the larger sanctuary sphere, see, e.g., 2 Kgs 11:3, 4–5, 8, 13. (Cp. similarly 2 Kgs 10:21, 23–25, on the Baal temple in Samaria.)

22. E.g., bāʾ without preposition.

23. For priestly service, see Exod 28:29, 35 (běbōʾô ʾel haqqōdeš); Lev 16:23 (ûbāʾ ʾahărōn ʾel ʾōhel môʿēd); Exod 28:30 (běbōʾô lipnê yhwh); Lev 16:17 (běbōʾô lěkappēr baqqōdeš); Ezek 44:27 (běyôm bōʾô ʾel haqqōdeš). For the entry of worshipers and others (e.g., aliens), see Lam 1:10 (bāʾû miqdāšāh); Ezek 44:9 (kol ben nēkār ʿerel lēb wěʿerel bāśār lōʾ yābôʾ ʾel miqdāšî); Isa 56:7 (wahăbîʾôtîm ʾel har qodšî).

24. In Hebrew, lōʾ yābōʾ pěṣûaʿ dakkāʾ ûkěrût šopkâ biqhal yhwh.

25. Lam 1:10 seems to allude to the exclusion of the Ammonite and Moabite from the assembly of Yhwh in Deut 23:4 (Eng., 3) and perhaps the partial exclusion of the Edomite in Deut 23:9 (Eng., 8). In any case, Lam 1:10 bears witness to an interpretive move to widen the scope of the exclusion to include the Babylonians (presumably; see 2 Kgs 25:9, 13–17), if not all aliens. The tendency to broaden Deut 23:4 (Eng., 3) is witnessed in later texts such as Neh 13:1–3, where it is understood to refer to all aliens, and Isa 56:3–7, where the original restriction and a broadening to all aliens is rejected. On Lam 1:10, see similarly D. Hillers, *Lamentations* (AB 7A; Garden City: Doubleday, 1972) 25.

26. In Isa 56:3–5, the eunuchs who observe Yhwh's Sabbaths and keep his covenant are urged not to despair: "I will give to them in my temple and within my walls a monument and a name better than sons and daughters. An everlasting name I will give to them, which shall not be cut off." The exact meaning of this passage remains unclear, though the mention of "a monument and a name" in Yhwh's house is striking. Does it mean that the writer rejects an apparent ban on the eunuch? This is clear regarding aliens in Isa 56:7: They may enter the sanctuary and participate in cultic rites. My guess is that the eunuch, too, is welcome according to this text, and the statement about the "monument and name" in the temple is meant to suggest this. This interpretation would provide some symmetry between v. 7 and vv. 3–5.

27. See especially v. 9, where the allusion to Deuteronomy 23 is clear: kol ben nēkār ʿerel lēb wĕʿerel bāśār lōʾ yābôʾ ʾel miqdāšî. Ironically, the original law in Deut 23:4–9 (Eng., 3–8) concerned only the exclusion of circumcised peoples from the assembly (the Ammonite, Moabite, Edomite, and Egyptian; see Jer 9:24–25 [Eng., 25–26]); uncircumcised peoples are not even mentioned in that context.

28. See the citations of Douglas's work in n. 5 above.

29. See further n. 26 above.

30. A number of scholars suggest or hint at this interpretation in passing, usually without argument. See, e.g., Levine, *Leviticus*, 145; and Caquot and de Robert, *Les livres de Samuel*, 403.

31. 11QTemp XLV 12–14 in Y. Yadin, *The Temple Scroll* (3 vols.; Jerusalem: Israel Exploration Society, 1983) 2.193. Yadin argued that the Temple Scroll derives its proscription not from 2 Sam 5:8b, but from Lev 21:17–23, expanding the prohibition on blemished priests there to apply to all Israelites. Though he mentions 2 Sam 5:8b, it is not clear to me how he thinks it fits into his developmental schema (1.289–90). Why the Temple Scroll does not also prohibit the lame is unclear, though Yadin argues that "blind" is intended to stand for all blemishes. See ahead for my similar argument regarding the possible function of "blind and lame" in 2 Sam 5:8b.

32. See m. Hag. 1:1; Mek., Mishpatim 20. The influence of 2 Sam 5:8b is not, however, explicit in either text. The Mishnah simply lists excluded categories of persons; the Mekilta develops justifications for each excluded category listed in the Mishnah on the basis of its rather loose reading of Exod 23:14, 17. The exclusion of the blind from pilgrimage is justified by quoting yērāʾeh ("he shall appear"/"be seen"); the exclusion of the lame is supported by quoting šālôš rĕgālîm ("three pilgrimage festivals," lit. "three feet"). My thanks to S. J. D. Cohen for pointing me in the direction of these two texts.

33. This seems to be the most likely meaning of gāzûl. Cp. Mic 3:2.

34. The inclusive intent of this text is communicated more clearly in the Hebrew, which employs a min . . . wĕʿad construction (literally, "from . . . to": "from man to woman, from child to infant, from ox to sheep, from camel to ass").

35. My thanks to David Konstan and William Gilders (in personal communications) for pointing out to me that the emblematic function of "blind and lame" may be due to the locus of each condition.

36. Thus, the verb ḥll as it is used in Lev 21:23 must mean "to profane" in that context; it cannot mean "to pollute," as it sometimes does elsewhere in H and other materials (on this, see my discussion in chapter 2 at n. 54, and chapter 3, n. 27). On the polluted priest and his separation from the holy foods, see Lev 22:1–9.

37. This means, presumably, the sanctuary, as in the texts of the earliest interpreters of Deut 23:2–9. On this, see my previous discussion in chapter 3.

38. The Hebrew of both of these texts is conveniently reproduced in Lohse, *Die Texte aus Qumran*, 50, 196.

39. The Hebrew reads kôl ʾîš ʿiwwēr lôʾ yābôʾû lāh kôl yĕmêhēmmâ wĕlôʾ yĕṭammĕʾû ʾet hāʿîr ʾăšer ʾănî šôkēn bĕtôkāh (11QTemp XLV 12–14, in Yadin, *The Temple Scroll*, 2.193. I have translated kôl ʾîš ʿiwwēr as a plural on account of the plural verb forms and possessive suffix that follow.) This interesting formu-

lation reflects the influence not only of 2 Sam 5:8b, but also of Num 5:3b and Deut 23:2–9. (I shall explore this in a future article.) Contrast the treatment of blindness and other blemishes in 1QS^a II 3–10 and 1QM VII 4–5, as discussed above.

40. Offering incense is represented as an elite and jealously guarded rite in Num 16:1–17:5 (Eng., 16:1–40). On this, see my discussion in chapter 1.

41. Laceration, tatooing, and certain kinds of shaving are condemned by D and H in Deut 14:1; Lev 19:27–28 (cp. 21:5 regarding priests specifically), though the language of blemish is not used of these acts. Deut 14:1 explicitly associates laceration and the shaving of a bald spot between the eyes with mourning; Lev 19:28 associates tatooing similarly and may have the same notion in mind when it proscribes shaving the corner of the head or beard. Many other texts mention shaving, and some, laceration, as normal, expected mourning rites (e.g., Jer 16:6, 41:5; Amos 8:10; Job 1:20).

42. E.g., Exod 12:44, 48; cp. Isa 52:1; Ezek 44:9, which prohibit the uncircumcised from entering the sanctuary.

43. My thanks to Victor Hurowitz for suggesting this point to me.

Conclusion

1. Note that the relationship of status to power may be less close in some cultures. For an example of this, see C. Geertz, *Negara: The Theatre State in Nineteenth-Century Bali* (Princeton: Princeton University Press, 1980) 62–63. On power and ritual, see C. Bell, *Ritual Theory, Ritual Practice* (New York: Oxford University Press, 1992) 169–223, esp. pp. 197–204 on theories of power, where Foucault and others are treated. Bell notes the variety of ways power has been defined (197). Unlike many who follow Foucault, I am unwilling to abandon the notion that power is exercised coercively; that it is something possessed; that some possess more of it than others. Yet, I believe that one can speak nonetheless of a relational, interactive dimension of power and find power manifest in resistance to coercion as well as in attempts to coerce.

2. Deuteronomistic cult centralization renders such a restriction impossible. See Deut 12: 15–19, 20–28, which allow for noncultic slaughter.

3. M. Foucault emphasizes the diffuseness of power in *The History of Sexuality, Volume I: An Introduction* (New York: Vintage, 1980) 93, as is often noted, though in significant ways my theory of power differs from his.

4. On the possible background of this text in the fifth century, see my discussion in chapter 3.

Appendix
The Idea of Holiness in the Holiness Source

1. See further Lev 11:44–45; 20:26; 22:32; Num 15:40.

2. The language is that of W. Zimmerli, " 'Heiligkeit' nach dem sogenannten Heiligkeitsgesetz," *VT* 30 (1980) 496. Zimmerli explores both constructions in some depth.

3. Here I assume that an idiom such as "I, Yhwh, sanctify you" ('ănî yhwh

měqaddiškem), which occurs in Exod 31:13; Lev 20:8; 21:8; 22:32, indicates that Israel is holy as a result of Yhwh's initiative, just as kî qādōš hû' lē'lōhāyw indicates the holiness of the priest in Lev 21:7. Obviously, I cannot accept the position of scholars such as Milgrom, who argue that the holiness of Israel in H is only potential and predicated on obedience to commandments. The idiom 'ănî yhwh měqaddiškem seems rather to suggest that Israel is continually being sanctified by Yhwh (cp. the similar idiom in Lev 21:23, concerning the sanctuary, which is surely holy). Furthermore, the same mix of a call to holiness and statements of fact about it is used of the priesthood in a text such as Lev 21:6–7, and the priests of that text are certainly sanctified (if their sanctification was not a fact, they could not present Yhwh's offerings; for Milgrom's argument, see provisionally *Leviticus 1–16* [AB 3; Garden City: Doubleday, 1991] 686–87). Kugler also concludes that the holiness of the people is an established fact in H, though with little argument ("Holiness, Purity, the Body, and Society: The Evidence for Theological Conflict in Leviticus," *JSOT* 76 [1997] 16 and passim).

4. E.g., Wright, "Holiness (OT)," 238.

5. Kugler has argued recently that H displays an ambivalent attitude toward the priesthood by emphasizing restrictions on priestly behavior (e.g., Lev 21:1–5) and by "democratizing" holiness ("Holiness, Purity, the Body, and Society," 25–26). I believe that severe priestly mourning restrictions are anything but an indicator of marginalization or reduced status; if anything, they betoken the priesthood's superior status, just as sole priestly access to holy foods does. Similarly, when P's Nazirite (Numbers 6) embraces a more restricted range of social behavior, her status is enhanced, not diminished! And the "democratization" of holiness evident in H does not suggest diminishment of priestly privilege in any concrete sense, as I have argued. Priestly holiness remains distinct from that of the people, as does priestly privilege, though I agree with Kugler that H holds the people to a higher standard of behavior as a result of their sanctification. Unfortunately, Kugler does not address the differences between priestly holiness and the sanctification of the people in H.

6. Exod 22:30 (Eng., 31); Deut 7:6; 14:1–2, 21; 26:19; 28:9; Exod 19:5–6, a D text (see M. Noth, *A History of Pentateuchal Traditions*, trans. B. W. Anderson [1948; Chico, CA: Scholars, 1981] 31 n. 112).

7. E.g., Exod 19:10, 14; Num 11:18; Josh 3:5; 7:13; 1 Sam 16:5; Joel 2:16; 2 Chr 30:17–18; cp. Isa 66:17. See further chapter 1 for discussion of this theme.

Index of Authors

Abrahams, I., 161n.87
Achtemeier, P. J., 168n.147
Alon, G., 161n.87
Anderson, B. W., 152n.10, 174n.6
Anderson, G. A., 124nn. 3, 5; 159n.69
Attridge, H. W., 153n.18

Barr, J., 130n.12
Barth, F., 165n.125
Baumgartner, W., 160n.72
Bell, C., 123n.2, 125nn. 8–10, 127n.28, 173n.1
Bendor, S., 157n.39
Berlin, A., 168n.147
Berreman, G. D., 8,126nn.18–19
Bertholet, A., 124n.3
Biran, A., 128n.1
Blenkinsopp, J., 163n.107, 164nn.114, 119
Bloch-Smith, E., 162n.95
Bourdieu, P., 123n.1
Brin, G., 135n.61, 155n.28
Brubaker, R., 169n.156
Buis, P., 167n.146
Buit, M. Du, 168n.146
Bultmann, C., 156n.36

Caplice, R. I., 168n.146
Caquot, A., 171n.19, 172n.30
Cardellini, I., 166n.133
Carmichael, C., 167n.144
Cartledge, P., 123n.1
Cazelles, H., 142n.1
Chirichigno, G., 165n.127
Clements, R. E., 133n.39
Clifford, J., 151nn.1–2
Clifford, R., 167n.141
Cohen, S. J. D., 152n.11, 153n.14, 154n.18, 156n.34
Cohn, R. L., 150n.1, 151n.4
Cole, J. B., 126n.18
Comaroff, J. and J., 125n.8,127n.28
Cook, G. A., 134n.41
Costecalde, C. B., 131n.13
Craigie, P., 167nn.141, 146, 168n.147
Cross, F. M., 127n.31,128n.36, 136n.62, 138n.78, 160n.75, 162n.91

Daube, D., 162n.98, 168n.150
David, M., 166n.139
Dion, P.-E., 156n.36, 159n.65
Dothan, J., 154n.19
Douglas, M., 108,131n.13, 142n.1, 143n.15, 144n.17, 170n.5
Driver, G. R., 167n.144
Duhm, B., 164n.114
Dumont, L., 123n.1,125n.9
Durkheim, E., 123n.1

Eilberg-Schwartz, H., 143–144n.15
Elliger, K., 164n.114

Falk, Z., 162n.93, 167n.144
Fallers, L. A., 8, 126nn.17–18, 23
Feigin, S. I., 167nn.141, 144
Feldman, E., 142n.1, 143n.15
Feldman, J., 131n.13, 145n.21
Finley, M. I., 8, 10, 126n.22, 127n.26
Fishbane, M., 160–161n.79, 161n.83, 162nn.90, 98, 100, 163nn.100, 102, 104–108, 164n.119
Fohrer, G., 148n.56
Foucault, M., 173nn.1, 3
Fox, M. V., 161n.84
Freedman, D. N., 128n.36
Frerichs, E. S., 151n.2
Friedman, R. E., 127n.31
Frymer-Kensky, T., 128–29n.4, 142n.1, 144n.16, 147nn.38, 43, 148n.52

Galey, J.-C., 123n.1
Galling, K., 160n.72
Gammie, J. G., 131n.13
Geertz, C., 9,126n.23, 173n.1
Gelb, I. J., 167n.141
Gennep, A. van, 123n.1, 165n.126
Gese, H., 133n.39
Gilman, S. L., 151n.2
Gittin, S., 128n.1
Goldingay, J., 124n.3
Goody, J., 125n.7
Gorman, F. H., Jr., 124n.3, 147nn.38, 43–44
Gourgues, M., 156n.36

Index of Biblical Citations

Qumran Texts

Other Ancient Texts

Rabbinic Materials

Other Ancient/Medieval Writers

Josephus